THE
ONE YEAR BIBLE
Story Book

Virginia J. Muir

KINGSWAY PUBLICATIONS

EASTBOURNE

Copyright © Tyndale House Publishers 1988

First published in the USA by Tyndale House Publishers, Inc, Wheaton, Illinois

First British edition 1990

This book contains the largest collection of artwork by Richard and Frances Hook ever to be produced in a single volume. Tyndale House gratefully acknowledges the following publishers for permission to print their Hook art:

Concordia Publishing House: the Richard Hook illustrations on pages 15, 19, 22, 24, 26-27, 40-41, 52, 53, 59, 77, 112-113, 123, 128-129, 144, 145, 186, 236-237, 250-251, 254, 270, 274, 340-341, 350, 351, 374 are from *My Good Shepherd Story Book*, copyright 1969 by Concordia Publishing House, St. Louis MO 63118, and are reprinted by permission.

David C. Cook Publishing Company: pages 193, 278, 282, 285, 287, 290-291, 296, 297, 298, 304-305, 309, 313, 314, 322, 331, 332-333, 339, 345, 348.

Standard Publishing Company: pages 94, 96, 124-125, 155, 164, 205, 260, 308.

Other artists:

Ron Ferris: pages 42, 45, 48, 61, 62, 72, 86, 105, 110, 116, 120, 127, 153, 156, 157, 180, 190, 200, 202, 206-207, 214, 222, 225, 230-231, 263, 266, 267, 294-295, 361, 365, 368.

Corbert Gauthier: pages 38, 63, 68, 70, 71, 74, 100-101, 102-103, 107, 114, 117, 133, 142, 163, 169, 172, 174-175, 185, 195, 199, 201, 212-213, 226, 233, 245, 246-247, 252-253, 257, 272-273, 301, 318, 323, 358.

J. H. Kibart: pages 88, 131.

Janice Skivington Wood: pages 373, 376, 377.

The One Year is a registered trademark of Tyndale House Publishers, Inc.

British Library Cataloguing in Publication Data
Muir, Virginia J.
  One year bible story book.
  1. Bible – Devotional works.
  I. Title
  242.5

  ISBN 0-86065-856-2

Printed in Yugoslavia for
Kingsway Publications Ltd, 1 St Anne's Road, Eastbourne BN21 3UN.
Reproduced from the original text by arrangement with Tyndale House Publishers, Inc.

CONTENTS

DECEMBER

FOREWORD

I wish this book had been available when my ten children were growing up. It is exactly what every parent needs. It gives your family the most important stories and people of the Bible in one year. The short daily readings are ideal for basic Bible knowledge that will be valuable throughout a child's entire lifetime.

The Bible is not only a great literary classic but is God's Word to you and to your family. It gives balance and inspiration for daily living and points its readers to God's provision for eternal life.

May God bless you and your children as you read and obey his Word day by day.

Dr. Kenneth N. Taylor

A VERY long time ago, God made the world. It was entirely different from the world we see today. It was dark and empty, and nothing lived in it—no people or animals or plants.

Then came six Creation Days. Here are the wonderful things that happened on each day:

DAY ONE—God said, "Let there be light," and light came. God called the light Day. At the end of the Day, darkness returned, and God called it Night.

DAY TWO—God placed the sky above the earth and called it Heaven.

DAY THREE—God divided the water that covered the earth into rivers and lakes and oceans. He made dry land appear between them. Then he made plants grow on the land.

DAY FOUR—God made the big bright sun to shine during the day. He made the moon and sparkling stars to shine at night.

DAY FIVE—God made fish and other sea creatures. Then he made water birds, like ducks and geese, and other birds, like robins and eagles, that live high in trees or on the ground.

DAY SIX—God made animals. He made huge ones, like elephants, and tiny ones, like mice. Some were beautiful, like the striped tiger. Others were funny-looking, like the anteater and the platypus. Some, like the cheetah, could run fast. Others, like the turtle, walked very slowly. And God made insects, some that flew, some that crawled, and some that jumped.

The World Was God's Creation

GENESIS 1–2

2

God Makes the First People
GENESIS 1–2

WHILE it was still Day Six, God decided to make a man—the very first man who ever lived. God took dust from the ground and formed it into a man's body. He breathed into it, and the man became alive and began to breathe. God named him Adam. Adam was different from the animals because he was like God himself.

God gave Adam a home in a beautiful garden called Eden. It was full of wonderful fruit trees. God said, "Adam, you may eat any fruit except the fruit from this one tree, called the Tree of the Knowledge of Good and Evil. If you even taste this tree's fruit, you will begin to die."

God put Adam in charge of the garden. He told Adam to give each kind of animal, bird, and insect a name. But in spite of all the animals around him, Adam still felt lonely. God knew it wasn't good for Adam to be the only person in the world. He needed a special human companion. So God put Adam to sleep, then took one of Adam's ribs and made a woman to be Adam's wife. (Adam later named his wife "Eve.")

So the earth and skies, plants and animals, and human beings were finished in six Creation Days. God looked around and was very well pleased with everything he had made.

On Day Seven, God didn't make anything. It was a quiet, holy day of rest, different from all the other days.

SOMEONE else was in the Garden of Eden besides God and Adam and his wife. It was Satan, an evil spirit who always tries to get people to do wrong things. Satan made himself look like a snake, or serpent. The snake asked the woman, "Did God tell you not to eat any fruit in the garden?"

"Oh, no!" she replied. "We may eat from every tree except the Tree of the Knowledge of Good and Evil. If we eat that fruit, we will begin to die."

"No, you won't!" Satan told her. "It can't hurt you at all. It's very good and will make you wise like God!"

Then the woman made a big mistake. She went over and looked at the tree. The fruit looked so good! She remembered that Satan had said it would make her wise, and she did want to be wise. Then she disobeyed God. She picked some of the fruit and ate it. She gave some to Adam, and he ate it too.

Later they heard God's voice calling them. They didn't answer. Instead, they hid among the trees, because now they were afraid of him. God called again. "Where are you, Adam?"

"I'm hiding," Adam finally replied. "I'm afraid of you."

"Why? Did you eat the fruit I told you not to eat?" God asked.

Adam blamed his wife. "The woman brought me some, and I ate it."

God asked the woman, "Did you really do that?"

"I did it because the serpent tricked me," she said.

What a weak excuse for disobeying God!

BECAUSE Adam and his wife listened to the serpent instead of to God, God had to punish them. But first, God spoke to the serpent. "From now on, you will have to crawl around on the dusty ground all your life. And you will always be a special enemy of the woman and her children. You will strike at their heels, but they will crush your head."

Then God told the woman that because she had disobeyed, she would have pain when her children were born.

God said to Adam, "Because you ate the fruit I told you not to eat, crops will no longer grow well for you. You will have to work hard to get rid of weeds and thorns. Then you will die and your body will return to the ground from which I made it."

It was after this that Adam named his wife Eve. Her name meant she would become the first mother of all the people who would later live on the earth.

Then came one of the saddest parts of the punishment. God made Adam and Eve leave the beautiful Garden of Eden forever. God explained that after they had eaten the fruit of the Tree of the Knowledge of Good and Evil, if they should then eat of the Tree of Life, they would live forever in their sinfulness. God put angels with swords at the entrance of the garden to make sure Adam and Eve would stay out.

AFTER Adam and Eve had to leave the garden, they had a baby boy named Cain. The next son was named Abel.

Cain became a farmer and Abel was a shepherd. When it came time to offer God a gift, Cain brought things from his garden and field, but Abel sacrificed a lamb on an altar.

God was pleased with Abel and accepted his offering. But God saw that Cain had disobedience in his heart, so he didn't accept Cain's grain and fruit. This made Cain very angry.

"Why are you so angry?" God asked him. "If you will do the right thing, I will be pleased with you, too. If you don't, you will always be in trouble because of your sin."

Cain became more and more angry with God, and he hated his brother because God had accepted Abel's sacrifice and not Cain's. One day he suggested that Abel go out to the field with him. There Cain attacked Abel and killed him.

God called to Cain: "Where is your brother?"

"How should I know?" Cain answered crossly. "Am I supposed to look after him all the time?"

Of course, God always knows everything we do, and he knew that Cain had killed Abel. He said, "Your brother's blood calls out to me from the ground. Now you must leave home and wander from place to place. You will live in fear. And your crops will never grow well."

ADAM lived for many years after Abel's death. When he was 930 years old, he died. His body was buried and became dust again, as God had said it would. He and Eve had had many children and grandchildren and great-grandchildren. Soon many, many people lived in the world.

One of them was Enoch. The Bible tells us Enoch walked with God. This is another way of saying he loved God and thought about him all the time. Enoch and God were friends, and Enoch pleased God by obeying him in every way.

When Enoch was 365 years old, God took him up to heaven while he was still alive! We don't know just how it happened, but we know Enoch didn't have to die like other people. God just took him away to live with him.

Enoch had a son named Methuselah, who lived to be 969 years old. We have never heard of anyone who lived longer than that, so we call Methuselah the oldest man who ever lived.

R. Hook

*A Good
Man in a
Sinful
World*
GENESIS 6

A S TIME went on, people in the world became more and more sinful. It seemed as if they just tried to think of wicked things to do. They didn't care about pleasing God or obeying him. God kept warning them, but they didn't pay any attention. This made God very angry with them. He said, "I'm going to destroy them by sending a great flood of water to cover the earth. The water will be so deep that everyone will drown. Not only will the people drown, but so will all the animals and snakes and birds and insects—everything."

But there was one man, named Noah, who loved God and served him. He did want to please God, so God wanted to save Noah and his family from the flood. He told Noah to build a very large boat. It would be as high as a three-story house and would have a long window reaching all around it, just under the roof. The boat would have plenty of room for Noah and his wife and their three sons (named Shem, Ham, and Japheth) and their wives. It would also have room for many, many animals—at least two of every kind, as well as birds and reptiles and insects.

NOAH did exactly what God told him to. He built the boat, sometimes called an ark, and made it just as long, as wide, and as high as God had said. It took him a long time to get it done—about a hundred years. Although Noah was several hundred years old, he was strong enough to do this work.

When the ark was finished, God told Noah it was time to gather the animals and enough food to take care of them for many weeks. Noah was to take a male and a female of some kinds, so baby creatures would be born. Of other kinds he was to take seven pairs—some for eating and some for sacrificing later on when they could all leave the ark.

Noah obeyed every part of God's instructions. He took his family and all the animals into the ark. About a week later, the flood began. Rain poured from the sky, and flood waters rose up from the earth—higher and higher, until there was enough water to make the huge ark float. Then every creature left outside the ark drowned—every man, woman, and child, and every animal, bird, reptile, and insect.

But because Noah and his family had obeyed God's warning, they were safe inside the ark, floating on top of the water.

RAIN kept falling for more than a month, but Noah and his family stayed dry inside their boat. How glad they must have been that they had listened to God and obeyed him!

Finally the rain stopped, and then—very slowly—the water began to go down again. Noah and his family stayed inside the ark for 150 days. That's five whole months! By that time the water had gone down enough for the boat to touch the ground, up in some mountains called Ararat. Still they stayed inside, waiting for God to let them know when it was safe to get out.

Noah sent out a raven, and it kept flying around until the ground got dry. Then he sent out a dove. The dove came back once, so Noah waited for about a week, then he sent it out again. This time it came back carrying an olive leaf in its bill. This showed Noah that the water had gone down to the level of the trees. After still another week, he sent the dove out once more, and this time it didn't come back. In a few more weeks the ground became dry enough to walk on. Then God said, "All right, Noah, it is time to leave the boat."

JANUARY

9

A Long Boat Ride

GENESIS 8

JANUARY

10

Dry Land at Last!

GENESIS 8–9

NOAH let all the animals and birds and snakes and insects out of their stalls and cages. They went out onto the dry ground. Then Noah and the seven other members of his family left the ark too. It must have felt good to walk on solid ground after riding in a boat for almost half a year!

The first thing Noah and his sons did when they left the boat was to build an altar and worship God. They thanked him for saving them from the flood. They sacrificed some of the extra animals they had taken on the boat. It made God happy that they wanted to worship him, and he was pleased with their sacrifice. God said to himself, "Even though people will disobey me again, I will never send another flood to destroy all the people and animals."

God told Noah and his sons to have many children, so the earth would again be full of people. He said from then on, animals and other creatures would be afraid of human beings, but people would be able to use them for food and for doing work.

Then God told Noah about his decision not to wipe out the people and animals on earth again with a flood. He said, "When it rains, don't be afraid of another flood, but look up at the sky. There you will see a beautiful rainbow. It will remind you of my promise to you and to your children after you."

22

After the flood ended and Noah and his family were living on dry land again, Noah's sons had many children and grandchildren. Sad to say, they behaved just like the people who had lived before the flood, doing things that displeased God.

Nowadays the people in the world speak many different languages—like Spanish, English, and German. But then, all people spoke the same language. They all wanted to live together in the same city, and they got the idea of building a huge tower that would reach far up into the sky. They said, "This tower will show how great we are. We can all stay together and not get spread out into the earth."

When they decided this, they were disobeying God's command to occupy the whole earth and take care of it. So God was displeased when he looked at the tower they were building. He decided to put a stop to their plan by making them begin to speak in different languages. That way they couldn't understand one another! This made them angry, and soon they gave up trying to work together and left the tower unfinished.

The tower they tried to build is called the Tower of Babel. The word "Babel" means "mixed up" or "confused." The languages were mixed up and so were the people! Finally, small groups who could speak to each other moved away from the ones who spoke another language, and so the people scattered to all parts of the earth.

JANUARY

11

The Tower of Babel

GENESIS 11

Long ago a man named Abram lived in a large city. Abram and his family were different from their neighbors because they believed in God. The others worshiped idols made of wood or stone.

One day God told Abram to leave his home and the idol-worshipers around him. God said he would lead Abram to a special country that would belong to Abram and his children. That country was Canaan, and because God promised it to Abram, we call it the Promised Land.

Abram believed God, so he took his wife, Sarai, and his young nephew, named Lot, and they started to Canaan. He also had many servants and animals. In those days having many animals was like having lots of money—so Abram was very rich.

When they got to Canaan, God said to him, "I'm going to give all this land to you and to your children forever." Abram said thank you to God by building an altar and sacrificing an animal on it.

The trouble with Canaan was that a famine was going on. A famine is a time when crops don't grow because there isn't enough rain, and many people starve to death. Abram didn't want that to happen to Sarai and Lot and his servants, so he took them into Egypt, where there was enough food. When the famine was over, they returned to the Promised Land to live.

As we know, Abram had very large herds and flocks of cows, sheep, and goats. Lot was rich too, with many animals in his flocks. Both men had servants who took care of their animals. The two groups of servants began to quarrel about the best fields and the best water supply for the animals. When Abram heard this, he said to Lot, "This is a large country. We don't need to live so close together that our shepherds have to fight over the pasture and the water. I will divide the land with you. Lot, you may have first choice."

Abram could have kept the best land for himself and his flocks because, after all, God had given it all to him. But he really wanted to be generous to his nephew. Lot was not as kind as Abram was. He quickly chose the best part, close to the river Jordan, where the fields would be well watered. But when he chose that part, he also chose to live in the wicked city of Sodom. Later on, Lot's selfish choice caused much trouble, as we shall see.

JANUARY

14

A Wonderful Promise

GENESIS 13

After Lot had moved away, God made some more wonderful promises to Abram. "Look all around you in every direction. I am going to give you and your children all the land you can see. Walk all around the countryside and look at the land that will be yours. Someday even that land Lot chose will be yours too.

"And I will give you many, many children and grandchildren and great-grandchildren. You will have as many descendants as there are bits of dust on the earth. They will become a great nation and I will bless them." That promise has come true, and today we call that great group of people the Jews, or Israelis. And the modern name for the Promised Land is Israel.

Abram moved to a place called Hebron and built another altar to the Lord. Each time he moved, he built a new altar so he would always have a place near him where he could worship God by making sacrifices.

About that time, four kings from nearby countries made war against the city of Sodom. They won the war and stole all the money, food, clothing, and jewelry. They even took some people to become their slaves—and Lot was one of the men they captured. When Abram heard that Lot was in trouble, he gathered his 318 servants and some friends and chased after the army. They caught up with the four kings and their armies and started to fight. In the end, God let Abram win. He was able to rescue Lot and all the other captives. As they returned to Sodom, Abram was met by Melchizedek, a powerful king who loved God. Melchizedek blessed Abram and prayed for him. Abram gave Melchizedek one-tenth of everything he had taken away from the enemy.

The king of Sodom was happy when he saw Abram returning with the captives! He said to Abram, "Give me back my people, but you can keep everything else for yourself—all the food, clothes, and jewelry." Abram said no, he had promised God he wouldn't keep anything for himself. He wanted everyone to know it was only God who had made him rich—not any other person.

Abram and Sarai were getting very old. They thought a lot about God's promise to make their children become a great nation. They wondered how that could possibly happen because they didn't have any children at all! They especially wanted a little boy, so Abram talked to God about it. God promised Abram that he and Sarai would have a son. God said, "I am your friend, and I will always protect you. Look up at the sky and see all the stars. Can you count them?"

Of course Abram couldn't count all the stars in the sky. No one can. But God said, "Not only will you have a son, but you will have so many grandchildren and great-grandchildren that their families will be like the stars—too many to count!"

Abram believed what God told him, and God was very pleased with him because he believed. Whenever we believe what God says, we make him happy.

Because she didn't have any children and was so old, Sarai became impatient for the son God had promised. She said her servant girl, Hagar, could be Abram's second wife so a baby could be born into the family. Hagar did have a baby boy, named Ishmael. But this wasn't the way God had planned for Abram and Sarai to get the promised son—and their disobedience brought much trouble into the family.

SEVERAL more years went by, and Abram was ninety-nine years old. Then God spoke to him again. God reminded Abram of all the promises he had made to him before and told him those promises would all come true. He said, "Your name won't be Abram any more. I want you to be called Abraham, because that means 'Father of Nations.' " Then God gave Sarai a new name too. She was to be called Sarah, which means "Princess."

Then God made a covenant with Abraham. A covenant is a very important agreement that God makes with people. Part of the covenant with Abraham was that God would allow Sarah to have a baby who would be the promised one to start Abraham's great nation.

Because Abraham thought he and Sarah were too old to have a baby, he laughed and said, "Surely you must mean that you are going to bless Ishmael!"

"I will bless him too," God replied, "but I really mean that Sarah herself will have a baby. You are to name him Isaac, which means 'Laughter.' "

JANUARY

18

*Heavenly
Visitors*

GENESIS 18

ONE hot day Abraham was sitting at the door of his tent. He saw three men coming. He invited them to rest for awhile. He brought water so they could wash their tired, dusty feet. Then he asked Sarah to prepare some food for them. Two of the men were angels and the third one was God, disguised in the form of a man.

While the guests were eating, the one who was God said, "Next year you and Sarah will have the promised son." Inside the tent Sarah heard this and laughed to herself about the idea of having a baby in her old age.

God said to Abraham, "Why did Sarah laugh? Doesn't she know that the Lord can do anything? She really will have a baby."

Sarah was afraid, so she lied. She said, "I didn't laugh." But God knows everything, so he knew she really had laughed.

When the three visitors left, Abraham walked with them toward Sodom. Do you remember who lived at Sodom? Yes, it was Lot, Abraham's nephew. God told Abraham he was planning to destroy Sodom to punish the people for their great sinfulness. Abraham didn't want Lot to be destroyed, so he said to God, "If there are fifty good men there, will you change your mind?"

God answered, "Yes, if there are fifty."

Abraham kept asking this, making the number smaller and smaller until he got to ten. God said he would leave the city alone if he could find even ten good men there.

Then Abraham stopped asking and went back home.

That evening, as Lot sat by the city gate, the two angels who had visited Abraham came to warn Lot about the trouble that was coming. They said, "Be sure that you and your wife and your daughters and their husbands all get out of Sodom. Do it quickly, because God is going to destroy the city."

Lot's sons-in-law didn't believe the warning and refused to leave. Lot took his wife and daughters and started to leave town. He hated to leave his comfortable home, but the angels grabbed his arms and hurried him along. "Don't look back at Sodom," they said. "Run to the mountains and hide."

Lot was afraid to go up into the mountains, so he begged the angels to let him stay in a small nearby city called Zoar. They said, "All right, but hurry up—run!"

Lot's wife knew she shouldn't look back at Sodom, but she disobeyed the order of the angels anyway. When she turned around for a last look, she suddenly turned into a big pillar of salt!

Lot and his daughters had no time to stop. They hurried on and left her there looking like a white statue.

JANUARY

19

The Angels Warn Lot

GENESIS 19

JANUARY

20

God Destroys Sodom

GENESIS 19

JUST as Lot and his daughters arrived at Zoar, the sun came up. At that very moment, God poured down fire on Sodom and a nearby city named Gomorrah. Everything in those cities and in the farm land around them burned up—all the buildings, people, animals, and plants.

Far away, where Abraham lived, he could see great billows of smoke rising from those terrible fires. Then he knew God had not been able to find even ten good people in Sodom, because God had promised to spare the city if he found ten people who were not wicked. Do you think God would have burned up Sodom if Abraham had asked him to spare it for just one good man—Lot?

The people in Zoar weren't much better than the ones in Sodom, and soon Lot became afraid of them. He decided he would be safer in the mountains, so he and his daughters lived in a cave. His daughters were not good women. They became the mothers of men who started very wicked tribes that made a lot of trouble for God's people many years later.

THE following year, exactly when God had told Abraham it would happen, Sarah had a baby boy. At last Abraham had the son who would start the great nation God had promised him. Abraham and Sarah remembered God's instructions and named the baby Isaac. Do you remember what that name means? It is "laughter" because they were so happy to have a son—and also, perhaps, because both Abraham and Sarah had laughed at the idea of having a baby when they were so old!

Isaac grew, as babies do, and one time Abraham gave a party for him. One of the children at the party was Ishmael, Abraham's older son, who had been born to Hagar, the servant woman. At the party he teased his half brother, Isaac, and this made Sarah angry. She told Abraham he should send Hagar and Ishmael away and not let them be in the family anymore. Even though it had been Sarah's idea that Abraham have a baby with Hagar, the servant-wife, Sarah had always been jealous of Hagar and Ishmael.

Even though Ishmael was not the son of God's promise, still he was Abraham's little boy, and Abraham didn't like to send him away. God said to Abraham, "It's all right. Let the boy and his mother go, and I will take care of them. Ishmael, too, shall become a great nation."

So Abraham packed a good lunch for Hagar and Ishmael, gave them water to carry with them, and sent them into the desert.

JANUARY

22

God Takes Care of Ishmael

GENESIS 21

DESERTS are very dry and hot. As Hagar and her son, Ishmael, walked through the desert, they quickly used up all the water Abraham had given them. Hagar didn't see a well anywhere, and she didn't know where to find any more water. She began to be afraid that Ishmael would die of thirst.

She found a little bush and had Ishmael lie down in its shade. Then she walked away and sat by herself, crying. Ishmael was crying too, because he was so hot and thirsty. Then the Angel of the Lord spoke to Hagar and said, "God has heard your son crying. Don't be afraid. Go back and comfort him." As she was returning to the bush where Ishmael lay, suddenly she saw a well! She filled up the water bottle and gave Ishmael a refreshing drink. Then he felt better, and they were able to continue their trip.

They made their new home in a place called Paran, and there Ishmael grew up. He became an expert with a bow and arrow. He married a girl from Egypt, and they had many descendants who became a great nation, as God had said they would. Just as Ishmael didn't get along well with Isaac, so Ishmael's descendants—we now call them Arabs—have never gotten along well with Isaac's descendants, the Jews. In fact, even today the Arabs and Israelis are often at war with each other.

ONE day God gave Abraham a very strange message. He told him to take his son Isaac, go up to Mount Moriah, and offer Isaac as a burnt sacrifice on an altar. Although Abraham loved his son very much, he didn't argue. He simply obeyed. Early the next morning he took Isaac and two servants and started up the mountain, carrying a knife, some wood, and some fire to light the wood on the altar. When they could see the place of sacrifice ahead, Abraham left the servants, and he and Isaac went on.

Isaac had often seen his father sacrifice a lamb, so he asked Abraham, "Father, we have the wood and the fire to light it, but where is the lamb we are going to offer?"

Abraham answered, "God will give us the lamb for sacrifice, my son."

When they arrived, Abraham built an altar and arranged the wood on it. Then he tied Isaac up and laid him on the wood. He raised the knife to kill Isaac, but at the last moment the Angel of the Lord said, "No! Don't hurt your son. I can see now that you really do love and trust me. You were even willing to give me your precious son of promise."

Just then Abraham saw a male sheep, called a ram, caught in a bush nearby. He sacrificed the ram to God on the altar and gave that place on the mountain a special name: "The Lord will provide." Then they went back home again. Abraham had passed God's test, and Isaac was spared.

JANUARY

23

Abraham Proves His Faith

GENESIS 22

S ARAH lived quite a few more years after Isaac was born, but when she was 127 years old, she died. Abraham and Isaac had loved her, and they missed her very, very much. Abraham bought some land from a man called Ephron, and there he buried Sarah.

Isaac was now a grown man and was thinking about getting married. Abraham didn't want him to marry one of the women who lived there in Canaan because they didn't love and worship God. So he decided to send his oldest and most trusted servant to look for the kind of person Isaac should marry. Abraham knew he had many relatives where he used to live, and among them would be the right wife for his son.

The servant said, "If the woman won't come here, shall I take Isaac back there to marry her?"

"No!" Abraham answered. "God told me that this is where we should live, and Isaac must stay here. If she won't come, I will forgive you for not being able to keep your promise. But please try to bring back a good wife for Isaac."

So the servant promised to do his best. He took many fine gifts with him and started his journey back to the place where Abraham's relatives lived.

THE servant arrived at Abraham's brother Nahor's village in the evening. He stopped near a well and had his camels kneel down. As he watched the women of the village come out to draw up water from the well, he asked God to help him find one who would be a good wife for Isaac. He decided on a test. He would ask one of them to give him a drink of water. If she said, "Yes," and offered to water all the camels too, she would be the right one.

As he was praying, a beautiful young woman came to the well and filled her water pitcher. Abraham's servant went to her and said, "May I please have a drink?"

"Yes, sir. And I will be glad to draw water for your camels, too—as much as they want to drink." And while the servant watched her carefully, she kept drawing up more and more water, until the camels had all had enough after their long, hot trip.

Seeing that she passed his test, the servant offered her some of the gifts he had brought and asked her who she was. Her name was Rebekah. He was pleased to find out she was the daughter of Bethuel, a son of Nahor. That meant she was Abraham's grandniece and Isaac's cousin! He asked if he might stay overnight at her father's home, because he wanted to ask her family to let her marry Isaac. Then he thanked God for helping him find Rebekah.

JANUARY

25

The Right Wife for Isaac

GENESIS 24

REBEKAH hurried home to tell her family about the man at the well. She showed them the jewelry he had given her. Her brother Laban went out to invite the visitor to their home. The servant was eager to tell them his story.

They all listened, amazed, as he told them he was their uncle Abraham's servant from faraway Canaan. He told how he had prayed that God would lead him to the right wife for Isaac. He said he had tested Rebekah, and she was the one he was looking for. "Will you let her go back with me?"

Rebekah's father and brother said, "We can see God brought you here. Yes, you may take Rebekah to be Isaac's wife."

The servant thanked God for this answer to his prayer. Then he gave Rebekah and her family the rest of the gifts—gold and silver jewelry and many beautiful clothes. He wanted to leave the next morning, but her mother and brother Laban said, "Oh, that's too soon! We want her to stay with us a few more days. But we'll ask her what she wants to do."

Rebekah said she would go at once, so her family gave her their blessing. Her childhood nurse went along, as well as several other servants. When they got to Canaan, the servant told Isaac the wonderful story of how he had found Rebekah. Then Rebekah became Isaac's bride, and he loved her very much.

AFTER awhile Rebekah had twin baby boys. The one born first was named Esau and the second one was named Jacob. Because Esau was the older one, he received the birthright. That meant that when his father would die someday, Esau would receive most of the family money and land. The younger twin, Jacob, would get only half as much of his father's property.

When they grew up, Esau became a skillful hunter. He would go out and kill wild deer for food. Isaac liked that deer meat, called venison, so he especially loved Esau. Jacob was a more quiet person, and he preferred to stay around home and help with the work. He was Rebekah's favorite son.

One day Jacob was cooking a big pot of stew. Esau came in from an all-day hunt, tired and hungry. When he smelled the stew, he said, "Oh, let me have some of that. It smells so good."

Jacob saw a chance to cheat Esau. "All right, I will if you will give me your birthright. Do you promise?"

Esau said, "Well, the birthright won't do me much good if I starve to death! Yes, I promise. You may have my birthright."

So Esau had a good supper. He was thinking so much about his hunger he didn't even care that he had traded something of great value for just a bowl of stew.

JANUARY

27

Esau Throws Away Something Valuable
GENESIS 25

28

Jacob Fools His Father

GENESIS 27

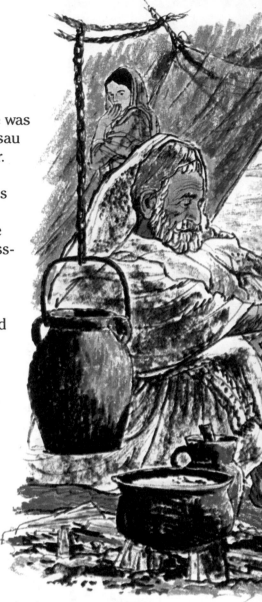

ISAAC was getting very old, and he was almost blind. One day he asked Esau to go hunting and bring back a deer. "Cook the meat in the special way I like. If you do, I will ask God to bless you."

Rebekah heard Isaac say this. She wanted Jacob to receive Isaac's blessing, so she thought of a way Jacob could trick Isaac. She told Jacob to bring in two young goats and she would cook them so that they would taste just like venison. When the meat was ready, she told Jacob to take it to his father.

"But Esau has a lot of hair on his arms and chest, and I don't. Father will know I am not Esau."

So Rebekah tied some of the goatskin around Jacob's arms and on his chest. He took the meat to his father and said, "Here is the delicious venison you wanted, Father. God helped me find a deer very quickly."

Isaac said, "Your voice sounds like Jacob's. Let me feel you to be sure you are Esau." He felt the goatskins on Jacob's arms and was satisfied. He ate the food and gave Jacob the blessing he had promised Esau. Then Jacob left the room.

Very soon, Esau came back from the hunt and cooked the real venison for his father. Then Isaac realized that Jacob had tricked him, but by that time it was too late. He had already given the special blessing to Jacob.

*Rebekah
Helps
Jacob
Escape*
GENESIS 27

AT LAST Esau could see just
how much he had lost through
his own thoughtlessness and
Jacob's trickery. This made him
furious with Jacob. "Not only did
he get my birthright," he growled,
"but now he has stolen the blessing I should have had. As soon as
our father dies, I'm going to kill
him, even though he is my
brother."

Someone told Rebekah about
Esau's threat. She called Jacob and
said, "Your brother really hates
you. You'd better go away for
awhile. Go to Haran and stay
with my brother Laban and my
other relatives until Esau's anger
cools down. I will let you know
when it is safe to come back."

Esau was married to two
Canaanite women who didn't
love God, and this had made his
parents very unhappy. In order
to get Isaac to let Jacob go to
Haran, Rebekah said, "We
certainly don't want Jacob to
marry one of the girls around here the way Esau did, do we?"

Isaac agreed, so he told Jacob to go to his grandfather
Bethuel's home and find a good wife among Rebekah's relatives
—possibly one of his uncle Laban's daughters. Of course this
was just what Rebekah had wanted him to say. Isaac blessed
Jacob and told him he would someday inherit the land of
promise, as God had promised Abraham and Isaac before him.
Then Jacob quickly packed up and started his trip.

30

A Stairway to Heaven
GENESIS 28

JACOB traveled toward Haran, where Bethuel and Laban lived. When he stopped for the night, he slept on the ground with a stone under his head for a pillow. He had a dream in which he saw a long stairway reaching from the earth to heaven. Angels were walking up and down on the stairway.

Then he saw the Lord and heard him say, "I am the God of Abraham and Isaac. I am going to make you a part of the great nation I promised them. You will have many children, and this land will be yours forever. I will take care of you wherever you go. Someday I will bring you back to this land. I'll never leave you."

When Jacob woke up, he was both excited and afraid because God had come to him in a dream. He got up and worshiped God at a sort of altar he made by setting up the stone he had used as a pillow. He poured oil over it as an offering. Jacob named that place "Bethel," which means "the house of God."

Then Jacob made a vow to God. A vow is a very serious promise. He promised that if God would indeed take care of him as he had said, and would bring Jacob back to the Promised Land, he would always love God and trust him. "I will worship you and give you one-tenth of everything you give me."

WHEN Jacob got to the eastern country where his mother's relatives lived, the first person he met at the village well was his cousin Rachel. She was one of the daughters of Laban, Rebekah's brother. Jacob helped her uncover the well and water Laban's flock of sheep. Then he told her who he was. She went to tell her father, and Laban hurried out to welcome Jacob.

Jacob stayed with Laban's family and helped with his sheep. After about a month, Laban said, "I don't want you to work for me for nothing. Tell me what you want me to pay you."

By this time Jacob was in love with his beautiful cousin Rachel. He told Laban he would work for him free for seven years, if Laban would let him marry Rachel. Laban agreed, and Jacob worked for seven years. At last it was time for the wedding.

When the wedding feast was over, Laban brought Jacob's bride to his tent after dark. When they woke up in the morning, Jacob found that Laban had tricked him and had given him Rachel's older sister, Leah, who was not the one he loved. He was angry about this, so Laban said, "It was important that the older girl be married first. Now you may have Rachel too, if you will work for another seven years." So Jacob was married to both sisters and continued to work for Laban.

JANUARY

31

Jacob Marries Leah and Rachel

GENESIS 29

FEBRUARY

1

Jacob's Secret Escape

GENESIS 29–31

LEAH had a servant girl named Zilpah, and Rachel had one named Bilhah. Jacob married both of them, too. His four wives bore him many sons, but his favorite was Rachel's son, Joseph. He wanted to go back to Canaan with his wives and children, but Laban didn't want him to leave. Jacob said, "I'll stay if you will give me some sheep and goats so I can have flocks of my own."

Laban did, and soon Jacob's flocks grew very large, making him a rich man. Laban's own sons became jealous of Jacob and grumbled about how rich he was. Soon Jacob found it wasn't very pleasant being with Laban and his family anymore.

Jacob realized he would have to leave Haran secretly, without telling Laban. So he and his wives gathered all the things they owned. They took all Jacob's flocks and left very quietly one day when Laban was out in the field, shearing his sheep.

Three days went by before Laban knew they were gone. He followed Jacob and his group, and when he caught up with them, he said he just wanted to say good-bye to his two daughters and his grandchildren. They camped together overnight, then they all told each other good-bye. Laban went back to Haran, and Jacob went on toward Canaan. On the way, he saw some angels, so he knew God was with him.

THE CLOSER Jacob got to his homeland, the more he wondered how Esau would feel about his coming back. It had been twenty years since Jacob had tricked Isaac and stolen Esau's blessing. Was Esau still angry with him? Did he perhaps even want to kill him? He decided to send messengers to Esau to tell him he was coming and that he wanted to be friends. He also

told them to tell Esau all about the things that had happened to him during the twenty years they had been apart.

The messengers came back and said, "Esau is coming out to meet you, and he has 400 men with him." That really scared Jacob! He divided his family, servants, and flocks into two groups. If Esau should attack, at least one group might be able to escape. Next, Jacob prayed that God would protect him from Esau's anger. He thanked God for all the good things that had happened to him in Haran, and for the riches he now had, even though he knew he didn't deserve them.

Then Jacob gathered many of his sheep, goats, camels, cattle, and donkeys—several hundred animals in all—as a gift for Esau. He sent servants ahead with groups of these animals to meet his brother. He thought a big present like that might make Esau less angry with him. Maybe they would be able to be friends after all.

JACOB especially wanted to protect his wives and children from harm in the fighting he thought might happen when he met Esau. So in the night he sent the women and children, with his personal possessions, across the river Jordan. They would be safer there.

When he came back to his camp alone, a Man came and started wrestling with him. They wrestled until early morning. When the Man saw that he could not overcome Jacob, he touched the hip joint of Jacob's leg and knocked it out of joint.

The Man said, "It is morning; let me go now."

Jacob answered, "I won't let you go until you bless me."

"What is your name?" the Man asked. So Jacob told him. "I'm going to change your name to Israel, which means 'one who struggles and prevails with God.' You will also be strong and prevail with men."

Jacob asked the Man his name. The Man would not tell him, but he did give him the blessing Jacob had asked for. Jacob knew then that the Man was the Lord in the form of a man. (He was the same Man who had come to Abraham to predict Isaac's birth and the burning of Sodom.) Jacob gave the place where they had wrestled a special name, Peniel, which means "the face of God." He said, "I saw God face to face, and yet my life was spared."

FINALLY the moment came for Jacob and Esau to meet. Jacob went on ahead of his family and servants and flocks. As he came close to Esau he bowed down seven times to show his respect for his brother. Esau ran to meet him and put his arms around him, hugging and kissing him. They were so glad to see each other that they both cried for joy.

When Esau saw Jacob's large family, he asked, "Who are all these women and children with you?"

Jacob replied, "These are the children God has given me." And he introduced his wives and children to Esau.

Esau asked, "And why did you send all those sheep and goats and other animals to me?"

Jacob said, "I sent them as a gift—to make you feel friendly toward me."

"Oh, no," Esau said, "I have all the flocks and herds I need. You keep them." But Jacob insisted, and finally Esau accepted them.

Esau offered to travel with Jacob the rest of the way, but Jacob was still a little bit afraid of him. He thought he'd be safer if Esau was out in front where he could keep his eye on him! He told Esau to go on ahead and he and his family would follow more slowly. And that's what they did.

So God answered Jacob's prayer and reunited him with Esau, and the brothers could be friends after twenty long years apart.

AFTER Esau left, Jacob traveled toward Canaan. He camped for a short time at Succoth, then entered Canaan and stayed for awhile at a city called Shechem. He bought a piece of land and built an altar. He called it "An Altar to the God of Israel."

Jacob's family didn't get along well with the people in Shechem, so Jacob was glad when God told him it was time to move on. God said, "Go to Bethel and build an altar." Jacob knew that place well because that's where he had dreamed about the

stairway to heaven. That's where God had promised to bring him back safely—and now God was keeping that promise.

Jacob built a great altar and made sacrifices to show God how grateful he was for his blessings. Again God told him about his new name, "Israel," and reminded him about the great nation God had promised Abraham.

They went on toward Bethlehem, but before they could get there, Rachel had another baby boy. They named him Benjamin. After the baby was born, Rachel died. Jacob was terribly sad because he had loved her so much. He buried her beside the road and then went on to see his father, Isaac, who now was very, very old. When Isaac died, Jacob and Esau buried him in the same cave where Abraham and Sarah were buried.

Esau took his family and moved to Edom, where his flocks would have more pasture. Jacob and his twelve sons stayed in the Promised Land.

BECAUSE Jacob loved Rachel best, and because her son Joseph had been born in Jacob's old age, he was Jacob's favorite child. Jacob gave Joseph special privileges and gifts, like a beautiful robe, bright with many colorful decorations. Of course this made the other sons angry, because they were so jealous of Joseph.

One day, when Joseph was seventeen years old, he told his brothers about a dream he had had. In his dream their bundles of grain bowed down to his bundle of grain. The brothers were angry about the dream. "If you think we would ever bow down to you, you can just forget it!" they growled. Now they hated Joseph more than ever.

Later Joseph had another dream, and he told this one to his brothers also. "I dreamed that the sun and the moon and eleven stars were bowing down to me," he said. This time his father heard about his dream too, and Jacob scolded him. "Now listen, what is this I hear about your dream? Do you mean that you think your mother and I and all your brothers will actually come and bow to you?"

Joseph's older brothers continued to be jealous and hateful toward him. Jacob thought a lot about Joseph's strange dreams and wondered why his son dreamed such things.

FEBRUARY

6

Joseph the Dreamer

GENESIS 37

JACOB'S sons took care of all his flocks and herds. One day they took the animals to Shechem to find good pasture. Jacob sent Joseph out to find them and bring back news about them. Joseph agreed to look for his brothers at Shechem, although it was a long walk. He wandered around the fields, hunting for them, but they weren't there.

He met a man who said, "Jacob's sons? Oh, they've left. I heard them say they were going to Dothan." So Joseph followed them to Dothan.

When his brothers saw him in the distance, they groaned. "Uh-oh! Look who's coming. It's that great dreamer! Let's get rid of him once and for all. When he gets here, we'll kill him and toss him into a well. We'll tell our father that a wild animal ate him. Then we'll see what becomes of all his big dreams about our bowing down to him."

The oldest brother, Reuben, didn't like the idea of killing his young brother. He said to his brothers, "Let's just put him into a dry well. Maybe he'll die in there without our having to hurt him ourselves." Reuben thought that later he could secretly get Joseph out of the well and send him home unharmed.

When Joseph arrived, his brothers grabbed the colorful coat Jacob had given him. They threw him into an empty well—and then they sat down to eat their lunch.

WHILE Reuben was busy somewhere away from the camp, the other brothers noticed a caravan of camels coming. Some Ishmaelites were on their way to sell spices and ointments in Egypt. Judah got an idea. "Listen," he said, "we don't really need to kill Joseph—after all, he is our half brother, the son of our father. Let's sell him to these traders. They will give us some money for him, and then they'll take him away so he can't bother us anymore."

So they pulled Joseph up out of the dry well and sold him to the traders for twenty pieces of silver. The traders went on toward Egypt. Soon Reuben came back to camp and looked for Joseph, but of course he was gone. Reuben was terribly upset. "What in the world are we going to tell our father? He will be brokenhearted if his favorite son doesn't come back with us."

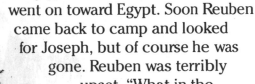

FEBRUARY

8

Joseph's Brothers Get Rid of Him

GENESIS 37

They decided to let Jacob think Joseph had been killed by a wild animal. They killed a goat and put a lot of its blood on Joseph's beautiful coat. They returned to Joseph and said, "We found this robe on the ground. Isn't this the coat you gave Joseph?"

"Yes, it is Joseph's coat. He must have been attacked by a wild beast and torn to bits. My dear, dear son is dead!" Day after day he grieved for Joseph. He said, "I will be sad about his death all the rest of my life."

9

*Joseph
Goes to
Jail*

GENESIS 39

THE TRADERS took Joseph to Egypt and sold him to Potiphar, an officer in the king's army. In Egypt all the kings were called Pharaoh, and Potiphar was the captain of Pharaoh's body-guard. Joseph worked in Potiphar's home, and he did his work so well that Potiphar was pleased and trusted him with more and more important jobs.

The only trouble was that Potiphar's wife liked Joseph too much. She tried to get Joseph to make love to her. Joseph knew this was very wrong, because she was his master's wife, so he refused. That made her furious, and she told lies about Joseph to get him into trouble. Potiphar believed his wife's lies and threw Joseph into prison.

Joseph did all the jobs the chief jailer gave him to do. He worked so well that the jailer put him in charge of the other prisoners. Joseph was a leader, even in jail.

One day Pharaoh became angry with two members of his staff—his baker and his butler, the man who served his wine. He put them into the jail where Joseph was in charge.

One night these men had strange dreams, and Joseph was able to tell them what their dreams meant. The baker was executed, but the butler was allowed to go back to the palace, which is exactly what Joseph had said would happen. Joseph said to the butler, "When you get out of prison, please ask the king to let me out too." Unfortunately, the man forgot all about asking Pharaoh to free Joseph.

TWO YEARS went by, and still Joseph was in prison. One night Pharaoh had a dream. First he saw seven fat, healthy cows come out of the Nile River. Then he saw seven thin, hungry-looking cows come and eat up the fat ones. The king woke up, but soon he went back to sleep and had another dream. This time he saw seven good ears of corn growing on a cornstalk. Then seven scrawny, withered ears grew on the same stalk and ate up the good ears. Again Pharaoh woke up and lay there worrying about his strange dreams.

He asked his wisest men what the dreams meant, but they didn't know. Just then the king's butler remembered Joseph and said, "O king, when I was in prison, I knew a young man who could tell what dreams meant."

Pharaoh sent for Joseph immediately and told him exactly what he had dreamed. He asked Joseph what it all meant. Joseph said, "I don't interpret dreams by myself; my God helps me understand them." Then Joseph said the dreams showed what would soon happen in Egypt. First there would be seven good years, with plenty of food. Then would come seven bad years, when the crops would dry up and the animals would go hungry.

Joseph suggested that the king put someone in charge of storing up corn during the good years so the animals and people would have enough to eat during the bad years. The king said, "Good! You are the right person for the job!"

R. Hook

11

Jacob's Sons Buy Grain

GENESIS 42

JOSEPH didn't have to go back to prison. Pharaoh had made him a great leader in Egypt. During the seven good years, Joseph made a rule that every farmer had to give some of his grain to the king. Joseph stored up all that extra grain in big buildings in the cities.

When the seven years of famine came, crops wouldn't grow. Soon the farmers had nothing to feed their animals or their families, and all the people and animals began to get hungry. They begged their king to help them. Pharaoh said, "I put Joseph in charge of famine relief. Ask him what to do." When the hungry people came to Joseph, he opened the barns and sold grain to them. Then they and their animals had enough to eat.

The famine was bad in the land of Canaan, too. Jacob's family desperately needed grain. Jacob said to his sons, "I have heard that the king of Egypt has plenty of grain stored up. Go there and buy some for us, or else we will starve." So all ten of Joseph's older brothers got on their donkeys and rode off toward Egypt—a trip that took many days.

When they got there, they asked where they could buy grain. "Go to the city and see our governor," was the answer. "He is in charge of the supplies."

FEBRUARY

12

Joseph's
Brothers
Don't
Recognize
Him
GENESIS 42

WHEN Jacob's sons found the governor, they didn't recognize him as their brother. Of course, he had grown older and had changed a lot since they had last seen him. Also, he was wearing Egyptian clothes and was an important government official. Joseph recognized them right away, and he was very glad to see them! But he pretended he didn't know them. They all bowed low to Joseph, and this was just what Joseph had dreamed when he was a boy.

Joseph asked sternly, "Where have you come from?"

They told him they were from Canaan and that they needed to buy food for their families.

"No, I can see you are spies, come to see how bad our famine is so you can bring an army against us," said Joseph, pretending to be very angry.

"Oh, no indeed. We are not spies. We are the sons of Jacob, a great man in Canaan, and we have another brother at home. There used to be twelve of us, but one brother died."

Joseph kept on pretending not to recognize them. He said, "There's one way I can find out whether you are telling the truth. I'll put you in jail, then I'll send one of you back to get your youngest brother." So he put all of them in jail for three days.

FEBRUARY

13

*Joseph
Sends for His
Favorite
Brother*

GENESIS 42

AFTER three days, Joseph let his brothers out of jail and talked to them again. "I've decided not to keep all of you in jail," he said. "I'll keep just one of you, and the rest shall return home with enough grain to keep your families from starving. But you must bring your youngest brother back here to me, so I'll know you have been truthful with me."

The men agreed to do this. They talked among themselves about the trouble they were having. "This is God's way of punishing us for the terrible thing we did to our brother Joseph," they said.

Reuben said, "Yes, don't you remember how I told you not to harm the boy—but you wouldn't listen to me. Now see what a mess we're in!"

They didn't realize that Joseph could understand their language and was listening to every word they said. When he heard them say they were sorry about the way they had treated him, he had to turn away for a moment to hide his tears. Then he told them he would keep Simeon as his prisoner until they brought their young brother from Canaan.

We know why Benjamin was Joseph's favorite brother. Not only were they the two youngest children, but they had the same mother—Rachel, who had died when Benjamin was born. Benjamin was Joseph's full brother instead of a half brother like the rest of the men, who had different mothers.

JOSEPH had his servants load bags of grain onto the brothers' donkeys. He told the servants to put the money his brothers had paid him into the bags but not to tell them it was there. The brothers started home. That night when they opened a bag to get some grain to eat, there was their money! This scared them because they didn't know how it got there.

When they got home and unloaded the grain, they found money in the top of every bag. This really frightened them. They told their father that the governor of Egypt would not let Simeon go unless they brought Benjamin back with them. Jacob said, "Oh, no! I lost Joseph a long time ago, and now Simeon is gone. You can't take Benjamin too."

But soon their grain was all gone. Jacob told his sons to go back and buy some more in Egypt. Judah said, "Father, we can't get any more grain unless we take Benjamin. Please let him go. I promise to take good care of him."

Finally Jacob agreed, and at last Joseph got to see Benjamin. He was so happy that he went into another room and secretly cried for joy.

He invited all the brothers to a dinner and seated them at the table according to their ages. They wondered how he could know so much about them. Joseph gave Benjamin five times as much food as he gave the others!

FEBRUARY

14

Joseph
Sees
Benjamin
GENESIS 43

JOSEPH asked the eleven brothers whether their aged father was still alive, and he was happy when they told him that Jacob was in good health.

Joseph had his servant fill all the men's bags with the grain they needed. And he had him put their money in the bags, as he had done before. Then he said, "Put my own silver cup on top of the grain in the youngest brother's bag, along with his money." And the servant did.

Very early the next morning the brothers started their trip home. They had not been gone long when Joseph told his servant to ride after them and accuse them of stealing his master's silver cup. "We don't know what you're talking about," they said. "We wouldn't think of doing such a thing. Go ahead and search us, and if you find it, we'll kill the one who stole it. Then the rest of us will go back and be the governor's slaves."

The servant said, "No, only the one who stole it will have to be a slave. The rest of you may go on home." So he searched through all the bags of grain, beginning with the oldest brother's and working his way down to Benjamin's. And sure enough, there it was in Benjamin's bag! Of course, they were all shocked. They rode back into the city with the servant and hurried to see Joseph about this problem.

WHEN Joseph saw his brothers bow-ing to him, he pretended that he thought Benjamin had stolen his silver cup. Judah spoke for the whole group. "What can we say? We are innocent but we can't prove it. This is a punishment for our past sins. We will all be your slaves."

"No, I don't want you all—just the one who had the cup in his bag."

"Oh, sir, we can't do that! We have told you about our elderly father. He lost the son he loved best. Now, if we go back without his youngest son, he will die of grief. Please let the boy go home with my other brothers, and I will stay in his place and be your slave forever."

Joseph saw how kind his brothers had become and how much they cared about their father. He couldn't stand to keep on fool-ing them about who he was. He sent all his servants away, and when he was alone with his brothers, he started to cry so hard that he could be heard all over the palace.

Then he said, "I am your brother Joseph! God spared my life so I could save you from dying in the famine. Yes, I really am Joseph! Now go back and tell my father I'm all right. Bring him here quickly because the famine is going to last another five years."

At first his brothers couldn't believe what he said, but finally they recognized him—and then what a happy reunion they had!

17

Jacob Moves to Egypt

GENESIS 45–46

PHARAOH soon heard that Joseph's brothers were there. He told them to take plenty of grain back to their father. Then he said, "Bring Jacob and all your wives and children to Egypt to live. I'll give you the best land in the whole country. Anything you want will be yours."

Joseph sent his brothers back with grain and many gifts for everyone. He gave each brother new clothes, but he gave Benjamin five changes of clothing and three hundred pieces of silver. The brothers returned to Jacob and told him the amazing news that his son Joseph—whom he thought had been killed by wild animals years before—was very much alive, and was a great ruler in Egypt. At first Jacob couldn't believe what they said. But when

he looked at all the gifts Joseph had sent, and his sons kept telling him about Joseph's life in Egypt, he began to realize it was true!

They packed up their belongings and started to move toward Egypt. Along the way, God spoke to Jacob. "Don't be afraid to go to Egypt. This is part of my plan. I'll be with you and your family there, and I will bring you back home again. And when you die, Joseph will be with you."

Because Jacob's new name was Israel, the Bible calls his family and descendants "Israelites" or "Israelis." Another name for them is "Jews." Jacob and sixty-six Israelis made the trip from Canaan to Egypt. Joseph and his two sons would make a total of seventy.

WHEN Jacob and his family got as far as Goshen, he sent Judah on ahead to let Joseph know they were coming. Joseph got into his chariot and hurried out to meet them. What a happy moment it was for Joseph and his father! They hugged each other and cried for a long time. Jacob said, "Now I will be able to die happy, because I have seen you again!"

Joseph took five of his brothers with him and introduced them to Pharaoh. "My brothers are all shepherds, and they have brought many flocks and herds from Canaan."

The king asked the men about their work. The brothers replied, "We have always been shepherds. We need good pastureland for our animals. May we live in Goshen, where our flocks will have plenty to eat?" One reason they wanted to live in Goshen was that people in most parts of Egypt didn't like shepherds and wouldn't welcome the Israelis.

Pharaoh said, "Yes, indeed. If Goshen is where you want to live, you are very welcome to make your home there. And if any of you are especially good shepherds, I will give you jobs taking care of my flocks, too." Then Joseph presented his father to the king. Pharaoh welcomed him kindly, and Jacob gave Pharaoh a special blessing.

So that is how Jacob's family got settled in Egypt. Joseph provided their food—the right amount for each household.

JACOB was 130 years old when he went to Egypt with his family. He lived there for seventeen years. Then he became very ill and would soon die. Joseph took his two sons, Manasseh and Ephraim, to see their grandfather. Jacob sat up in bed and blessed his grandsons. He surprised Joseph by saying that the younger boy would be greater than the older one.

Then Jacob called all of his sons to come and receive his blessing: The sons of Leah—Reuben, Simeon, Levi, Judah, Issachar, and Zebulun; the sons of Bilhah the slave-wife—Dan and Naphtali; the sons of Zilpah the slave-wife—Gad and Asher; and the sons of Rachel—Joseph and Benjamin. Jacob understood his sons and gave each one the blessing that was just right for him.

Finally Jacob asked his sons to take his body back to Canaan and bury him in the family burial cave. Then he lay down and died. Joseph cried with sorrow over his father's death. Pharaoh gave him permission to take Jacob's body to Canaan.

Joseph's brothers thought Joseph might turn against them, now that Jacob was no longer alive. But Joseph said he would never do that. He said, "You thought you were harming me when I was a boy, but God turned that harm into good for all of us."

Joseph lived in Egypt all the rest of his life. When he died, he asked that his bones be taken back to Canaan. Four hundred years went by before that happened. Meanwhile, his body was kept in a coffin there in Egypt.

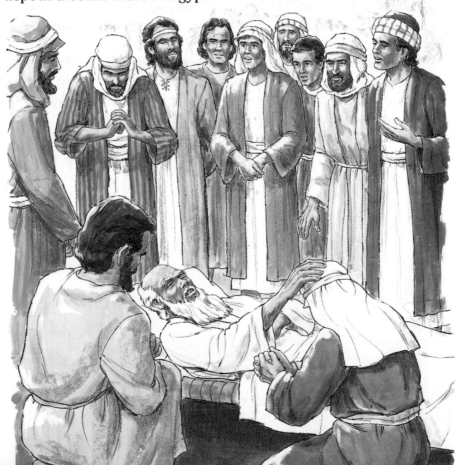

AFTER Jacob and Joseph had both died, their families kept growing. Many, many years went by, and their children and grandchildren and great-grandchildren were so many that it was almost impossible to count them. That is just what God had said would happen, when he had promised Abraham that his descendants would become a great nation.

After several hundred years, a Pharaoh was ruling who didn't know anything about Joseph, that great leader who had saved Egypt from starvation and had served the country so faithfully. This new Pharaoh was worried about what a large nation the people of Israel had become. He thought they might get to be so powerful that they would turn against Egypt and help Egypt's enemies.

Even though Pharaoh was a little bit afraid of the Israelis, he also worried that they might decide to go back where they had come from and he would not have them to work for him anymore. So he ordered all the Egyptians to make the Israelis their slaves, to work in their fields and build their houses. The Egyptians treated the people of Israel cruelly and made them work very hard. They had to toil long hours on the farms. The builders had to carry heavy loads of bricks. Because they were slaves, they were prisoners in the land of Egypt. But God had promised to take care of them, and he always keeps his promises. More and more Israeli children were born and the nation continued to grow.

21

The Baby in the Floating Basket

EXODUS 2

WHEN Pharaoh saw how the Israeli families were growing, he sent a terrible message to the midwives. They were the women who helped the Israeli mothers when their babies were born. Pharaoh told them to kill the baby boys as soon as they were born. The midwives knew this was wrong, so they disobeyed Pharaoh, and God blessed them because of it. Then Pharaoh told his own people to take the baby boys away from the Israelis and throw them into the Nile River. The babies would either drown or be eaten by crocodiles. This was a sad and frightening time for the people of Israel.

Once a man and his wife, both of the family of Levi, had a baby boy—their third child. Of course they loved their little son, so they hid him, hoping no Egyptian would find out about him and take him away to be killed. When the baby was three months old, he was getting too big to hide. His mother tried to think what to do to keep him safe.

She decided to weave a basket and make it waterproof by coating it with tar. Then she put her baby boy into the basket and hid it among the tall grasses at the edge of the river. There the little basket floated on the water. The baby's older sister, Miriam, hid nearby to watch the basket and see what would happen to her baby brother.

PHARAOH had a daughter who went out, with several of her servant girls, to bathe in the Nile River. As they were walking along the river bank, the princess noticed the basket floating among the reeds. She sent one of her maids to pick the basket up out of the water and bring it to her.

When she looked inside the basket, she was amazed to see a beautiful baby boy! She said, "Oh, this must be one of the babies of the Israeli slaves. Some mother has hidden him here so he won't be killed." The baby was probably hungry by this time, and he began to cry. This made the princess feel sorry for him, and she wanted to keep him from being harmed. "I'm going to adopt this baby as my own," she said.

Just then Miriam, the baby's big sister, decided it was safe to come out from her hiding place. She went to the princess and said, "Would you like me to get one of the Jewish women to nurse him while he is so small?"

Pharaoh's daughter said, "Yes, please do." So Miriam went home and got her mother. The princess said, "Take this baby home and nurse him for me. I'll pay you for taking care of him."

So the baby's mother got to take care of her own little boy until he was old enough to go to live with the princess and be her adopted son. The princess named the little boy Moses.

FEBRUARY

23

Moses Escapes

EXODUS 2

E VEN though Moses grew up in the royal family, he never forgot that he was really one of the people of Israel. He kept in touch with his own parents and with his brother and sister. One day when he went to visit his people, he happened to see an Egyptian hitting one of Moses' Israeli relatives. This made Moses terribly angry. He looked around to be sure no one was watching, then he killed the Egyptian and buried his body in the sand.

The next day he saw two Israeli men fighting with each other. He said to the one who was in the wrong, "What is the matter with you? Why are you hitting your own Israeli brother like that?"

The man answered him angrily, "That's none of your business! It's not your job to be my judge. Do you plan to kill me, the way you killed that Egyptian yesterday?"

When Moses heard that, he realized someone had seen his crime and that he would be in trouble. Sure enough, Pharaoh tried to find Moses so he could arrest him and execute him for murder. But Moses escaped in time. He hurried away to a place called Midian. There he saw some men being unkind to several young sisters who wanted to water their father's sheep at a well. Moses helped the girls. Their father, Reuel, was grateful to Moses, so he hired him to work as a shepherd. After awhile, Reuel let Moses marry his daughter Zipporah.

WHILE Moses was living in Midian, the people of Israel were suffering as the slaves of the Egyptians. They cried out to God for help, and he heard them. He remembered all his promises to Abraham, Isaac, and Jacob, and he decided it was time to rescue his people.

One day Moses was out in the fields, tending his father-in-law's sheep. Suddenly he noticed something strange. A bush was on fire, but it didn't burn up. He went closer to look at it, but then he heard a voice speaking to him out of the bush.

"Moses!" the voice said.

"Yes? Who is it?" Moses answered.

"I am God—the God of Abraham, Isaac, and Jacob. Don't come any closer. Take off your shoes, because this is holy ground." Moses was afraid to look at God, so he put his hands over his face.

"I have heard my people in Egypt crying for help," God said. "I want to rescue them and take them out of Egypt. I have chosen you to go to Pharaoh and tell him to let my people go. You are to lead them back to the land of promise."

"Oh, no!" Moses replied. "I would never be able to do that."

"You can do it, because I will be with you," God said.

Moses said, "If I tell the people you have sent me, they will ask, 'What is the name of this God?' What shall I say?"

God answered, "Tell them 'I AM' has sent you to them."

FEBRUARY

24

The Bush That Kept Burning

EXODUS 3

EVEN though God promised Moses he would help him with the people of Israel and with Pharaoh, Moses still was afraid to accept the job God wanted him to do. He thought the people would never believe him when he said God had talked to him. And certainly Pharaoh would not want to let the slave-nation of Israel leave Egypt.

Finally God showed Moses just how powerful a God he served. God asked Moses, "What do you have in your hand?" Because Moses was a shepherd, he was carrying a shepherd's rod. God said, "Throw the rod down on the ground."

Moses obeyed, and right away the rod turned into a live snake. Moses was afraid of it and jumped away from it. Then God said to him, "Grab the snake by the tail."

Carefully, Moses picked up the snake. Immediately it turned into a rod again. God said, "When you do that miracle, the people will believe I sent you. Now do another miracle. Put your hand inside your robe, next to your chest."

When Moses did this and took his hand out again, it was covered with the disease leprosy.

"Now do it again," God ordered. Moses did, and this time, when he took his hand out of his robe, the leprosy was all gone and his skin was healthy. "Now, if the people don't believe the first miracle, they may believe the second—then they will listen to you."

GOD told Moses one more thing he could do to prove he was God's messenger. He could take some water from the Nile River and pour it out on the ground, and it would turn to blood. But he was still afraid, and he found another excuse not to go. He said, "O Lord, I'm not a powerful speaker. I never have been." God said, "Listen, Moses. Who do you think made your mouth and all the other parts of your body? I did! And I can make you a good speaker if you will only trust me."

But Moses still didn't want to go. He said, "No, Lord. I think you should find someone else to do this job."

Then God became angry with him. He said, "All right, I'll send someone else with you. Your brother, Aaron, is a good speaker. I'll send him along to speak for you. You can tell him what to say, and he will deliver the messages. But I am going to give you the ability to talk well, too. Now take your shepherd's rod and get going!"

Moses got his father-in-law's permission to leave his work as a shepherd and go to visit his people. He took his wife and sons and started the trip. Before he left, God said, "The Pharaoh who wanted to kill you has died. Don't be afraid to go, because no one in Egypt wants to hurt you anymore."

R. Hook

27

*Pharaoh's
Hard
Heart*

EXODUS 4–5

GOD told Aaron to go and meet Moses at Mount Horeb. The two brothers were happy to see each other after so many years apart while Moses was in Midian. Moses told Aaron what God wanted them to do. He told him about the miraculous signs, too. Together they went to the leaders of the people of Israel and gave them God's message, and Moses showed them the wonderful miracles.

The elders of Israel did believe that God had sent Moses and Aaron. They were very thankful to hear that God had not forgotten them. They bowed down and worshiped the Lord.

Then came the harder part! Moses and Aaron had to go and tell Pharaoh what God had said. They said, "The Lord God of Israel has sent us to you with this message: 'Let my people go, so they can make a special trip out into the desert to worship me.' "

Pharaoh was not impressed. He said, "Oh, really? Who is this God, and why should I pay any attention to him? I am not going to let the Israelis stop their work to take a trip. Now get out of here!"

Then he ordered the supervisors to make the slaves work even harder than before. He said, "Don't give them any more straw. They must make just as many bricks as ever, but they must find their own straw to make the bricks hold together. We'll keep them so busy they won't have time to think about trips to the desert!"

THE Israeli slaves suffered greatly as their cruel masters
made them work harder and harder. They couldn't gather the
straw they needed and still keep making as many bricks as they
had when their masters furnished the straw. As the work slowed
down, the masters beat them and said they were just lazy.

The slaves blamed Moses and Aaron. "You got us into this
mess," they said angrily. "Everything is much worse for us since
you went to Pharaoh and asked him to let us go. You've made
Pharaoh hate us, and if he kills us all, it will be your fault!"

Moses talked to the Lord about this. "I thought you were going
to rescue your people," he said. "But they are in worse trouble
than before. I wish you hadn't gotten me into this."

The Lord told Moses again that if he would just be patient, he
would see how well God would take care of the Israelis. God said,
"Tell the people not to give up hope." Then he said they should
try again with Pharaoh.

So Moses went back to Pharaoh and asked again that the
slaves be released. That time Aaron threw down his rod and it

became a snake. But when
Pharaoh called his magi-
cians, they were
able to do the
same miracle.
Then
something
exciting
happened:
Aaron's
snake swal-
lowed up all
the magi-
cians'
snakes!
Still
Pharaoh
was too
stub-
born
to let
the
slaves
go.

1

Big Trouble for Egypt

EXODUS 7–8

AGAIN God told Moses to speak to Pharaoh, so Moses met him the next morning by the river. Moses repeated his message from God, but Pharaoh said no. Then the Lord told Aaron to point his rod over the river. Aaron did this and then struck the water. At that very moment all the water in the river—and all the other water in Egypt—changed into blood.

The fish all died, and the people of Egypt had no clean water to drink. This went on for seven days. The only way they could get any water was to dig holes in the ground. Pharaoh's magicians imitated the miracle, but they could only make more blood out of water. They could not make fresh water out of the dirty water. Do you think this terrible experience made Pharaoh change his mind? No, he still refused to let the people go.

The next week Aaron pointed his rod again, and thousands of frogs appeared. They filled the whole country. They got into the Egyptians' homes, their food, their beds—everywhere! Again the king's magicians tried to do something, but they could only make more frogs! Pharaoh begged Moses and Aaron to get rid of the frogs. "If you do," he said, "I will let the people go to the desert."

"When shall I do this?" Moses asked.

"Tomorrow," Pharaoh answered.

So the next day all the frogs died. Smelly dead frogs were everywhere. But Pharaoh changed his mind and broke his promise to Moses.

GOD used Moses and Aaron to bring more troubles to Egypt. God kept giving Pharaoh chances to let the people go. Each time, Pharaoh said he would, then at the last moment he would break his word.

God made the dust turn into very unpleasant insects called lice. They got all over the people and made them miserable. Then swarms of flies came down upon the Egyptians. The next punishment was a disease that killed the flocks and herds of animals.

Then God told Moses to throw ashes into the air. As the ashes settled onto people's skin, awful sores called boils broke out all over them. Next he sent a violent storm, with thunder, lightning, and hailstones that destroyed the crops and hurt the people.

Pharaoh tried to make a deal with Moses to let only the men go and leave the women and children in Egypt. But Moses wouldn't agree. That time God sent a great swarm of locusts that flew in and ate up every plant, tree, and blade of grass. The king said he would let the people go if Moses got rid of the locusts. But he didn't keep that promise either.

Next God sent a terrible, thick darkness over Egypt. For three days people were afraid to move, because they couldn't see a thing. None of these bad things happened in Goshen, where the Israelis lived. Pharaoh said, "Take the people, but leave the animals behind." But Moses said that wasn't what God had told them to do. So again Pharaoh refused to let them go.

MARCH

2

Frightening Punishments

EXODUS 8–10

FINALLY God said to Moses, "Now you will see how I will deal with Pharaoh. I'm going to send one final, dreadful punishment. When it is over, he will be begging you to take my people and go. But first, tell my people to ask their Egyptian friends and neighbors to give them pieces of gold and silver jewelry." Although Pharaoh had treated the Israelis so badly, most of the people of Egypt liked them and greatly respected Moses, their leader.

So Moses went to Pharaoh one more time and said, "This is what God is going to do to you and your people. He is going to come in the middle of the night, and the firstborn son in every home will die. Your own son will die, Pharaoh, along with all the other firstborn. Every Egyptian family will be in deep sorrow. But no Israeli child shall die. You will soon see that the Lord God thinks differently about his own people than he does about your people. The Israelis are very special to God, and he will take care of them. All your government officials will be begging us to leave the country. Then I will take my people and go."

By this time Moses' face was red with anger. He turned and hurried out of the palace. He already knew that Pharaoh would not listen to him. God had hardened the king's heart so he could show everyone his own power and glory.

MOSES and Aaron's next job was to tell the people of Israel what God wanted them to do. They had to get ready for the night when God would visit the homes of the Egyptians and kill the firstborn sons. Here are the instructions God gave them:

1. Each family should kill a perfect, one-year-old lamb or baby goat.

2. They should use a certain weed as a brush and paint some of the lamb's blood on each side and over the top of their front door.

3. Then they should roast the lamb and eat it, along with bitter-tasting herbs and hard bread made without yeast.

4. They must eat all of it that night and not save any for the next day.

5. While they ate it, they were to wear their traveling clothes and their sandals and carry a walking stick.

Then God made a wonderful promise to his people. He said, "When I go through the land, killing the firstborn of the Egyptians, I will see the spots of blood on your doors. That will show me that you have obeyed my instructions, and I will pass over your homes and not kill your firstborn sons."

He said that from then on, they were to do this ceremony on a certain day every year in memory of his goodness to them. The annual celebration should be called "the Lord's Passover," because he had passed over their homes when he saw the blood on the doors.

MARCH

5

Pharaoh Lets the People Go

EXODUS 12

THE PEOPLE of Israel followed all the instructions God gave them. At midnight everything happened just the way God had said it would. The Lord passed through the nation of Egypt, and the firstborn in every family died—from Pharaoh's oldest son to the first son of the lowest prisoner in the jail. Even among the animals, the firstborn cattle died.

All the Egyptian people, including Pharaoh and his government leaders, got up in the middle of the night to see what had happened. They were all heartbroken to find that in every Egyptian home, someone had died. The sound of their crying filled the whole nation.

Pharaoh knew this tragedy had happened because he had not listened to the warnings of Moses and Aaron. Quickly he called them to his court and said, "Hurry and leave my country! Take all your families and all your flocks and herds of animals. Get out quickly and worship your God any way you want to. But before you go, please bless me."

The Israelis asked their Egyptian friends and neighbors for gold and silver jewelry, and the Egyptians gladly gave it to them. Then the people of Israel packed up all their things and lined up to start their trip—600,000 men, plus all the women and children. Do you remember how many people Jacob (or Israel) brought to Egypt with him 430 years before? Yes, about seventy. God had certainly kept his promise to make them grow into a great nation.

LED by
Moses and Aaron, the
people of Israel started their long journey back to Canaan, the
Land of Promise. As they had promised Joseph many years
before, they took his bones with them from Egypt. The Lord told
Moses to have the people camp by the sea. He said, "Pharaoh is
going to change his mind again and chase your people. I will
show everyone how great I am. I will protect you from Pharaoh's
army as they chase you." Moses obeyed, and the people made
camp by the sea.

When Pharaoh heard that the people of Israel had really left
and that they did not intend to return, he was sorry he had let
them go. He said, "We have let a lot of valuable workers get away.
We must get them back." He called together all his army,
hundreds of chariots with their drivers, and many cavalry
soldiers with their horses. And this great military force chased
the Israelis.

When the people saw the Egyptians coming, they were angry
with Moses for putting them in danger. But Moses said, "Don't
worry; God will rescue us." And he stood by the sea and raised
his rod over the water. Then God divided the water, opening up
a path right through the sea. He also brought a cloud down
around the Israelis so Pharaoh's soldiers couldn't find them. The
people of Israel escaped from Pharaoh by walking across the sea
on the dry path God had made.

MARCH
7
*Pharaoh's
Soldiers
Drown*
EXODUS 14–15

PHARAOH'S huge army was not far behind the people of
Israel. The soldiers were able to see the path on which the
Israelis had started to cross the sea, so they followed them. The
chariots and horsemen went between the great walls of water
that were piled up on each side of the path. Then God slowed
them down by sending problems. Wheels started falling off their
chariots, so that they dragged along the ground. The soldiers
became frightened because they could see God was for the
Israelis and against the Egyptians.

As soon as the last person in Moses' group was safely across
the sea, God told Moses to raise his rod over the water again. By
this time all the Egyptian soldiers and horsemen and chariots
were crowded together on the path through the sea. As Moses
lifted his rod over the sea, the waters on each side came crashing
down on the path. The whole Egyptian army drowned. Not one
single soldier escaped. As the Israelis watched from the other
side, they could see the bodies of their enemies washed up on
the shore.

Then the people of Israel realized how good God had been to
them. They had great love and respect for him and also for his
servant Moses. Moses led them in singing a beautiful song of
praise to the Lord. Here are some of the words they sang: "The
Lord is my strength, my song, and my salvation. He is my God
and I will praise him."

As the people traveled, they forgot how good God had been to them. They got thirsty, but the only water they could find was bitter. They complained to Moses about it, and he asked God what to do. God said he should throw a tree into the bitter water. Instantly the water became good to drink. But later, when they were hungry, they blamed Moses. They grumbled, "At least in Egypt we had enough to eat."

When God heard this, he said to Moses, "I am going to send food for all the people. They will have meat in the evening and bread in the morning. Then they will remember that I am the Lord their God."

That evening a large number of birds called quail flew into the camp, so the people had all the meat they could eat. The next morning, after the dew had dried up, the ground was covered with thin white flakes that looked a little like bread. The people asked, "What is it?" In their language, the word for "what is it" was manna, so that is what we call that special food God sent.

The Lord told Moses, "Every morning each family should gather a certain amount—just what they need for one day. Don't try to save it for the next day, or it will spoil. On the sixth day, pick up enough for two days, and it won't spoil. I won't send any food on the Sabbath because it is a special, holy day."

MARCH

9

Water from a Rock

EXODUS 17

THE MANNA kept coming each morning, except on the
Sabbath, for forty years—all the time that the people of Israel
were traveling on their way back to Canaan. Each morning it was
a reminder of God's loving care.

When they came to a place called Rephidim, they were near
Mount Horeb. That was where Moses had seen the bush burning
and had heard God telling him to get his people out of Egypt.
The people had used up all the water they were carrying. They
were getting very thirsty, but no one could find any water. They
became angry with Moses and said, "It's all your fault. You took
us away from Egypt and brought us to this desert place. Now we
are all going to die without water."

Moses asked God what he should do. "I think they are going
to throw stones at me and kill me if I don't get water for them."

God told Moses to take the people to Mount Horeb. "Go to the
rock I will show you. Then take your rod—that same rod with
which you struck the Nile River—and hit the rock. Immediately,
water will pour out." Moses did exactly what God told him to do,
and water flowed from the rock. There was plenty for all the
people to drink.

WHILE the people were still at Rephidim, an army from Amalek attacked them. They had to fight back to protect themselves and their property. Moses chose a very brave man named Joshua to lead Israel's army. He said, "Joshua, choose the fighting men you need and go out to fight against the Amalekites. I will stand on a hill and watch. Aaron and Hur will be with me. I'll hold up my rod and point it out over the army. As long as I hold it there, God will give you and your soldiers a victory."

This worked fine. While Moses held the rod up, the people of Israel defeated the Amalekites. But sometimes his arm got so tired he had to lower the rod to his side. At those times, the Amalekites started to win the battle.

Aaron and Hur thought of a way to help Moses. They rolled a big rock over to him and he sat on it. They stood one on each side of Moses, and held up his arms, so that the rod was always pointing out over the battlefield. And they stayed there all day. Finally, when the sun went down, the battle was over, and the army of the people of Israel had won.

God told Moses he would someday destroy all the people of Amalek. Then Moses built an altar and named it "The Lord is my battle flag." He said, "God will always be at war against the Amalekites."

MARCH

10

Joshua Leads the Army

EXODUS 17–18

11

God Calls Moses to the Mountain

EXODUS 19

AFTER the war with the Amalekites, the people of Israel continued to travel. About three months after they left Egypt, they came to Mount Sinai, and there God told them to camp for awhile. He told Moses to climb up into the mountain to talk with him.

God said, "Tell the people how much I love them. Remind them how I rescued them from Egypt and have taken care of them along the journey. Among all the people in the whole world, they will always be my special servants—a holy nation. Go back and tell them these things."

So Moses gave the people God's message. They all promised to obey God and be his special people. Then God told Moses that all the people must prepare themselves for a time when God would send them important instructions and rules. They must wash their clothing, and they must be very careful not to sin. They must get their hearts ready to hear what God would tell them. They would hear a trumpet call, and they would know that God was ready to speak to them through Moses. Only Moses was allowed to go up into the mountain. Anyone else who went up would die.

The trumpet sounded and smoke rose from the mountain. The mountain began to shake and the trumpet call got louder. All the people stood around the foot of the mountain while Moses climbed up to meet God.

12

Command-ments about Loving God

EXODUS 20

GOD met Moses up there on Mount Sinai and told him how he wanted the people of Israel to live. First he gave Moses ten important rules that we call the Ten Commandments. The first four of those rules tell how men and women and children should feel about God himself.

1. *I am Jehovah your God. You shall not worship any other god.*
   Our God made us and loves us, and he wants us to love and worship him. This commandment warns us not to believe in any false gods as some people do.

2. *You shall not bow down and worship any kind of idol.*
   When this commandment mentions idols, it means more than just statues of wood or stone or plaster. Each of us can easily begin to love something more than we love God. It might be money or nice clothes or special friends. These things can get to be like idols. God says to worship only him.

3. *You shall not take the name of God in vain.*
   This means that when we use God's name we should do it respectfully, because he is a holy God. We must not swear or say God's name in a careless or irreverent way.

4. *You shall keep the Sabbath as a holy day.*
   God created everything in six days, and on the seventh day he rested and didn't do any work. He wants us to keep one day as a special day in which we worship him and don't do our usual work.

MARCH
13
*Command-
ments about
Loving
Others*
EXODUS 20

THE REST of the commandments tell us how we should behave toward other people.

5. *Honor your father and your mother.*
   God says we must respect our parents and obey them willingly. God promised long life to those who keep this commandment.

6. *You shall not commit murder.*
   Murder is always wrong. In the New Testament the Lord also warned us that hating others and wishing they were dead is like having murder in our hearts.

7. *You shall not commit adultery.*
   This commandment is about sexual sin. When a man and a woman sleep together when they are not married to each other, that is adultery. We must also keep our thoughts and words pure.

8. *You shall not steal.*
   We must never take anything that belongs to someone else and keep it for our own. If we have done this, we must give it back or pay for it.

9. *You shall not tell lies.*
   We must be very sure everything we say is exactly true and that we don't hide the truth by keeping quiet when we should speak.

10. *You shall not covet anything that belongs to your neighbor.*
   Coveting is wishing we could have things that belong to other people. God wants us to be content with what he has given us.

After giving Moses the Ten Commandments, God told him more than six hundred more rules he wanted the people of Israel to obey—rules about getting along well with one another, being clean and healthy, taking care of property, and keeping their lives pure so they could please God.

WHEN Moses gave the people all God's rules, they promised to obey. Then God called Moses back to the mountain so he could give him pieces of stone with the Ten Commandments carved on them. This time Moses took Joshua with him, and they were on the mountain for forty days and nights.

God told Moses he wanted the people to build a special place in which to worship him. He described it to Moses very carefully and even gave him a pattern to follow. Because the people were traveling, the building had to be easy to move, so God said it must be a tent that could be taken apart and carried. This building was to be called the Tabernacle.

Then God described the kind of furniture that should go into the Tabernacle. One of the most important pieces would be the Ark of the Covenant—not the kind of ark that is a boat like the one Noah made, but a beautiful chest made of wood and then covered with gold. The cover of the chest, or Ark, would be called the Mercy Seat. They were also to make a table, a lampstand with seven lamps, and altars on which offerings would be made and incense burned.

God gave Moses a list of the materials he would need and told him to ask the people to provide the different materials as a gift to God. Moses would need gold, silver, bronze, beautiful cloth, wood, oil, spices, incense, and jewels.

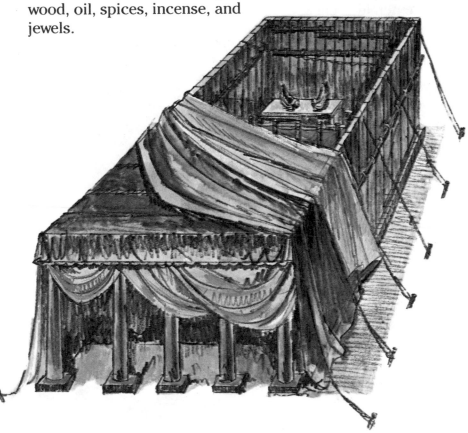

GOD appointed Aaron and his family to be in charge of the worship that would take place in the Tabernacle. Aaron would be the High Priest, and his four sons would help him. It would be the priests' job to sacrifice the animals the people of Israel brought as offerings to God.

God wanted the priests to have special clothing to show they had been especially chosen for their work. Aaron's clothes would be the finest. He would wear an embroidered robe covered by a blue coat. Around the hem of the coat would be bells and blue, purple, and scarlet decorations in the shape of pomegranates. Over the coat he was to wear a cloth vest, called an ephod, which had twelve kinds of jewels sewn on the front. The jewels should be a ruby, a topaz, an emerald, a carbuncle, a sapphire, a diamond, an amber, an agate, an amethyst, an onyx, a beryl, and a jasper. Each jewel represented one of the tribes of Israel.

Aaron was to wear special shirts and undergarments. On his head he should wear a linen turban that had a gold plate on the front of it, with the words "Holiness to the Lord."

Aaron's sons were also to wear robes, sashes, and turbans. God told Moses to have a special dedication ceremony for the priests. He was to put oil on their heads and pray that they would be good priests and leaders of worship.

GOD gave Moses more details about the way he was to dedicate Aaron and his sons for the priesthood in the Tabernacle. He was to prepare three kinds of bread, made without yeast, and bring a young bull and two rams that were perfect. He was to

have Aaron and his sons bathe at the entrance of the Tabernacle. Then Moses should dress them in the clothing God had described. He should pour oil on Aaron's head. That was a ceremony people used then to show that a person was chosen for a very special work for God.

Next they should offer first the young bull and then the rams as offerings to God. They were to do certain things with the different parts of the animals' bodies, following God's detailed instructions. The meat and the bread were symbols or signs of obedience, setting Aaron and his sons apart as different from all other people. They were priests in the house of God—the Tabernacle.

This ceremony was to be repeated every day for seven days. As offerings were made on the altar, the altar was dedicated to God and became a holy place of offering and worship. God said that if all these instructions were followed carefully, he would always live among the people of Israel and be the Lord their God. That was the very reason he had brought them out of Egypt.

Moses was still up on Mount Sinai all this time that God was telling him about the Tabernacle and the priests. Finally, God gave Moses the tablets of stone on which God himself had written the Ten Commandments. The people had been waiting down at the foot of the mountain for more than a month. They were becoming very impatient and beginning to wonder if Moses was ever going to come back.

Some of them went to Aaron and said, "Something must have happened to Moses. Now we don't have anyone to tell us what God says. Please make us a new god to take care of us and lead us on our journey." Already they seemed to forget that they had recently promised to obey the commandment against worshiping any false god or idol.

Aaron was disobedient too. He agreed to do this terrible thing they asked. He said, "Give me your gold jewelry." They did, and he melted it all down and formed it into the shape of a calf. The people worshiped the calf-idol—then they had a feast and got drunk. They committed sexual sins, breaking another of God's commandments that they had promised to obey—the one about adultery.

Of course, God was able to see everything they were doing. He spoke to Moses about it and said, "Hurry down the mountain and see what your people are doing. They are worshiping an idol and are breaking many of my laws. I feel like destroying all of them because of their sin."

WHEN God threatened to destroy his people, Moses answered, "Oh, no, Lord! Please don't do that. If you do, the Egyptians will hear about it. They will say you tricked the Israelis into leaving Egypt just so you could wipe them out. Remember the promise you made to Abraham, Isaac, and Jacob—that you would make them a great nation and would give them the land of Canaan for their own? Please forgive the people and bless them as you promised."

God listened to Moses and changed his mind about destroying his chosen people. Moses went on down the mountain, carrying the stone tablets on which the Ten Commandments were written. As he got close to the camp, he heard the sound of the wild party the people were having. When he saw what they were doing, he was terribly angry with them. He threw the stone tablets down on the ground so hard that they broke.

Then he melted the gold calf-idol. When the gold had hardened, he ground it into powder. He put the powder into the water and made the people drink it.

Moses was angry with Aaron, too, because he had made the idol for the people. Aaron tried to make excuses. He said, "The people insisted I give them a new god. I put the gold into the fire and the idol just happened to come out." Of course, that wasn't true. God punished the people for their sin of disobedience, and many of them died.

MARCH

18

Moses Destroys the Idol

EXODUS 32

MARCH

19

*New
Tablets
and a New
Agreement*

EXODUS 33–34

GOD was so disappointed in his people that he said he wouldn't go with them into the Promised Land. They would have to get along without him. But Moses begged the Lord to change his mind. He said, "If you are not with us, how will all the people of the world know we are special to you? If you don't go with me as I lead the people, I don't think I can do it!"

God replied, "All right. You have pleased me, and I think of you as my friend. Because you ask it, I will go with you to Canaan. Now, prepare two more tablets of stone, just like the ones you broke. Bring them up to the mountain tomorrow."

Moses obeyed, and the next day he went alone to the mountain, taking the new tablets. God met him there and made a new covenant, or agreement, with him. He said that if the people would start obeying him faithfully, he would do wonderful things for them. He told Moses not to make any peace treaties with their enemies in Canaan, because God himself would see that they were destroyed.

God also told Moses more about how the people should worship and about feasts they should have to celebrate the goodness of God. Moses promised to keep the agreement. Then God wrote the commandments again. Moses went down the mountain and joined his people. Because he had been with God, his face was shining, but he didn't even realize it.

NOW it was time to start to build the Tabernacle according to the instructions God had given Moses during the forty days he was on Mount Sinai. Moses invited all the people to bring gifts that could be used in the building and furnishing. The people responded very eagerly, bringing earrings, bracelets, and precious jewels. They gave valuable oil for the lamps and beautiful cloth for the various hangings. Finally they had brought so much that Moses had to tell them to stop! Everything that went into the building and furnishing of the Tabernacle was the very best and most beautiful that could be found or made. They wanted God's house of worship to be perfect.

Certain workmen were chosen to make the furniture. A skillful workman named Bezaleel made the Ark of the Covenant—the wooden box covered with gold—with its gold cover, called the Mercy Seat. This was the most important piece of furniture in the Tabernacle because it was a symbol of God's presence with his people.

The workmen made the table, the altars, the lampstand and the lamps, and all the cloth hangings. Moses inspected everything to be sure it all was exactly like the pattern God had given him. Then God said it was ready to be put together and used.

M OSES supervised the workers as they put the Tabernacle together. They set up the Ark, into which Moses had put the tablets with the Ten Commandments. Then they put a curtain around it, because it was to be the Holy of Holies, a place where only the High Priest could ever go. They put all the other pieces of furniture exactly where God had said they should go. Around the courtyard they hung the cloth curtains on poles, to enclose the whole Tabernacle area.

Ever since they had left Egypt, the people of Israel had always been able to see a great pillar of cloud in front of them every day, leading them along. At night the cloud glowed red, as if it were on fire, so it could be seen in the dark. Now this great cloud came and covered the Tabernacle.

From then on, during the rest of their journey to Canaan, whenever the cloud lifted up and moved, the people knew they should pack up the Tabernacle and move along with it. When the cloud stayed in the same place, the people stayed too.

When the Tabernacle was finished and everything was in place, God's glory filled the place. It was so bright that Moses couldn't even go into the Tabernacle.

GOD told his people just how they should worship him. Aaron and his four sons were to be leaders in this worship. The clothing the priests wore and everything they did had a special meaning.

God said that when the priests and the people followed his instructions, his glory would appear to them and he would accept their offerings. The priests were to build a wood fire on the altar to burn up their sacrifices. But if the people or the priests did not follow God's rules, God would not accept their sacrifices and he would punish them.

One thing the priests had to do was to put some incense in special cups on top of fire they got from the altar. At first everything went well. The people brought their sacrifices, and the priests offered them before the Lord. God sent his glory upon them, even sending fire from heaven to burn up the sacrifice. All the people shouted for joy and fell down on their faces before God.

But soon Nadab and Abihu, two of Aaron's sons, got ideas of their own about how they wanted to do things. They didn't follow the rules but put a different kind of fire in their incense cups. Immediately God punished their disobedience by sending fire from heaven to kill them. God told Aaron and his other two sons not to show any grief, because Nadab and Abihu had been fairly punished for their sin.

GOD was interested not only in his people's spiritual lives and their worship in the Tabernacle. He also cared about their health, so he made special rules about what they should eat. Those rules included lists of many kinds of animals, fish, and birds. The ones they had permission to eat were called "clean," and those they were forbidden to eat were called "unclean."

Animals: The main rule was that they should eat only those animals that chewed a cud and had divided hooves. Some animals that might have tasted all right were still called unclean, because they didn't meet both of those requirements. For instance, although pigs have divided hooves, they are called unclean because they don't chew a cud.

Fish: Fish that had both fins and scales were clean; those that had smooth skins or no fins were unclean.

Birds: God gave them a list of the birds they were not to eat. We see from that list that the unclean ones were what we call "raptors," or birds of prey. Some of those are eagles, vultures, and hawks.

Insects: Insects that fly, crawl, or walk were declared unclean. Those that jump—like grasshoppers—were clean.

Small animals: Little animals that moved around on the ground were all called unclean—creatures like lizards, rats, and reptiles.

Not only were the Israelis not to eat all the unclean creatures, but they were told not even to touch their dead bodies. God wanted to keep all disease and infection out of the Israeli camp.

AFTER giving many more instructions about keeping healthy, God then told Moses just what Aaron, the High Priest, should do in the Tabernacle. One of his most wonderful privileges was that he was the only person who was allowed to go into the inner room of the Tabernacle, where the Ark of the Covenant was kept. This was called the Most Holy Place. Even Aaron could go in only once each year, on the Day of Atonement.

First he had to bathe himself carefully and put on simple white clothing. He had to make an animal sacrifice for his own sins and the sins of his family. Only then could he go into the Most Holy Place.

MARCH

24

Aaron's
Special
Work
LEVITICUS 16

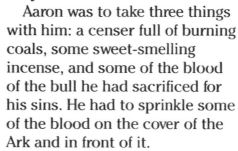

Aaron was to take three things with him: a censer full of burning coals, some sweet-smelling incense, and some of the blood of the bull he had sacrificed for his sins. He had to sprinkle some of the blood on the cover of the Ark and in front of it.

Then he made a sacrifice for the sins of all the people of Israel and put some of that blood on the Mercy Seat also. The important things to remember about this ceremony were that a blood offering had to be made and that only the High Priest could do it.

While all these things were happening, the people of Israel were to stop their work and spend the day thinking about how sorry they were for their sins. If they were truly sorry, they would be forgiven.

GOD wanted his people to be like himself. Since God is fair, kind, loving, honest, pure, and holy, that is how his people were to be also. God helped them understand how to be like that; he gave them instructions about getting along with other people and keeping both their hearts and their actions pure.

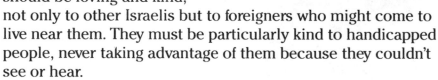

For instance, he taught them to leave some of their grain and grapes in the fields so poor people could have some too. He said they should never steal or tell lies. If they owed other people money, they should pay it as soon as possible. They should be loving and kind, not only to other Israelis but to foreigners who might come to live near them. They must be particularly kind to handicapped people, never taking advantage of them because they couldn't see or hear.

God said, "You must never, never imitate the terrible things your ungodly neighbors do, especially when they worship their false gods by sacrificing their own children." And he said not to be like those evil people who had wrong kinds of sexual relationships with others.

He made it very clear that his people were to be different from other people in the world, because they were his chosen ones— chosen to show God's character and his glory to everyone they met. So he set very high standards for them and expected them to obey him perfectly.

JUST as we have special religious holidays now—such as Christmas, Good Friday, and Easter—so the people of Israel had special holidays that God told them to observe. Of course, the one they had most often was the Sabbath, the day on which they didn't do any work, but rested and gathered together for worship. God had told them to do this in memory of the way he rested after creating the world and everything in it.

Three of their most important holidays were these:

1. *The Passover.* This was to remind them of how God passed over the homes of his people on that terrible night when he killed the firstborn children of the Egyptians and helped his people escape from slavery in Egypt.

2. *The Harvest Festival.* This was a day of thanksgiving after all the crops had been gathered into the barns and storehouses. The people were to praise God for sending rain and sunshine on their farms and gardens.

3. *The Tabernacle Festival.* This was a reminder to God's people of the way they were living as they traveled from Egypt to Canaan, the land of promise. For a whole week they were to move out of their regular houses and live in huts formed from tree branches woven together.

At each of these celebrations, the people were to bring gifts to God—olive oil for the lamps in the Tabernacle and fresh bread to put on the gold table.

JUST as the people of Israel observed a Sabbath day of rest
every week, so they also had a Sabbath year every seven years.
That year they didn't plant any crops but let the land rest completely. And the people rested from their work all through that
year. After seven of those Sabbath years had gone by—that is, a
total of forty-nine years—God gave them a great year of special
celebration on the fiftieth year. It was called the Year of Jubilee.

During that year the people didn't grow crops. Still, they had
plenty to eat, because they had been able to save food from the
year before, when their crops were better than usual. Also, if they
had had to sell any of their land to pay their debts, on the Year
of Jubilee they would get their land back. That was a reminder
to them that all the land really belonged to God and was theirs
only as his gift.

The Israelites were told to be especially kind to each other
and to foreigners among them during that year. God said, "Don't
cheat anyone or take advantage of other people. If any of your
fellow Israelis have become your slaves because they owed you
money, you must let them go free." Of course, all the people were
very glad when it was time for a Year of Jubilee, because so
many good things happened to them during that year!

THE PEOPLE of Israel stayed near Mount Sinai for a long time. Finally—more than a year after they had left Egypt—the time came for them to move on. God told Moses and Aaron to count all the people who could be soldiers, and the total was 603,550! That number included men from every tribe except the Levites. The Levites had the special job of looking after the Tabernacle and were not to fight in wars.

The Levites had to take the Tabernacle apart when it was time to move. They also had to carry the different parts of it as they were traveling. Most of the parts of the Tabernacle were carried in wagons, but several pieces had to be carried on the shoulders of Levites—the Ark, the lampstand, and the gold and bronze altars. When the Cloud stopped and the people stopped to make camp, the Levites put the Tabernacle together again.

They also were the ones who made all the sacrifices when the people brought animals as their offerings to God. They carried wood to burn and water for washing—and then they had to carry the ashes away from the altars after the sacrifices were burned.

When Moses and Aaron counted the people in the tribe of Levi, they found there were 8,580 of them. All of them were to be workers in the Tabernacle, helping the rest of the Israelis worship the Lord God. It was a great privilege to be a Levite and work in the Tabernacle.

MARCH

28

The Levites Work in the Tabernacle

NUMBERS 1–4

THE PEOPLE left Mount Sinai and traveled for three days. Then the Cloud stopped and the people camped. Right away they started complaining to Moses.

"We haven't had a decent meal since we left Egypt. Oh, the food was so good there—meat and fish and such good vegetables! But now all we have is this manna. It isn't nearly as good, and we're getting so tired of it!"

The Lord heard them grumbling, and this made him angry with them; after all, he had rescued them from terrible trouble and had led them safely away from their cruel masters. Moses was discouraged by his people's bad attitude, too. He said, "Lord, why did you give me this awful job of leading such a stubborn, ungrateful group of people? If they are going to behave like this, I'd rather die right now!"

God said that he would appoint seventy helpers for Moses so he wouldn't have to do everything himself. Then God told Moses that he would send meat to the people for a whole month.

"They will have all they can eat; in fact, they will get so tired of it that they will hate the sight of it! That will teach them not to complain all the time."

He sent a great flock of quail that flew into the camp, blown along by a strong wind from the ocean. The people had plenty of meat, but some of them got sick and died as a punishment for their complaining.

IT WAS bad enough when the people of Israel complained about what Moses did, but worse yet, his own brother and sister began to criticize him. Although Moses was a very humble man, Miriam and Aaron were jealous of his position of leadership, and they talked against him. "Is Moses the only one who can speak for God? Why couldn't he speak through us, too?" And they also criticized him because he had married a woman who wasn't an Israeli.

When the Lord heard this, he called Moses, Aaron, and Miriam to the door of the Tabernacle, and he met them there, surrounded by the Cloud. He said to Aaron and Miriam, "Moses is the one I chose for this task, and you should be afraid to criticize him. I speak directly to him, face to face."

Then God left, very angry with Aaron and Miriam. As the Cloud moved away, Miriam's skin suddenly became white with the disease of leprosy. When Aaron saw that, he told Moses he was

sorry about criticizing him, and he begged him not to let Miriam have the terrible disease of leprosy. Of course, Moses didn't want his sister to have leprosy either, so he begged God to heal her.

God said that she must stay outside the camp for seven days, and then she would be healed and could come back. She and Aaron had learned a lesson the hard way.

THE PEOPLE of Israel had now come close to the borders of Canaan, the Promised Land. God said to Moses, "Choose one man from each of the twelve tribes and send that group into Canaan to look it over carefully. Tell them to check out the people to see whether they are many and powerful, and whether the cities are strongly protected. Also find out whether the land is good for farming and whether there are lots of trees. Tell the spies to bring back some samples of the fruit of the land."

The twelve spies were gone for forty days. They explored various parts of Canaan and brought back some grapes from the Valley of Eshcol. One bunch of grapes was so large that two men had to carry it on a pole that rested on their shoulders. They also brought back pomegranates and figs, showing what good land it was.

When the spies returned, most of them said, "Yes, it is a fertile and beautiful land. See what wonderful fruit we brought back as samples. But the people who live there are very large and fierce. We really can't win if we try to drive them out of the land."

But two of the spies didn't agree. Caleb and Joshua said, "God has promised to give us this land, so we don't need to be afraid of the huge people. It's a wonderful country, and we should march right in and start to live there. We can trust God!"

WELL, when the Israelis heard both sides of the spies' report, they chose to believe the ten who thought they would be wiped out if they fought with the fierce tribes in Canaan. Once more they started to complain about Moses' and Aaron's leadership. They shouted to each other, "If only we had stayed in Egypt or had died in the wilderness! We were better off in Egypt. Let's choose a new leader who will take us back."

Again Caleb and Joshua tried to remind them of God's promise of victory, but the people wouldn't listen. Then, suddenly, the glory of God appeared in the camp, and God spoke to Moses:

"That's it! I've heard enough. How long will these people rebel against me? I'm going to wipe them out with a plague. Moses, I'll make *you* a great nation instead of them."

Moses said, "Oh, no, Lord! If you do that, everyone will think you couldn't take care of your people. Please forgive our sins and let us continue to be the great nation you promised Abraham."

God decided to listen to Moses and give the people another chance. However, their punishment was that instead of getting to go right into Canaan, they had to go back into the wilderness and wander around for forty years—a year for each of the forty days the spies had explored Canaan. The ten unfaithful spies were struck dead, but Caleb and Joshua were rewarded for their faith.

APRIL

1

Punishment for Disobedience

NUMBERS 14

YOU would think the people would stop complaining about Moses, but it wasn't over yet. A Levite named Korah and three of his friends stirred up more trouble. They got 250 important leaders of the people to join them in a rebellion against Moses and Aaron. They went to Moses and said, "We are tired of your ordering us around. You are no better than the rest of us, so why should you tell us what to do? And why should Aaron get to be High Priest?"

Moses prayed, then he answered them, "All right, we'll find out whether God has really chosen us. Come back tomorrow with fire in your incense burners, and we'll see what God has to say about this."

So on the next day they were back with their censers. All the people of Israel gathered around to stand with Korah and the other rebels. Then the Lord spoke to Korah: "Aren't you satisfied to be a worker in God's house of worship? Must you try to take the place of God's appointed servant?"

Then Moses warned the great crowd of people to get away from Korah and the rebels. He said, "Now God will show who should be your leaders. He will open the earth, and Korah and his family will be destroyed." As soon as he finished speaking, the earth opened and swallowed up Korah and his rebellious friends.

WHEN KORAH and the other rebels were swallowed up by the earth as God's punishment for their sin, the rest of the people of Israel were afraid. They ran away so they wouldn't be killed too.

The next day, as they thought about what had happened to Korah, they became angry and started criticizing Moses and Aaron again. They blamed them for what had happened to Korah. While they were muttering and grumbling, they suddenly saw the Cloud over the Tabernacle—the Cloud that showed that God was present in all his glory.

Then God's voice spoke, saying, "I'm going to destroy these stubborn people."

But Moses and Aaron prayed for them and tried to stop the sickness God sent to the people. Before they could get it stopped entirely, almost 15,000 people had died.

God said, "Now I'll put an end to all this grumbling against my chosen leaders. Moses, tell the chief of each tribe to bring a wooden rod with his name carved on it. The rod from the tribe of Levi should have Aaron's name on it. Put them in front of the Ark in the Tabernacle. The true leader's rod will sprout buds."

Moses followed God's instructions. The next day Aaron's rod had not only buds on it but also blossoms and ripe almonds! From that time on, Aaron's rod was always kept in the Tabernacle. Whenever anyone complained, Moses showed him the rod.

APRIL

3

Buds, Blossoms, and Fruit

NUMBERS 16–17

4

*Moses
Loses
His
Temper*

NUMBERS 20

NEXT, the people moved on to the Zin Desert. There Moses' sister, Miriam, died and was buried.

After awhile they ran out of water, and the people blamed Moses as usual! They whined, "Why didn't you just kill us along with Korah? That wouldn't be any worse than dying of thirst."

God told Moses and Aaron to take Aaron's rod and stand in front of a certain rock. "Speak to that rock, and water will gush out."

Moses went to the rock, but then he lost his temper. He shouted, "You stubborn rebels! Must I get water for you all the time?" Then he hit the rock twice with the rod. Immediately water gushed out, and all the people and animals had plenty to drink.

But God said, "You didn't obey me exactly. Because you struck the rock instead of speaking to it, you and Aaron may not enter the Promised Land. Another leader will take the people into Canaan."

Soon the Lord told Moses it was time for Aaron to die. He said, "Take Aaron and his son Eleazar up into Mount Hor." When they got there, God told Moses to remove Aaron's priestly clothing and put it all on Eleazar. He did this, and then Aaron died. Moses and Eleazar came back down the mountain and joined the people, who were waiting at the foot of the mountain.

"Now Eleazar is the High Priest," Moses told the people. "God has appointed him to take Aaron's place." The people of Israel mourned for Aaron for thirty days.

BY NOW the people had been traveling for almost forty years, and everyone was getting very tired and discouraged. Once again they took their anger out on Moses. "We don't have enough water and food, and we are sick and tired of eating manna," they grumbled.

Again God became angry with them for their ungrateful attitude. He punished them this time by sending a lot of poisonous snakes into the camp to bite the people. Many of those who were bitten died of the poison. The people were sorry then that they had complained, so they ran to Moses and cried, "Oh, please pray that God will take the snakes away and save our lives."

Moses asked the Lord to help his people. God's answer was, "You must make a snake out of bronze and fasten it on the top of a long pole. Raise it up high over the camp where people can look up at it. Everyone who looks up at the bronze snake will be healed of snakebite and will not die." Moses did this, and many lives were spared.

Once more the Israelis needed to go through some land belonging to a powerful king of the Amorites. Moses asked King Sihon to let them travel through his land. Like the other kings, Sihon refused, and he attacked the Israelis at a place called Jahaz. But the Israelis won and were able to go anywhere they wanted to in the land of the Amorites.

APRIL

5

Bitten by Poisonous Snakes

NUMBERS 21

APRIL

6

The Talking Donkey

NUMBERS 22

WHEN the Israelis came near the plains of Moab, the king there, whose name was Balak, became frightened. He had heard what they had done to the armies of the Amorites! He sent messengers to offer money to a man called Balaam if he would curse Israel. (Cursing someone means asking God to do something terrible to him.)

Balaam wanted the money, so he saddled his donkey and went with the king's messengers. Of course, God didn't want anyone to curse his special people, so he sent an angel to stop Balaam. The angel stood in the road in front of Balaam with a sword in his hand. Balaam couldn't see the angel, but his donkey could. The donkey turned away and left the road. Balaam didn't understand, so he beat the donkey.

The angel then waited for Balaam at a place in the road where there was a wall on each side. When the donkey saw the angel again, she pressed up against the wall, crushing Balaam's foot. This made him angry, so he hit her again.

The angel met them again, and this time the donkey fell down under Balaam. Again Balaam beat her. This time an amazing thing happened; the donkey spoke words to Balaam, asking, "Why have you beaten me three times?"

Then the Lord let Balaam see the angel, and he was sorry he had treated the donkey so badly. The angel said he should go on to see King Balak but that he should say only what God told him.

BALAAM went on with Balak's messengers, and the king came out to meet him. "At last you are here," he said.

Balaam said, "Yes, but I'll speak only what God puts in my mouth."

The next day he told Balak to build seven altars and prepare seven bulls and seven rams for sacrifice. He and King Balak each sacrificed one of the bulls and one of the rams. Then Balaam went off alone to ask God what he should say about Israel. God sent him back, and when Balaam spoke, everything he said was a blessing upon the people of Israel.

This made Balak really angry. He took Balaam to a different place, and they built seven more altars and made sacrifices. Again Balaam asked God's advice, and again he was allowed to speak only good things.

Balak said, "Listen, maybe you can't curse them, but at least don't *bless* them! They are my enemies!"

The same thing happened once more, and at last Balak said, "I give up. Go on home, but don't expect any pay. It is your God's fault that you didn't earn the money I offered you!"

Balak thought of another way to bring trouble upon Israel. He gave a big party to honor Canaanite idols. He invited Israeli young people to come, and soon they started to worship the false gods along with the Canaanites. As Balak had expected, this made God angry, and he sent a disease upon his people that killed thousands of them.

APRIL

7

Curses Turn to Blessings

NUMBERS 22–24

8

The View across the River

NUMBERS 25–36

THE FORTY years of wandering were now almost over. Before God could let the people go into the Promised Land, he had to check to be sure all of the older generation had died, so he had Moses count the people again. Caleb and Joshua were the only older people allowed to go into Canaan. That was because they had been faithful, trusting spies.

But because the people of Midian had led many of the Israelis into idol worship, God said his people must make war on Midian. So they did, and they killed all the Midianites and kept their animals—72,000 oxen, 61,000 donkeys, and 675,000 sheep. Then they burned down all the cities and country estates.

When the war was over, God's people were very thankful to him, because not a single one of the Israeli soldiers had been killed. To show their gratitude, they brought an offering of all the jewelry they had taken from the Midianites during the battle. Moses and Eleazar, who was the new High Priest after Aaron died, accepted the jewelry and put it into the Tabernacle as a thank offering to God.

Then, at last, the people of Israel stood on the banks of the Jordan River, which separated them from the Promised Land. They looked across the river into Canaan and thanked the Lord that it was almost time to enter the land.

THE PEOPLE of Israel were camped beside the Jordan River, waiting for the right time to go across. The tribes of Reuben and Gad and half of the tribe of Manasseh came and asked Moses for permission to make their permanent homes on that side of the river, instead of across the river where the other tribes would be settling.

Moses was angry with them for suggesting such a thing. "What's the matter? Are you so much afraid of the wicked people over in Canaan that you want to avoid a war with them? Do you want the other tribes to do your fighting for you?"

"Oh, no, that's not it at all," they replied. "We have been looking around at the land here on this side of the river, and we think it would be a wonderful place for our flocks and herds. There's plenty of pastureland. What we want to do is to leave our families and our animals here. We men will come across the river with everyone else, and we'll fight right beside you until the Canaanites are all destroyed. Then we can come back here and settle down with our families."

Moses thought it over, and he asked the rest of the tribes what they thought about it. Everyone agreed that the two and a half tribes could have the land they wanted, if they would help wipe out the Canaanite enemies first.

APRIL

9

The People Are Divided

NUMBERS 32

MOSES kept telling his people about plans for the future, when they would be living in Canaan. He himself couldn't go into the Promised Land, of course, because of his disobedience when he struck the rock to get water.

One of the things he told them was that certain cities were to be given to the Levites for their special use. Each of those cities was to have plenty of pastureland around it, for the flocks.

Other special cities, Moses said, were to be called Cities of Refuge, or Cities of Safety. Those cities were places where someone who had accidentally killed someone else could run to for safety. A relative of the dead person might try to get revenge on the killer. That person was called an avenger. But once a killer was inside a City of Safety and had told his story to the judges there, an avenger could not harm him. The killer had to stay in the City of Safety until after the death of the High Priest. Then he could go back to his original home, and no one could punish him for the accidental killing.

Of course, if someone killed another person on purpose, that was a murder. The Cities of Safety were not intended to protect murderers but only those who had not meant to cause another person's death.

BECAUSE he wasn't going into Canaan, Moses made a long speech to his people, reminding them of all the things that had happened to them since they left Egypt. He didn't want them ever to forget God's goodness to them during the past forty years.

Moses had seen how easily the people forgot God's instructions and how often they disobeyed God. He repeated all the commandments to them, trying to get them to remember just how God wanted them to live. He said, "Don't forget: You must never worship any other God. Don't make idols or worship them. Don't use God's name carelessly, and always keep the Sabbath Day holy. Honor your father and mother. You must never murder, or commit adultery, or steal, or lie. And you must not desire anything that belongs to someone else—his wife, or house, or land, or servants, or animals."

Then he reminded them about all the other 613 rules—about health, food, cleanliness, relationships with other people, holiness before God, and worship in the Tabernacle. And he repeated what they had learned about all the feasts and festivals they were to observe, each one a reminder of good things God had done for them.

Finally he told them that Joshua was to be their new leader. Then Moses climbed up to the top of Mount Nebo and looked across the river at the Promised Land. And there Moses died at the age of 120.

APRIL

11

Moses'
Long
Speech
DEUTERONOMY

12

*Joshua
Becomes the
Leader*

JOSHUA 1

AFTER Moses died, Joshua took over the job of leading the
people of Israel. Joshua had been Moses' assistant, and he
was also one of the two faithful spies who had brought back a
good report from Canaan and had encouraged the people to
trust God for safety.

God said to Joshua, "Get the people ready to cross the Jordan
River. I will keep my promise to give you all the land you walk on,
many miles in each direction. Don't be afraid to go into Canaan,
because I will always be with you and will take care of you wherever you go. Just be sure to obey me and be brave."

Then Joshua told the people to get ready to cross the river
three days later. He reminded the tribes of Reuben and Gad and
the half-tribe of Manasseh that although their wives and children
could stay on the east side of the river, the men must go across
with the other tribes and help them get rid of the wicked and
hostile Canaanites, as God had directed them. Later, when the
wars were over, they could come back and join their families and
go on being herdsmen in the wonderful pasturelands on their
plots of land.

All the people promised to obey Joshua and to follow him,
because he was the one God had chosen to be leader. And they,
too, encouraged him to be full of courage as they all entered
Canaan.

JOSHUA decided to send in two more spies for a last look around before he took the thousands of Israelis into Canaan. The two spies very quietly crossed the river and went to an inn owned by a woman named Rahab. They had thought they would stay there overnight, but the king heard a rumor that spies had come to Jericho, so he sent some men to capture them.

Rahab got word that the king's men were coming, so she hid the two spies under some piles of grain that were drying on the roof. When the king's men came, she told them the spies had been there but had already left. "Hurry," she said, "you might still be able to catch them before they leave the city."

Then she went to the two spies and said, "I know what your soldiers have been doing to hostile armies everywhere you have gone. You must worship a very powerful God. I know your God will give you the victory over Jericho. I want you to save me and my family, because we have helped you today."

The spies said they would do that. They told her to hang a red rope in the window of her home. When the people of Israel captured the city, they would see the red rope hanging from her window and they would know that was where Rahab and her family lived. They said she and her family must stay inside the house. If they went outside, that would cancel their agreement.

14

*Crossing
the River*

JOSHUA 3

THE SPIES returned to the camp, and the people gathered by the Jordan River, ready to cross. The next morning Joshua told the priests who were appointed to carry the Ark to go first. As they stepped into the water, the river stopped flowing, and the priests walked on dry ground into the middle of the river. They stood there, holding the Ark, while all the rest of the people crossed the river.

God told Joshua, "Choose twelve men, one from each tribe, to go out into the middle of the riverbed and pick up twelve large stones. They are to carry them to the far bank of the river. Have them do this while the priests are still in the middle of the riverbed."

When everyone was safely across and had gone up on the banks, the priests continued to walk on across the riverbed. As soon as they stepped up on the banks, the water started to flow again!

The people made a camp at a place called Gilgal. They used the twelve stones from the riverbed to build a monument. Joshua said, "Someday your children and grandchildren will ask, 'What is that stone monument for?' Then you must tell them all about this wonderful day when God opened up the waters of the Jordan River and let his people walk across on dry land. He did this to show you, as well as the whole earth, how powerful he is."

THE PEOPLE of Israel were very, very happy to have arrived in Canaan. They had been looking forward to this for many years. One of the first things they did was to celebrate the Passover. Every year they celebrated the night when they were freed from Egypt and the Angel of the Lord passed over their homes when he came to kill the firstborn in the Egyptians' homes.

They were glad to find some corn growing in the fields there in Gilgal, because they were very tired of eating manna. They didn't have to eat manna any more, because it stopped appearing on the ground the very next morning, now that they were in a country where they could find food and could start growing crops.

Joshua knew that one of his biggest jobs would be to capture Jericho and occupy it. As he was thinking about how he and his army could successfully make war on Jericho, suddenly a Man appeared to him, holding a sword in his hand. Joshua asked him, "Are you for us or for our enemies?"

The Man replied, "I have come as the Commander-in-Chief of the Lord's army."

This let Joshua know that the Man was really the Lord himself, so he fell down and worshiped him.

Then the Commander said to him, "Take off your shoes. You are standing on holy ground." The Lord had said the same thing to Moses when he appeared to him at the burning bush many years before.

THE COMMANDER of the Lord's army told Joshua that although the people of Jericho had closed and barred the city gates to keep the Israelis out, God would give Joshua the victory. And he told him exactly how to win the battle. Joshua agreed to obey what the Lord told him to do. This is how it worked:

Joshua lined up his soldiers and they marched all the way around the city wall. The priests went with them, carrying the Ark of the Covenant. Out in front of the Ark walked seven priests who were blowing trumpets. The army and the priests did this once each day for six days.

On the seventh day everyone got up especially early and started the marching earlier than usual, because that day they marched around the walls of Jericho seven times instead of just once. As usual, the seven priests blew on their trumpets all the time they were marching. At the end of the seventh time around, the priests gave a final loud blast on their trumpets and Joshua called to his soldiers, "Give a great shout, for the Lord has given you victory over the city!" The soldiers shouted loudly, and the walls fell down with a great crash!

The soldiers marched right into Jericho and captured it, but they remembered to take care of Rahab and her family, because she had helped the spies. Then the army burned the city down, but they put valuable things, like gold and silver, into the Lord's treasury.

THE NEXT place Joshua wanted to conquer was a town called Ai. He sent some scouts to find out how well fortified Ai was. The scouts came back and said, "We won't have any trouble taking Ai. Only a few soldiers are protecting it, so we don't need to send our whole army. Two or three thousand men will be plenty."

Joshua sent three thousand men, but the soldiers at Ai defeated them easily, killing thirty-six of them. Others died while the Israeli troops were in retreat. Joshua's army was terrified by this defeat, and Joshua fell on his face and asked God, "Why in the world did this happen? Did you bring us into Canaan only to let us be defeated by our enemies? Now the Canaanite tribes will no longer respect our God, and they will attack us and wipe us out."

God replied, "Get up! This has happened to you because of sin in your camp. Someone disobeyed by taking some of the loot from Jericho instead of destroying everything as I commanded. Have everyone appear before me, and I will point out the guilty one."

So the people came before the Lord and he showed that the guilty one was a man named Achan, from the tribe of Judah. Achan then confessed, "I did steal some silver, some gold, and a beautiful robe and hid them in my tent."

APRIL

17

Why Did Ai Defeat Israel?

JOSHUA 7

18

Punishment for a Thief

JOSHUA 7

JOSHUA sent some men to search Achan's tent, and there were all the stolen goods, buried in the ground under the tent. The men brought all of it to Joshua. Then Joshua gathered Achan and his family and all of their flocks, together with the stolen gold, silver, and clothing. Joshua said to Achan, "What you have done has brought trouble to all of us. Now the Lord will bring disaster to you."

Then all the men of Israel threw stones at Achan and his family until they were dead. Their bodies were burned and then buried under a big pile of stones. That place became known as "The Valley of Trouble."

The Lord said to Joshua, "Now you will be able to defeat the army at Ai. This time you must destroy all who live there, but your people may keep the gold and silver instead of putting it into my treasury." So Joshua and his army attacked Ai again. This time he took all his soldiers. He sent 30,000 of them around behind the city while the rest attacked from the front. When the soldiers of Ai came out to fight the attackers, the 30,000 men set the city on fire.

The men of Ai were trapped between the burning city and the Israeli army, and they could not get away. Joshua's army completely destroyed them. They did keep the loot for themselves, for God had told them it would be all right.

THE KINGS of the Canaanite tribes were afraid of the Israelis when they saw what they did to Jericho and Ai. They banded together, planning to attack them. But one of the neighboring tribes, the people of Gibeon, tried another way to protect themselves.

They sent a group to see Joshua. They loaded their donkeys with worn-out sacks and old, brittle wineskins, and they carried moldy bread with them. The men wore patched-up sandals and ragged old clothes, so Joshua would think they had been traveling for a long, long time.

When they came to the Israeli camp, they said to Joshua, "We live a long way from here. We want you to make a treaty with us."

Joshua told the Gibeonites, "I can't make a treaty with you because you may be one of my neighboring tribes. God has said I must destroy all of the heathen Canaanite nations because he has given this land to us."

The Gibeonites answered, "Oh, no. We're from far away, and we came just because we have heard what a powerful God you have, and we want to be your friends. You can tell how far we have come, because our clothes and sandals were all new when we left, and this bread was fresh, right out of the oven."

Joshua should have asked the Lord's advice about this, but he didn't. He believed the Gibeonites and signed the treaty, and the Israeli leaders approved it.

A FEW days later Joshua found out the Gibeonites really were a neighboring Canaanite tribe. He asked them, "Why did you trick me that way?"

The men of Gibeon said, "We heard about the victories your army was winning, and we were afraid. We wanted to keep you from attacking us. Now do to us whatever you think best."

The people of Israel wanted to kill them, but Joshua said, "No, we must honor our treaty." And he made them slaves who would chop wood and carry water for the Tabernacle.

When the king of Jerusalem heard about the treaty, he was worried because Gibeon was a large and powerful city. He called on four other kings to help him make war on Gibeon. When they began their siege, the Gibeonites sent for Joshua. "Please come and fulfill your treaty with us by helping us fight our enemies."

Joshua took his whole army and went to help Gibeon. The Lord promised to help him defeat the large combined army of the five nations. One way he did this was to send big hailstones that actually killed more soldiers than the Israeli army did! Then Joshua prayed, "Let the sun stand still over Gibeon and the moon over the Valley of Aijalon."

God answered that prayer, and for almost a whole day and night, the sun and moon stood still and Joshua could finish defeating the five kings and their armies. Such a thing had never happened before, and it has never happened again.

DURING all their travels in the wilderness, the people of Israel had been carrying the Tabernacle around with them. They would set it up when they stopped and pack it up when they moved on. Now that they had entered the Promised Land and were going to settle down, the Tabernacle could stay in one place all the time. They chose the city of Shiloh, near the center of their new land, and the priests and Levites carried the Tabernacle there and set it up for the last time.

In the wilderness the tribes of Israel had become tired of traveling. Now they were getting tired of fighting to clear out the wicked Canaanite tribes from the Promised Land. But still more enemy tribes remained to be defeated. Joshua called the people together and reminded them that there was still land to be conquered and occupied. He sent out some scouts and asked them for a written report and some maps showing where their enemies were.

Then Joshua drew straws to find out just what part of the land should go to each tribe. He told them, "God says you must finish the task of driving out the heathen tribes. And he will help you gain the victory over them."

Again God said the priests and Levites would not have farmland like the other tribes, because their work was in the Tabernacle. But they could have special cities—forty-eight of them—where they could live with their wives and children.

NOW it was time for the people of Reuben, Gad, and Manasseh to go back to their land on the east side of the Jordan River. Joshua thanked them for helping the other tribes fight for their land. He said to them, "Be sure to love the Lord and serve him faithfully." When they got to the river, they built an altar that looked just like the one at the Tabernacle in Shiloh.

Because God had said there must be only one place of sacrifice, the other tribes were upset, and they sent the High Priest to scold them. But the eastern tribes said, "Why, we aren't making another place of sacrifice. This is only a monument to express our gratitude to God and to remind all of us that we are Israelis just as much as you are on the west side of Jordan." Then everyone understood, and no one was angry anymore.

Joshua was getting very old, so he called all the people together and made a speech, reminding them of all God's wonderful care. "He has given you this beautiful place to live and has driven out your enemies so your homes can be peaceful. Be sure that you never forget to love him and worship as you should. My family and I are always going to serve the Lord."

And all the people replied, "Yes, we will all serve him forever. We will never worship false gods or idols." And Joshua set up a big rock near the Tabernacle to remind them of that promise.

SOON after that, Joshua died at the age of 110. The people buried him on a hillside. Then they buried the bones of Joseph, which they had brought from Egypt many years before. The Israelis had served the Lord all through Joshua's lifetime, and they kept on being faithful to God as long as the elders of Israel were alive—all those who had lived through the wilderness journey and the occupation of Canaan.

Some of the Israeli tribes went on fighting the Canaanites for the territories God had promised them. But gradually they became careless about doing just what God had instructed. They didn't destroy all the cities and they didn't break down all the idols and heathen altars.

APRIL

23

Israel Needs New Leaders

JOSHUA 24—JUDGES 3

In some parts of Canaan, the Israelis made friends with some of the wicked tribes. Some of them even married young people from the enemy nations. Of course, this caused a lot of trouble and led the Israelis to worship the heathen gods of the Canaanites. When God saw what was happening, he sent troops to defeat the people of Israel and make them slaves. Then they said they were sorry and would try to follow the Lord again.

Each time this happened, God would forgive them and give them a strong leader to help them do the right thing. These leaders were called "judges," and the Book of Judges is their story. It tells us about fifteen judges who tried to guide Israel in following the Lord.

24

The First Judges

JUDGES 1–3

WHEN the people of Israel turned away from God and started to worship Baal and Asherah, some of the false gods of the Canaanites, God was angry. He stopped protecting them, and soon they became slaves of the king of a district called Mesopotamia. For eight years they served this king, but finally they remembered their true God and prayed that he would help them.

The way God helped them was to choose a strong leader to rescue them. The leader, or judge, was Othniel, the younger brother of Caleb, one of the two brave and faithful spies in Moses' time. God sent his Spirit to Othniel, and Othniel saved the Israelis from the king of Mesopotamia. For forty years they obeyed God and had peace in the land.

When Othniel died, the people began to forget God again. This time they became subjects of a Moabite king named Eglon, and they had to pay heavy taxes to him. God sent another judge to help them—Ehud, a Benjaminite. Ehud went to see King Eglon and pretended he needed to talk to him alone. The king's aides left, and then Ehud stabbed Eglon with a dagger. By the time the king's men found Eglon, Ehud had escaped. He called Israel together and led them in war against the Moabites. Israel won, and for eighty years they had peace.

The next judge was Shamgar, and he helped them get victory over the Philistines. But after awhile the people forgot God again.

FOR about twenty years the Israelis had to serve King Jabin. The head of his army was a cruel man named Sisera, who had nine hundred iron chariots, which shows how huge his army was. When God sent a leader this time, he chose a woman. The people of Israel used to come to Deborah, a prophetess, and she would settle their problems with wise decisions.

Deborah sent for Barak and said, "God wants you to lead his people in a campaign against General Sisera. God will give you the victory."

Barak was afraid Sisera was too strong. "I can't go to war unless you go with me."

Deborah said, "All right, I'll go, but everyone will give me the credit instead of you." They gathered an army of ten thousand men and marched into the battle.

God sent confusion and panic into the enemy forces, and Barak's troops destroyed every one of them—except Sisera, who jumped out of his chariot and ran. He escaped to the camp of some allies of King Jabin. A woman named Jael invited him to hide in her tent. She gave him a drink of milk and covered him with a blanket so he could rest. When Sisera was asleep, Jael crept in and killed him by hammering a sharp tent peg through his head.

When Barak came by, chasing Sisera, Jael showed him Sisera's body. From then on, Barak's army kept getting stronger, and soon Jabin and his people were completely destroyed.

APRIL

26

God Chooses Gideon as Leader

JUDGES 6

AFTER forty peaceful years, Israel again started to worship false gods. The Lord sent the Midianites against them, and for seven years the people suffered terribly. They hid in mountain caves to escape the Midianites' cruelty. Their enemies stole their crops and flocks, leaving them hungry and poor.

At last they cried to God for help, and he chose a leader named Gideon. Gideon was threshing his last bit of grain secretly in a grape press. The Angel of the Lord appeared and said, "The Lord is with you, mighty warrior!"

Gideon replied bitterly, "If the Lord is with us, why are we in all this trouble? This 'great God' I've always heard about has gone off and left us to the mercy of Midian. Besides, I'm not a mighty warrior. I'm just a farm boy."

"I'm telling you that God will use you to get your people out of this trouble," the Lord answered.

"How can I be sure you are telling the truth? Wait here, and I'll bring you an offering." Gideon went and got goat meat, broth, and unleavened bread.

The Lord told him to put the bread and meat on a rock and pour the broth over it. The Lord touched it with his walking stick, and fire flamed up from the rock, burning up the offering. Immediately the Lord disappeared. Gideon was afraid he would die because he had seen the Lord, but the voice of the Lord said, "Don't worry. You won't die." Gideon built an altar there and called it "Peace with God."

THAT night the Lord told Gideon to tear down his father's altar to Baal and break down the idols. "Then build an altar to the Lord and sacrifice a young bull from your father's herd. Use one of the idols as wood for the fire on the altar." Gideon was afraid, but he knew he better obey the Lord. He did these things in the dark so no one could see him.

In the morning the village men were amazed at what they saw. "Who did such a thing?" they asked. When they found out it was Gideon, they said, "He must die because of what he did to Baal's altar and the idols."

But Gideon's father spoke up for him. "Why are you defending Baal? If he's a real god, he can take care of himself." So the men left Gideon alone.

God sent his Spirit to Gideon, and he called the men of Israel together to fight against the Midianites. He asked the Lord for a sign to prove he would help. "I'll put some wool on the barn floor. In the morning, if the wool is wet and the floor dry, I'll know you are with me."

In the morning, the floor was dry but the wool was so wet Gideon could wring a bowlful of water out of it! Gideon asked the Lord for one more sign. This time he wanted the floor to be wet and the wool dry. And the Lord did just as Gideon asked.

GIDEON gathered about 32,000 men to fight the Midianites. The Lord said, "If you use that many soldiers, everyone will think you won by military power instead of by my power. Send home all who are fearful about the battle." About 22,000 of them went home. Then God said, "You still have 10,000, and that's too many. Take them down to the edge of the water, and I'll show you how to choose the right ones."

Gideon did this, and then God said, "Let them drink water from the spring. You will see that they do it in two different ways. Those who pick up water in their hands and lap it like dogs are the ones you should take to battle. Others will get down on their knees and drink from the spring. Send that group home."

Only three hundred of the soldiers drank from their hands. The Lord said, "I'll conquer the Midianites with those three hundred men."

Gideon gave each soldier a trumpet and a pitcher containing a lighted lamp. He said, "When we get close to the Midianites' camp, we will blow our trumpets, break our pitchers, and shout,'The sword of the Lord and of Gideon!' " When they all broke their pitchers and shouted, the Midianites were frightened. The noise and lights made them think there were more soldiers than there really were.

Gideon's army defeated them totally and captured their two kings. At last Israel was free of the cruel Midianites, and Gideon led a peaceful nation for forty years.

ONCE there was a brave Israeli soldier named Jephthah.
Some of his relatives quarreled with him, and he decided to
move away to another country. Later the Ammonites attacked
Israel, trying to get back the land the Israelis had taken from
them. Israel needed a strong leader to be general of the army.
They sent for Jephthah, but he didn't want to come. He replied,
"You didn't want me around in peace time, but now that you're
in trouble, you ask me to come back!"

The men promised that if he would win the war, they would
make him king. So he finally agreed to come.

Jephthah made a vow—that is, a serious promise to God—
that if the Lord would help him win the victory, he would offer
to God the first thing that came from his house when he got
home. This was a foolish thing to say, because he had no way of
knowing whether the first thing that came out would be an animal or a person—and God had strictly forbidden Israel to make
human sacrifices like the wicked nations around them.

Jephthah won the war, but when he got home, the first thing
that came out of his house was his own dear little daughter!
Now, God would have excused him from his vow, since it was
against the Law to sacrifice one's child, but Jephthah kept his
word. For many years, the young women of Israel had a time of
mourning for Jephthah's daughter.

30

A
Miracle
Baby

JUDGES 13

DURING one of the times Israel sinned against God, the Philistines ruled over them for forty years.

Manoah and his wife were a couple in the tribe of Dan. They had not been able to have any children, but one day the Angel of the Lord came to the wife and said, "At last you are going to have a baby. Don't drink wine or eat anything unclean. When the baby comes, he is to be a Nazirite, a special servant of mine. He must not drink wine or cut his hair or beard. He will free Israel from the Philistines." Then the Angel disappeared.

Manoah's wife told him what had happened. Manoah prayed that God would send the visitor back, so he could ask him questions. The Angel returned, and this time Manoah got to talk to him too. Neither Manoah nor his wife realized who their visitor was, and they asked him his name. He said, "Don't ask my name. It is a secret."

Manoah prepared some meat and grain for a sacrifice. When he put it on the altar, a fire sprang up and burned the sacrifice. Then the Angel of the Lord went up to heaven in the flames! Manoah realized they had seen the Lord, and he was afraid. But his wife said, "Don't worry. He didn't come to hurt us."

She did have the baby, as the Angel had promised. They named him Samson and dedicated him to God's service.

WHEN Samson grew up, he fell in love with a Philistine woman and wanted to marry her. His parents wanted him to marry an Israeli girl, but he insisted, so they went to her home to arrange it. On the way, they were attacked by a young lion. God's Spirit gave Samson strength to kill the lion with his bare hands.

On another trip to the girl's home, Samson stopped to look at the carcass of the lion he had killed. Bees had made a hive in it, and it was full of honey.

Samson had to give a wedding feast. He challenged thirty young men to a contest. "I'll ask a riddle," he said. "If you guess the answer, I'll give each of you some new clothes. If you cannot answer it, you must give me all the clothing."

"All right," they said, "what's the riddle?"

" 'Food came out of the eater and sweetness came out of the strong.' " Samson said.

Samson's bride begged him to tell her the answer. She cried and cried until he finally told her. At the end of the contest the young Philistine men answered, "What is stronger than a lion, and what is sweeter than honey?" Samson could see that his bride had told them the answer. Her disloyalty made him angry. He gave the young men the clothing he had promised, but then he deserted his new wife and went back to Israel.

MAY

1

Samson Kills a Lion

JUDGES 14

MAY

2

*Samson
Punishes
His
Enemies*

JUDGES 15

AFTER awhile, Samson wasn't angry with his Philistine wife anymore, so he went to see her. Her father said, "I thought you weren't coming back, so I let your best man marry her." This made Samson so violently angry that he went out and caught three hundred foxes. He tied their tails together and fastened a burning torch to each pair. The foxes ran through the fields of the Philistines, setting fire to all their crops.

When the Philistines found out why he had done this to their fields, they killed the girl and her father. That made Samson angrier than before. He attacked the Philistines and killed many of them. Then he stayed for awhile in a cave in the territory of Judah. The Philistines chased him and asked the people there to help them capture him. The men of Judah went to the cave and told Samson he had to stop doing things like that to the Philistines. They wanted to turn Samson over to the Philistines, so Samson said, "Just don't kill me yourselves."

"No, we won't." They tied him up with some new ropes and took him to where the Philistines were waiting. They came toward him, shouting. Then the Spirit of God made him very strong again, and he easily broke the ropes and got free. He grabbed the jawbone from the body of a dead donkey and used it to kill a thousand Philistines.

Samson was Israel's leader for twenty years.

SAMSON had a girlfriend named Delilah, who was not loyal to him. The Philistines promised her a lot of money if she would find out why Samson was so strong and would help them capture him.

She kept begging Samson to tell her the secret of his great strength. He teased her by telling her he would be weak if he was tied up with leather bowstrings. So she tied him up and then said, "The Philistines are coming after you!" But he snapped the leather thongs easily and got away.

Delilah tried again, and this time Samson said he could be tied with new ropes. But again he broke the ropes with no trouble. Delilah was upset because he had lied to her, so he said, "Well, if you weave my long hair into a loom, I can't get away." But again he got loose very easily.

She nagged and complained until he finally broke down and told her his secret. "I am strong because I am a Nazirite and have never had my hair cut. If it were cut, I would be no stronger than other men." This time she could tell he was telling the truth, so she sent for the Philistines.

They brought the money they had promised her and hid nearby while Delilah got Samson to take a nap. While he was asleep, she had a barber come and cut off his hair. Then she called, "Samson! The Philistines are coming!" And this time he couldn't escape.

MAY

3

An Unfaithful Girlfriend

JUDGES 16

MAY

4

Samson's Enemies Capture Him

JUDGES 16

THE PHILISTINES captured Samson and took him to a prison in Gaza. They blinded him and bound him with bronze chains. He had to grind the grain for the prison. Now, there's one thing that's sure about hair: it keeps on growing. And Samson's hair began to grow again while he was in prison!

The Philistines decided to have a big celebration and make sacrifices to their god Dagon, because they thought he had helped them capture Samson. The people got drunk and shouted, "At last that terrible Israeli who caused us so much trouble is in our hands. Hey, bring him out here so we can see how the old 'hero' looks now!"

Samson was brought from the prison, led by a young boy. Samson asked the boy to put him in the center of the temple—which by now was crowded with thousands of jeering Philistines. "Put one of my hands on each large pillar," he told the boy. Then Samson prayed, "O God, please give me back my strength just one more time, so I can punish the Philistines for taking away my sight."

Then he started to push very hard on the two pillars. He cried out, "Let me die with the Philistines!" And the temple collapsed, crushing all the people, including Samson himself. In his death he killed more Philistines than he had during his whole life. Then Samson's brothers came to get his body, and they buried him beside his father, Manoah.

ONCE, during the time of the judges, a famine brought hunger upon the people in the tribe of Judah. A man named Elimelech took his wife and two sons and moved to Moab to find food. After awhile Elimelech died, leaving his widow with her two sons, Mahlon and Chilion. When the boys grew up, they married Moabite girls named Orpah and Ruth. Sad to say, both of the sons died too, leaving Naomi without any men to care for her.

She heard the famine was over, back in Judah, so she decided to take her daughters-in-law and return home. Along the way she changed her mind about taking the young women and tried to send them back to Moab. Orpah agreed to go, but Ruth insisted upon going on with her mother-in-law. She said, "Don't make me go back. I want to stay with you and your people. And I want to worship your God."

So Naomi agreed, and they went on to the city of Bethlehem, which had been her hometown. The village women saw her coming and asked, "Isn't that Naomi?"

"Don't call me that," she said. "That name means 'pleasant.' Things haven't been pleasant for me. My name should be 'Mara,' because that means 'bitter,' and my life has really been bitter. I went to Moab with a husband and sons, but I come back without them. God has turned his back on me."

Naomi and Ruth

RUTH 1

MAY

6

*Ruth
Works
in the
Fields*

RUTH 2

NAOMI and Ruth had arrived in Bethlehem just at the beginning of the barley harvest. They needed food, so Ruth offered to go out and find a field where the owner would let her pick up grain that the reapers dropped as they were working. The Law said that kind of grain had to be left for the poor. Naomi agreed, and Ruth went to work in the field of a farmer named Boaz. Ruth didn't know it, but Boaz was closely related to Naomi's dead husband.

Boaz saw Ruth in the field and asked, "Who is that new girl?" When he learned she was Naomi's daughter-in-law, he wanted to help her, because he had heard how kind she had been to Naomi. He told Ruth she was welcome to come to his fields every day and take all the grain she wanted.

He said, "Stay close to my servant girls. Have lunch with us, and be sure to get a drink from our water jar when you get thirsty."

Boaz told his farm workers to "drop" extra grain for Ruth on purpose and also to treat her respectfully. At the end of the day Ruth had gathered about a half-bushel of grain to take home. Naomi was amazed when she saw it. "What farmer has been so kind to you?" she asked. When she learned it was Boaz, she realized he was a rich relative of Elimelech's. She told Ruth to keep going to his field to gather grain every day.

RUTH kept on working in Boaz's field all through the barley and wheat harvests. One day Naomi explained to her who Boaz was. She told her to go to his threshing floor that night and to lie down quietly by his feet. "Wait to see what he will do," she said.

Ruth did just as Naomi said. When Boaz woke up and saw Ruth lying at his feet, he was surprised. "What do you want?" he asked.

"Please cover me with your garment, because you are my close relative," said Ruth. She was asking him to show that he would accept his responsibility, as her nearest relative, to marry her and protect her. That was the custom among the people of Israel.

Boaz said, "I would like very much to marry you, but I know a man who is even morc closely related to you than I am. I'll ask him if he wants to marry you. If he doesn't, I will gladly become your husband." In the morning, before dawn, Boaz sent Ruth home with a gift of grain, and he went to see the other relative.

The other man said he could not marry Ruth, so Boaz took her as his wife. After awhile God sent them a baby boy, whom they named Obed. Naomi was a happy grandmother, helping to take care of the baby.

When Obed grew up, he became the father of Jesse and the grandfather of King David.

MAY

7

Ruth and Boaz Are Married

RUTH 3–4

JOB was
a very rich man
who lived in Uz. He had a wife
and a large family—seven grown-up sons
and three daughters. He worshiped God and tried to
please him every day. His flocks and herds were huge, with
thousands of animals.

When Job's sons had birthday parties and invited their sisters
to their homes, Job always made special sacrifices for them. Just
in case they had done something they shouldn't, Job asked God
to forgive them.

One day, God was talking to Satan, the evil tempter. Satan told
God he thought Job obeyed God only because he was rich and
had a lovely family. God said, "You may test him by taking away
those things."

So Satan sent terrible trouble to Job. First his oxen and donkeys were stolen by enemies. Then fire burned up his sheep and
their shepherds. Next, another tribe took his camels and killed
their herdsmen. Worst of all, a terrible windstorm collapsed his
oldest son's home, where all the brothers and sisters had
gathered. All ten of them were killed when the roof caved in.

Job was heartbroken. But all he said was, "God gave them and
now God has taken them away. I still love him and praise him."

Then Satan said to God, "Well, Job is still faithful to you because he is healthy." So God gave Satan permission to make Job
ill. Job felt terrible because he had big sores all over his body.

WHEN Job became sick, his wife asked him, "Why don't you curse God for letting all this happen to you?"

Job said, "That's a foolish thing to say! God has given me many blessings. Why shouldn't I have trouble, too? Even if he killed me, I wouldn't curse him."

Three friends of Job's came to visit him. Their names were Bildad, Zophar, and Eliphaz. For several days they didn't say anything, but finally they started to tell him what they thought about his illness. They said he was having so much trouble because he had sinned and offended God. "Probably you stole something or were mean to poor people. Perhaps you haven't been praying enough. These troubles must be a punishment for disobeying God," they insisted. Day after day they sat and accused him of sinning.

"No, I really haven't done anything wrong," Job protested. "I've always tried to live right and please God. I can't think of any way I've made God angry with me. And you aren't making me feel any better by saying all those things! A fine bunch of comforters you are!"

At last Job got tired of suffering so long, and he complained that God was being unfair to him. Then his friends said, "See, you *are* sinning! We *said* you must be doing something wrong!" And they argued with Job all the more.

10

God Blesses Job Again

JOB 38–42

FINALLY God said, "That's enough! You don't know what you are talking about. Job, let me ask you some questions, and you answer if you can. Where were you when I made the world? Can you possibly understand how wonderful my creation is—the lightning, the snow, the hail, the beautiful stars?" And he described the animals and told how he takes care of them, giving them food and protecting them. He said, "Do you think you are wise enough to do all those things? You forget you are just a man, and I'm the great God of the universe!"

Then Job told God he was sorry for being so impatient and not understanding God's ways. He said, "Lord, I've heard about you all my life, but now I really know you. I've seen how wonderful you are, and now I despise myself. I am so sorry I acted like that."

God also told Job's three friends he was angry with them for saying such foolish things to Job when he was in trouble. God told them to take seven bulls and seven rams to Job and ask him to make a sacrifice for their sins. "If my faithful servant Job prays for you, I will forgive you."

Then the Lord gave Job back his health and more riches than before. He even gave him and his wife ten more children—seven sons and three daughters, the same number as before. Job lived 140 more years and was very happy with his children, grandchildren, and great-grandchildren.

JONAH was one of the people God chose to do a special job for him. God said, "I want you to travel to Nineveh and preach about the trouble I'm going to send to them. They are so wicked that I'm going to destroy them."

Now, the city of Nineveh was a beautiful place, with great houses and temples and gardens. But the people were very evil. Not only did they not love God and honor him, but they were terribly cruel to other people. Everyone knew how violent the Ninevites were, and no one wanted to risk making them angry.

Jonah knew he might be killed if he went to Nineveh, so he decided he wouldn't deliver God's message. Instead, he went down to the port city of Joppa and bought a ticket to sail to Tarshish, clear across the Mediterranean Sea, about as far away from Nineveh as he could get! He boarded the ship and fell asleep down in the hold, thinking he was hiding from God.

Out on the Mediterranean Sea, a terrible storm came up suddenly and the sailors were terrified. The captain found Jonah asleep and said, "How can you sleep? Get up and pray to your God to save us."

Then the sailors tried to find out whose fault it was that they were in trouble. They decided it was Jonah's fault, and he knew they were right. "Yes, you'd better throw me overboard. Then the storm will stop." Jonah knew what he had done!

MAY

11

Jonah Disobeys God

JONAH 1

MAY

12

*Jonah
and the
Fish*

JONAH 2–4

THE SAILORS hated to throw Jonah into the sea, but it was either that or have their ship sink. They threw him overboard, and right away the storm stopped and the water was still. And what happened to Jonah? Well, God had sent an enormous fish to swim close to the ship. When Jonah fell into the water, the fish opened its huge mouth and swallowed him whole, without hurting him.

Jonah was alive inside the fish for three days and nights. He had plenty of time to think about what he had done, and he was sorry about disobeying God. He prayed, promising God he would do as he said, so God made the fish swim close to land and spit Jonah out. Then God gave Jonah another chance to preach to Nineveh, and this time Jonah did it.

He shouted to the Ninevites, "Forty days from now, God is going to destroy you because of your sin." He was amazed to find that the king of Nineveh and his people all believed him and were sorry for their wickedness. They asked God to forgive them and spare their lives, and he did.

This didn't please Jonah at all. He had really wanted God to destroy the Ninevites because that's what they deserved for being so cruel. He was actually disappointed when they were forgiven. God scolded Jonah for having such an unforgiving attitude.

IN THE TRIBE of Ephraim, a man named Elkanah lived with his two wives, Hannah and Peninnah. Hannah was his favorite wife, and he loved her especially. But she was not able to have any babies, so she was very sad. Peninnah had several children. This made her think she was better than Hannah, and she made fun of Hannah and treated her unkindly.

Each year Elkanah took his wives and Peninnah's children to the Tabernacle at Shiloh to make his sacrifices and worship God. He would give gifts to Peninnah and her children, but he gave only one gift to Hannah, since she didn't have children. Year after year Peninnah would say cruel things to Hannah, and Hannah was terribly unhappy. She couldn't eat or sleep, and she would cry bitterly because she couldn't have a baby.

One evening while they were in Shiloh, Hannah went to the Tabernacle to pray. She stood there telling the Lord about her sadness, and she promised him that if he would give her a baby boy, she would let her son serve God in the Tabernacle.

Eli, the High Priest, watched her as she prayed. Because it looked as if she was muttering to herself, he thought she had been drinking. He scolded her for being drunk, but she said, "Oh, no! That's not it. I was just praying for something I want very much."

Then Eli said, "Oh, I see. Well, may God give you exactly what you prayed for!" Hannah went home feeling much better.

MAY

13

Hannah Prays for a Son
1 SAMUEL 1

SOON Hannah had a baby boy, and she named him Samuel, a name meaning "I asked the Lord for him." She and Elkanah were very happy, but they didn't forget Hannah's promise to God. When Samuel was old enough, they took him to the Tabernacle and left him there to help Eli. Eli really needed him, because his own sons were not faithful in their duties as priests.

Each year Samuel's parents visited him, and as he grew bigger, Hannah brought him new clothes she had made for him. God blessed Hannah and Elkanah with three more sons and two daughters.

One night as Samuel lay in bed, he heard a voice calling his name. He thought it was Eli, so he went to see what he wanted. Eli told him he had not called. "Go back to bed," he said.

Again Samuel heard the voice. "Samuel! Samuel!" it called. Again he went to Eli and asked what he wanted.

"I didn't call you, my boy. Go back to bed, and next time you hear the voice, answer, 'Speak, Lord. I'm listening.'"

Samuel obeyed. When he heard the voice again, he said, "Yes, Lord. Speak, and I'll listen." God gave him a message for Eli about how he was going to punish the disobedient sons, Hophni and Phinehas.

Samuel hated to tell Eli bad news, but he had to do it.

Eli said, "The Lord must do what he thinks best."

AS SAMUEL grew up, God talked to him often, and Samuel always listened and then told the people what God had said.

Once the Israelis went to war with the Philistines. The battle didn't go well, and the enemy killed 4,000 Israeli soldiers. The people thought that if they took the Ark with them to the war, the Ark would give them a victory. Hophni and Phinehas went into the battle with the Ark. But neither the people nor the priests asked God's advice about what they were doing. It was just their own idea.

When the Philistines heard about the Ark, they were terrified, because it represented God, and

they thought the Israelis would win. So they fought harder and defeated the Israelis, who ran to their tents. Hophni and Phinehas were killed, and the Philistines captured the Ark.

A young soldier ran back to Shiloh to take word of the disaster. He told Eli, "Your two sons have been killed and the Ark of the Covenant has been stolen by the Philistines."

When Eli heard that terrible news, he fell over backward. The fall broke his neck, and he died. Eli had been a priest in Israel for forty years.

The Philistines took the Ark to Ashdod and set it right beside the idol of their god Dagon, in Dagon's temple.

MAY

16

*God
Brings
the Ark
Back*

1 SAMUEL 5–7

T HE PHILISTINES left the Ark in Dagon's temple and went to their homes. In the morning they looked in, and there was the image of Dagon lying on its face in front of the Ark! They set it up again and went away. The next morning the idol was not only lying in front of the Ark, but its head and hands had been broken off.

While the Ark was there, God sent much trouble to the Philistines. They had an epidemic of a terrible disease. Finally they figured it out. "We are being punished by the Israelis' God because we stole the Ark. We've got to get rid of it, or we'll all die!"

The leaders talked it over and decided to send it to Gath. But when it got there, the people of Gath started dying of the same disease. So they took it to another city, but when those people saw it coming, they said, "Oh, no! Now we'll die too. Send it back to the Israelis, or soon our whole nation will be destroyed by illness."

So they sent it back on a cart pulled by cows, and when the Israelis saw it coming, they were overcome with joy. They broke up the cart for firewood and sacrificed the cows on an altar, thanking God for returning the Ark. Then they made a bad mistake; they opened the Ark and looked inside, which was forbidden. A lot of them died as result of that disobedience.

F OR twenty years the Ark stayed at a place called Kiriath Jearim. The people of Israel wondered why they couldn't defeat the Philistines once and for all, and Samuel told them it was because they were sinning by having some idols in their homes. He begged them to be sorry for their sin and to get rid of the idols, so they did. Then God gave them victory over the Philistines, who didn't attack them again for a long time.

Samuel led the people faithfully all his life. When he got old, he appointed his sons to be judges in his place. But his sons were as bad as Eli's sons; they were dishonest and unfair. So the leaders of Israel said to Samuel, "You are too old to be our judge now, and your sons are bad men. They aren't at all like you. We want you to get us a king to rule us. Other nations have kings. Why shouldn't we have one too?"

Samuel didn't like that idea, but he asked God what to do. God said, "Go ahead; give them what they want. But warn them about what will happen if they have a king."

So Samuel agreed to get Israel a king, but he said, "You'll be sorry! A king will rule over you and take your money and the best of your crops and herds—even your sons and daughters. You will be like slaves."

The people refused to listen. "We don't care. We still want a king to help us defeat our enemies!"

GOD promised to help Samuel find the right king. He said, "Tomorrow I'll send you a man from the tribe of Benjamin."

Meanwhile, a young man named Saul was helping his father by hunting for some lost donkeys. Saul was a handsome fellow, much taller than other men. He and a servant tramped around for a long time, looking for the donkeys.

Finally Saul said, "We'd better give up and go home. Father will be worried about us."

His servant replied, "Before we go, let's ask the man of God who lives here if he can help us find the animals."

So they went to the town where Samuel lived. Some girls told them where to find the prophet. Samuel saw them coming, and immediately God said to him, "There! That's the man I promised to send to be king."

Samuel told Saul who he was, and then he said, "Don't worry about your father's donkeys. Someone else has already found them. Now, you are going to be very great in Israel!"

Saul said, "I'm from the smallest of the tribes— Benjamin. And my family is very unimportant. How can I possibly be 'great'?"

Samuel explained to Saul that God had chosen him to be king. He poured oil over Saul's head. That was the way people showed that God had appointed someone for special service. Later Samuel announced to the entire country that Saul was to be their king, and all the people shouted, "Long live the king!"

THE AMMONITE army attacked Jabesh, an Israeli city. When the elders of the city asked for a peace treaty, the cruel Ammonite general said, "I'll make peace with you—but I'll put out every man's right eye!"

The elders replied, "Give us seven days to get help. If we fail, we'll surrender." They sent messengers to beg other Israelis for help. A messenger came to Saul's town, and the citizens started crying. Saul came in from plowing and asked why everyone was sad. When he heard the story, the Spirit of God came into him. In anger he killed two oxen, cut them up, and sent a piece to each of Israel's tribes with a message. "This is what I'll do to all your oxen if you don't come and help the people of Jabesh!"

They sent soldiers in a hurry—330,000 of them! Saul led them into a great battle and totally defeated the Ammonites.

Then Samuel spoke to the people. "There! I've given you the king you wanted. And I've been your leader since I was a child. Tell me, have I ever taken your money? Have I ever been selfish or dishonest?"

The people all answered, "Oh, no. Never!"

Samuel reminded them that they had sinned by insisting upon having a king. To prove it, he asked God to send a sign—a heavy storm that damaged their crops and threatened their lives. He said, "God will reward you if you obey, but punish you if you don't."

20

*Saul
Disobeys
the Lord*

1 SAMUEL 13

AFTER Saul had been king for a couple of years, he and his son, Jonathan, took 3,000 men and attacked an outpost of Philistine soldiers at Geba. When the news reached the rest of the Philistines, they got together their whole huge army, including thousands of chariots and a large cavalry, and marched against Israel.

The Israelis were terrified, because they didn't have the forces to fight such a vast army. They ran away and hid in caves, behind rocks and bushes, and down in pits and wells. Some of them even crossed the Jordan River to get away from the Philistines.

Saul and some of the soldiers waited at Gilgal, because Samuel had told him he would come there in seven days to make sacrifices and ask God's advice. When Samuel didn't come on time, Saul decided to make the sacrifices himself, though he had no right to do that.

Just as Saul finished the offering, Samuel arrived and asked, "What do you think you're doing?"

"Well, you didn't come when you promised, and our enemies are about to wipe us out. I thought I'd better make the burnt offering myself."

Samuel shouted, "That was really stupid! If you had done the right thing, God would have let you and your family be kings forever. But now God is going to take away the kingdom and give it to someone who will be obedient!" Then Samuel went away, and Saul was left there with about six hundred soldiers.

ONE day Saul's son, Jonathan, said to his armor bearer, "Listen, let's sneak across the valley and go up to the Philistine camp. I don't care how many of them there are. The Lord might do some kind of miracle and let us get rid of them!"

The other young man said, "I'm with you! Let's do it!"

Jonathan said, "This is what we'll do when they see us. If they call, 'Get away from here or we'll kill you!' then we'll stop. But if they say, 'Come up here and fight with us!' we'll know that's God's way of letting us know he is going to help us win."

When the Philistine soldiers saw the two young fellows, they yelled, "Well, will you look at that! The Israelis are crawling out of their holes! Come on up here, and we'll give you a fight!"

Jonathan and his friend climbed up the rocks and started fighting. They killed about twenty men, and the other soldiers became afraid. Soon the whole army was in complete panic, which became even worse when God sent an earthquake. The Philistine soldiers were so confused that they started killing each other as they all tried to run away!

Over in the Israeli camp, Saul's sentries could see that the Philistines were disappearing, so the Israeli soldiers came out of hiding and ran after them— and God gave them a great victory.

WHEN Saul heard that God was going to give Israel a new king, he felt terrible. When Samuel started to leave him, Saul grabbed Samuel's robe, and it tore. Samuel said, "That's just the way the kingdom is going to be torn out of your hands!"

Saul asked Samuel to worship with him one more time, and he did. Then each one went to his home, and that was the last time in their lives they ever saw each other.

God told Samuel to stop feeling sorry for Saul. "Go to Bethlehem and see Jesse. I've decided on one of his sons to be the next king. Invite Jesse to worship with you when you make an offering."

Samuel did as God said. He looked carefully at Jesse's sons when they came with their father to worship. They were all fine, strong men, but God said to Samuel, "None of these is the one I've chosen. Remember, I don't choose people because of the way they look. I decide because of what's in their hearts."

Samuel asked Jesse if he had any other sons. Jesse said, "Only David, my youngest. He's in the field, taking care of my sheep."

"Call him," Samuel ordered. David came in, a handsome young fellow with red cheeks and bright eyes.

"That's the one!" God said to Samuel. So Samuel poured oil on David's head, showing everyone that he was to be the next king. And God sent his Spirit into David's heart.

WHEN Saul proved to be a disobedient king, God took his Spirit away from him. Then God allowed a bad, tormenting spirit to come into his heart and upset him terribly. When that happened, Saul would become nervous, sad, and fearful.

Everyone tried to think of a way to cure the king. Saul's advisors suggested that music might make him feel better. "Let's find someone who can stay here in the court and play the harp for you when the evil spirit makes you feel bad." And Saul liked that idea.

One of the servants said, "Oh, I know a brave young warrior who plays the harp beautifully. He is David, one of the sons of Jesse. He learned to play the harp out in the fields while he was watching his father's flock of sheep. He's a good musician, and the Lord is with him."

Saul asked Jesse to send David to try out for the job. Jesse agreed and sent David to Saul, along with a lot of gifts. Saul liked David right from the start and appointed him to be his personal musician. Each time Saul felt the evil spirit coming into his heart, he asked David to play the harp. The music would calm Saul down and make him relax. Then the troublesome spirit would leave him for awhile.

When Saul wasn't needing him, David would spend time helping Jesse with the sheep, and Saul would almost forget about him.

MAY

24

*Goliath
Frightens
the
Israelites*

1 SAMUEL 17

ISRAEL'S old enemy, the Philistines, decided to attack again, so the two armies got ready for war. The Philistines were in the hills on one side of a valley, and the Israeli army on the other side.

This time the Philistines had a very scary soldier in their army. He was a real giant—more than nine feet tall. (He wouldn't even have been able to stand up straight in the rooms most of us have in our houses!) And he was amazingly strong—strong enough to wear metal armor that weighed about two hundred pounds! He had a bronze helmet, and even his legs were covered with metal. He carried a big, thick spear with a twenty-five-pound tip. Another soldier walked in front of him, carrying a big shield to protect him.

Goliath wasn't afraid of *anybody.* He walked around in the valley, laughing at the Israeli soldiers. He shouted. "You don't *all* need to get killed. Send out just one soldier to fight with me. If he can kill me, the Philistines will be your servants. But if I kill him, then you will have to serve us! Come on, isn't anyone brave enough to fight me?"

Even though Saul was a very tall man, he was afraid of Goliath, and so were all his soldiers. No one had the courage to walk out into the valley and tangle with a giant! So they all stayed in their camp while Goliath kept daring them to fight.

DAVID'S older brothers were among Saul's soldiers. One day Jesse said to David, "I want you to go over to the battlefield and take some food to your brothers. Bring back a note from them, letting me know how they are getting along."

David got someone else to take care of the sheep, and off he went to the army camp. Since no one would go out to fight Goliath alone, the armies were lining up for an all-out battle. David found his brothers, and as they were talking, Goliath shouted out his daily challenge.

When David heard this, he asked the Israeli soldiers, "Who is this heathen fellow who dares to talk like that to the army of the living God?"

The soldiers explained, and they told David that whoever killed Goliath would receive a big reward and would be allowed to marry Saul's daughter. Some of the men told Saul what David had said, so Saul sent for him.

"Cheer up," David said to the king. "I'll kill Goliath for you."

"Not likely!" said Saul. "You're just a young man, and that giant has been a warrior all his life."

David said, "And I've been a shepherd all *my* life. God has given me strength to kill wild animals that were trying to attack my sheep. Why, I've killed a lion and a bear with my bare hands! The same God will help me kill the giant."

MAY

25

David
Hears
Goliath's
Challenge
1 SAMUEL 17

WHEN Saul saw how brave David was, he said, "Well, go ahead—and God bless you." He offered his armor to David, but when David tried it on, it was far too big and heavy for him, so he didn't wear it.

David picked up five smooth stones and put them into his shepherd's bag. With his slingshot in his hand, he walked out to meet Goliath. The giant took one look at David and roared, "Why, you're just a boy! What do you think I am, a dog that you can chase with a stick? Come on out here, and I'll feed you to the vultures!"

David called, "You are depending on your heavy weapons, but I'm depending on the Lord of the armies of heaven. He will let me kill you, and when I've cut off your head, everyone will know it was because of my God's power."

Then David ran toward Goliath, swinging his sling. He let a stone fly, and it hit the giant right in the forehead, killing him instantly. Then David used the giant's own sword to cut off his head.

When the Philistines saw their greatest warrior fall dead, they turned and ran away in terror. The Israeli soldiers chased them all the way back into their own territory, killing many of them.

Saul asked his men, "Who is that young fellow, anyway?" They reminded him that David was Jesse's son, and Saul made him an officer in his army.

DAVID became a very successful soldier in Saul's army, and he was a great hero. After he killed Goliath and was on his way home, women came out and sang and danced, shouting, "Saul killed thousands of the enemy, but David has killed tens of thousands!" Of course this made Saul very angry. He was jealous because David was so popular. He began to worry about David's taking the kingdom away from him.

The next day the evil spirit came back and bothered Saul again. He got upset and talked wildly. David began to play the harp to try to quiet Saul, but Saul threw a spear at David. David dodged it and wasn't hurt. This happened again, but again David jumped aside, and the spear missed him.

Saul thought that if he couldn't get rid of David that way, he would send him out to fight Philistines, and maybe he would get killed. Saul said, "I promised you my oldest daughter for killing Goliath, but first you must go out and win a a battle." While David was out fighting, Saul gave that daughter to another man.

David came back unharmed. He and another of Saul's daughters, Michal, wanted to get married, but Saul said, "No, first you must kill one hundred Philistines." David went out and killed *two* hundred of them, so Saul had to let Michal marry him. And the people loved David more and more.

MAY

27

Saul Is Jealous

1 SAMUEL 18

28

David's Best Friend

1 SAMUEL 18, 20

AFTER David killed Goliath, he met Saul's son, Jonathan. David and Jonathan liked each other right away and became the best of friends. They agreed always to be loyal to each other.

When Saul began to hate David, David asked Jonathan why the king wanted to kill him. Jonathan replied, "Oh, I don't think he really would kill you—but I'll find out for sure and let you know."

David said, "Well, you may not know it, but King Saul would like to see me dead. Tomorrow is the feast of the new moon. I'll stay away from the court, and you can find out what your father thinks of me."

"All right," Jonathan answered. "If he's as angry as you think, I'll come out here and shoot some arrows into the field. I'll call to my helper, 'The arrows are farther out in the field.' Then you will know you are in danger."

As they parted, David and Jonathan made a promise that they would always take care of each other's families, even if either of them should die. This is the way they showed their great love for each other.

At the feast, Jonathan found out that his father was really jealous enough to kill David, so he went out to the field and gave the signal he and David had agreed upon. David told him a sad good-bye and left that area to escape from Saul.

DAVID left Saul's court so quickly and quietly that he didn't take his weapons. He didn't even have any food with him. He went to Nob, where the Ark was being kept, and visited Ahimelech, the High Priest. And he told Ahimelech a lie, which, as we will see, led to great trouble for many people. He said, "I'm here alone because Saul has sent me on a secret mission. I need some supplies for my men who are waiting for me near here. Do you have any bread?"

Ahimelech answered, "I don't have any regular bread, but I can give you some of the special bread from the altar, if you and your men have been obeying the Law."

"Oh, yes, we have," said David. "And do you have a sword I may use? My business for the king made me leave so quickly that I couldn't bring my own sword."

"Well, the only sword here is the one that belonged to Goliath. You could take that one, I suppose."

"Fine! That's the best one I could possibly use!" David answered.

While David was talking to Ahimelech, a man named Doeg—one of Saul's cattleherders— happened to be in the Tabernacle. He overheard their conversation. Doeg hurried back to Saul's court and told him he had seen David at Nob, talking to the High Priest.

WHEN Doeg told Saul what he had seen at Nob, Saul was very angry and blamed Ahimelech for helping David. He sent for Ahimelech and the other priests from the Tabernacle. He yelled at Ahimelech for helping David escape and giving him supplies. Ahimelech said, "That's not fair! I didn't know he was lying to me; I believed everything he said. I thought I was doing the right thing to help the king's son-in-law—such a respected member of your family and your army."

But the king was too angry to listen to Ahimelech. He roared at him, "Don't make excuses! You are going to have to die—you and all your family and the other priests, too." He ordered his soldiers to kill the priests, but the soldiers were afraid to harm God's appointed priests, so they refused.

Then Saul ordered Doeg to do it, and Doeg obeyed. He killed eighty-five priests, then went to Nob and killed Ahimelech's relatives and his livestock. Only one son, Abiathar, escaped. He found where David was hiding and told him what had happened to Ahimelech and the other priests. When David heard the story, he was heartbroken to think that his selfish lie had caused such terrible trouble. He was sorry he had not trusted God to take care of him instead of lying to protect himself. He said to Abiathar, "Stay with me, and I will always take care of you."

DAVID had been gathering other men who wanted to help him—his brothers and some other fellows who didn't like serving Saul. Soon he had about four hundred followers who were loyal to him. David heard that the Philistines were causing trouble again, so he asked God if he should take his little "army" to fight them. God said yes, so they had a battle at Keilah. David's men won, and they kept the Philistines' cattle.

When Saul heard about it, he said, "Aha! Now I can catch David while he's in the city of Keilah." David heard that Saul planned to come after him, and he asked the Lord whether he was in danger. The Lord said he was, so David and his army, which had now grown to six hundred, left the city and traveled around, hiding wherever they could.

From then on for a long, long time, Saul kept trying to find David so he could kill him. But God always warned David in time for him to escape. More than once David had a chance to kill Saul, but he wouldn't do it, even when his own men urged him to.

"No," David said, "it would be wrong for me to do anything to harm the man God has chosen as king."

Once David and his men found Saul and his soldiers sleeping in a cave. David crept up quietly and cut off a bit of Saul's robe without waking him. But he would never actually hurt the king.

MAY

31

David Spares Saul's Life

1 SAMUEL 23–24

FOR awhile David and his men lived in a desert area where there was a rich sheep owner named Nabal. David's soldiers were friendly with Nabal's shepherds and were careful not ever to steal any of Nabal's sheep. Once David sent this message to Nabal:

"We have always been kind to your shepherds and have never harmed your flocks. Now we are in need of some supplies, for it is a feast time for us. Would you be so kind as to give us whatever food you can spare?"

Nabal was a mean, unpleasant man, and he answered crossly, "Who does that David think he is? Why should I give my valuable food to someone who may be a runaway or a criminal for all I know? Forget it!"

This answer made David angry, so he told one-third of his men to stay in camp to guard their supplies, while the rest put on their swords and went to teach Nabal a lesson.

While they were on the way, one of Nabal's shepherds hurried to Nabal's wife, Abigail, who was not at all like her husband. She was gentle and kind, as well as being very beautiful. The shepherd told her how kind David's men had been to them and how honest they were. Then he told Abigail how rude Nabal had been to David's messenger.

Abigail realized they were in danger because of Nabal's insults, so she quickly thought of a plan. Could she save them from David's anger?

ABIGAIL got busy right away, preparing some food for David and his men. She gathered two hundred loaves of bread, two large containers of wine, five sheep ready for cooking, two bushels of roasted grain, a hundred cakes of raisins, and two hundred cakes of dried figs. She loaded all this onto donkeys. She sent servants on ahead, and she followed.

Abigail met David as he approached Nabal's farm. She got off of her donkey and bowed low before him.

She said, "Sir, I apologize for my husband's rudeness. He is a wicked, foolish man. If I had known about your messengers' visit, I would have sent food immediately. Now, please forgive us and accept what I have brought for you and your men. I know God has blessed you and will make you the king of Israel. Surely you would not want to have Nabal's death on your conscience."

David's heart was touched, and he answered, "Of course I accept your apology. I'm glad you talked to me before I saw Nabal, or we would have killed him for sure. Thank you for your gift. Go back home in peace."

Abigail went home, and the next day she told Nabal how she had prevented David from killing him. He was so shocked that he became very ill and couldn't move. Ten days later, he died.

When David heard that Nabal was dead, he sent his men to bring Abigail to his camp, and they were married.

*David
Refuses
to Kill
the King*

1 SAMUEL 26

ONCE when Saul was looking for him, David took his nephew Abishai and very quietly crept over to Saul's camp at night. They saw Saul asleep on the ground, with Abner, his general, beside him. The other soldiers lay around them in a circle, to protect them. Saul's spear was stuck into the ground beside his head.

Abishai whispered to David, "God has given us a good chance to get rid of your enemy. I'll tip-toe over and run his spear through him, and then . . ."

"No, indeed!" David answered. "God made him king, and I would be doing wrong to kill him. Someday God will deal with him. Let's just take his spear and the water bottle there beside him, and get out of here."

They did, and no one saw or heard them. When they were a safe distance away, David shouted, "Hey, Abner! Wake up! You haven't been taking very good care of the king. Where is his spear that was beside his head—and his water jar? Some bodyguard you are!"

Saul recognized David's voice, and he called, "Is that you, David, my boy?"

"Yes, my lord. Tell me what I've done to deserve your anger. I would never hurt you, but you have driven me away from my home."

Then Saul told David he was sorry. He said, "Come on home now and I won't hurt you." But David didn't trust Saul, so he just left the spear there and went away.

DAVID realized that Saul might chase him forever, so he asked Achish, a Philistine leader, for a city to live in. In return, David and his soldiers would help Achish with his wars. David and his men took their families and settled in the city of Ziklag. Then Saul stopped hunting for them.

After awhile some of the Philistines prepared to attack Saul's army. Saul asked God what to do, but God would not answer. Saul used to get advice from the Lord through Samuel, but Samuel had died. Saul wanted to try to talk to Samuel's spirit, but he himself had made a law against trying to get messages from the dead. He was so desperate that he disguised himself and went to Endor, where there was a woman who thought she could talk to dead people.

He told her he wanted to talk to Samuel. She said, "The king has forbidden this. I'll get into trouble." But he talked her into it. Even she was surprised when Samuel appeared! Then she guessed that her visitor was the king, and she was terrified.

Saul asked Samuel what he should do about the Philistines. Samuel said, "I can't help you. You got yourself into this when you disobeyed God. Now God will give David the kingdom. And when you fight with the Philistines, they will win—and tomorrow you will be dead, too."

Saul was sick with fear, but the woman gave him food to eat. Then he was strong enough to leave.

JUNE

4

Saul Calls Samuel's Spirit
1 SAMUEL 28

*David
Defeats
the
Amalekites*

1 SAMUEL 30

DAVID and his men expected to fight against Saul's army, right along with the Philistines. But some of the Philistine leaders didn't trust him. "He'll probably desert and go back to Saul when we start fighting. We don't want him with us." So David took his men back to Ziklag, but they found that a terrible thing had happened. The Amalekite army had come and burned the city and had stolen the women and children—including David's own two wives.

David asked God, "If I catch up with the Amalekites, can I defeat them and get our families back?"

God said, "Yes, go! You will get back everything they have stolen."

So David and his men started out. Along the way, two hundred of the soldiers were too tired to go on, so they stayed behind. The rest of the soldiers soon caught up to the Amalekites and fought fiercely with them for a day and a night. At last they killed almost all the enemy and were able to take their wives and children and property home, along with livestock they took from the Amalekites' camp.

When they rejoined the two hundred who had stayed behind. some of David's men said, "They don't deserve any of the loot, because they didn't help with the fighting."

David said, "No, that's not fair. Those who stay with the equipment are just as important as those who fight. After all, the Lord is the one who gives us the victory!"

JUST as Samuel had told Saul, the Philistines were too strong for Israel's army. They overpowered the Israelis and killed many of them, including Saul's sons, Jonathan, Abinidab, and Malchishua. Then a Philistine soldier shot an arrow that wounded Saul very badly. He said to his armor bearer, "Please kill me, so that the Philistines don't capture me and torture me."

But his armor bearer couldn't bring himself to do that, so Saul made himself fall against the point of his own sword, and that killed him. When his armor bearer saw what Saul had done, he felt so bad that he too fell on his sword and took his own life. The Philistines chased the Israelis out of their towns and occupied them. What a sad day for God's people!

When the Philistine soldiers went out into the battlefield to steal things from the bodies of the dead soldiers, they found the bodies of Saul and his sons. They cut off their heads and displayed them on the wall of one of their cities to show their disrespect for the Israeli king.

When the Israelis heard that, they came and took away the bodies. They cremated them and buried the ashes, then they mourned for their king for seven days.

JUNE

6

Israel's First King Dies

1 SAMUEL 31

IN SPITE of all the trouble between David and Saul, David was sorry when he heard that Saul was dead, and he wrote a sad song of mourning.

David asked God, "Is this the right time for me to move back to Judah?" and God said yes. So he and his six hundred men and their families all went back and settled in the city of Hebron. Right away the leaders of Judah crowned David king of their tribe.

Meanwhile, Saul's army commander, Abner, chose Saul's son Ish-bosheth to be king of the other tribes of Israel. So God's people were divided into two groups, each with its own king. For several years they fought many battles, each trying to take control of the whole nation.

Gradually David's group became stronger than the Israel group. After awhile Abner and Ish-bosheth had a quarrel, and Abner offered to surrender all of Israel's forces to David. "But in exchange, you must make me the commander of the combined army," he told David.

Now Joab, one of David's chief soldiers, hated Abner, so without out David's knowing it, he murdered Abner. Then two of Ish-bosheth's army captains killed Ish-bosheth and bragged about it to David. David was angry, because he had wanted always to be fair to everyone in Saul's family, so he had the assassins killed.

With Ish-bosheth dead, all the people of Israel said they wanted David to be their king, too, so his kingdom was united at last.

WITH the army of Israel united and strong, David drove the Jebusites out of the city of Jerusalem. Then he made it his capital city, and ever since then it has been the capital of the Israelis. Next, David won wars against the Philistines, and with the Lord's help he wiped most of them out.

Now David wanted to get the Ark back where it belonged, so he and 30,000 soldiers went to the town where it had been held for many years. They put the Ark on a new ox-cart, and two men—Uzzah and Ahio—walked beside it. When they went over some rough ground, one of the oxen stumbled. Uzzah put out his hand and held the Ark steady.

God had said that men must never touch the Ark. They must move it by lifting it with poles that went through some rings on the side of the Ark. So when Uzzah touched the Ark, God was angry with him and struck him dead right there. This upset David and he said, "I'm afraid to keep on moving the Ark. We'll leave it here, at the home of Obed-edom."

The Ark was there for three months, and during that time God greatly blessed Obed-edom and his family. When David saw that, he decided it was time to go back and get the Ark and take it home.

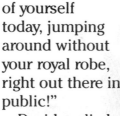

DAVID went to the home of Obed-edom and got the Ark. He and the people with him started the trip to Jerusalem. They were so happy that they sang and danced and shouted for joy as they traveled along. Every few steps they would stop, and David would sacrifice a bull and a calf, in thanksgiving to God.

As they entered Jerusalem, David danced and sang more than anyone else, while trumpets were blown to announce their coming. His wife Michal, the daughter of Saul, watched the procession from the window. When she saw the way David was acting, she thought it was disgusting.

At last the Ark was back where it belonged, and David made more sacrifices. Then he blessed the people in the name of the Lord and gave each man and woman a gift of bread, raisins, and dates.

When all the people went to their homes, David went home to give blessings to his own family. But Michal didn't feel like celebrating. She spoke to him in a nasty way: "You really made a fool of yourself today, jumping around without your royal robe, right out there in public!"

David replied, "Look, I was dancing before the Lord, not to get the attention of people. God chose me to be king instead of any of your father's sons, and he made me the leader. I would be willing to look even more foolish than I did today, to express my thanks to God!"

DAVID thought a great deal about his dear friend Jonathan, who had been killed in the same battle with his brothers and his father, Saul. David missed him and wanted to do something to honor his memory. He remembered how he and Jonathan had promised to take care of each other's families in case either of them should die. David sent for Ziba, an old servant of Saul's, and asked him, "Are any members of Saul's household still living? I made a vow to be kind to them."

The servant said, "Yes, one of Jonathan's sons is alive. He is Mephibosheth, who was crippled when he was a little boy. His nurse dropped him, and the fall injured both of his feet."

So David sent for Mephibosheth, who came rather fearfully and bowed to David. "Don't be afraid of me," David said. "I loved your father, Jonathan, and I want to be kind to you for his sake. I'll give back your family's land, but I want you to come and live here at the palace with me and eat at my table."

Then David said to Ziba, "I've given all of Saul's land to Mephibosheth. Now I want you and your family to farm Mephibosheth's land so his family will have plenty of food. But he is going to live at the palace as my guest for the rest of his life."

JUNE

10

David's Kindness to Jonathan's Family

2 SAMUEL 9

Oxxx NE year David's army was at war with the Ammonites. David usually fought along with his soldiers, but that spring he stayed in Jerusalem. One night he couldn't sleep, so he walked around on the roof of the palace. From there he could see into a nearby home where a beautiful woman was bathing. David learned that she was the wife of Uriah, one of his army officers. Her name was Bath-sheba.

David sent for her, and when she came, he slept with her as if she were his wife. She went home, but soon she sent word to the king that she was pregnant.

David didn't want anyone to know he was the father of the baby. He tried to get Uriah to go home, so it would look as if he had been with his wife and the baby was his. But Uriah wouldn't go. He said, "My duty is to my country and to the army."

David decided to get rid of Uriah so he could marry Bath-sheba. He told General Joab to send Uriah into a part of the fighting where he would almost certainly be killed. So Joab put Uriah in the front line and then pulled the other soldiers back, leaving Uriah to die.

Joab sent the news to David, and David said to the messenger, "Well, that's the way it goes. Some get killed and some don't."

Then David married Bath-sheba, and soon she had a baby boy.

GOD was greatly displeased with David because he had coveted another man's wife and had committed adultery and murder. God sent a prophet named Nathan to talk to David about his sins.

Nathan told David this story: "Once two men were neighbors. One was very rich and had many sheep and cattle. The other was poor; he had only one little ewe lamb. The poor man's lamb was a beloved pet, almost like one of the family. Once the rich man had a guest. Instead of killing one of the sheep from his own large flock, he stole the poor man's lamb and cooked it for his guest's dinner."

David was terribly angry. He said, "Why, a selfish man like that should be killed, but first he must give the poor man four lambs to pay for the one he stole."

Nathan said, "David, you are that rich man. God has been good to you. He saved you from Saul and made you king over Israel and Judah. You have everything you need. Why have you done this great sin of stealing Uriah's wife and then murdering him? Now you shall always live in fear of war, and your family shall become rebellious."

David confessed that he had sinned against God. Nathan said that because he was sorry, he would not have to die, but Bathsheba's baby would die. In a few days the baby became very sick, and although David prayed for him, he died.

13

A Rebellious Son

2 SAMUEL 13–14

DAVID had married several women, so he had children who were half brothers and sisters. Some of them were jealous of one another and quarreled a lot. One time David's oldest son, Amnon, hurt the sister of his half brother, Absalom. This made Absalom furious. When he had a chance, he told his servants to kill Amnon—which, of course, made him a murderer just as if he had done the killing himself. Absalom had to run away to keep David from punishing him, and he stayed away for three years.

David had been angry with Absalom, but gradually he began to miss his son. Joab persuaded him to allow Absalom to return home. But David said Absalom would have to stay in his own home and not come to see him.

For two years Absalom lived in Jerusalem but didn't get to see his father. Finally he asked Joab to get David to change his mind. So David let Absalom come to see him.

This did not heal the trouble between them. Absalom didn't forgive his father for not accepting him, so he decided to try to get the kingdom away from David. He was a fine-looking young man, with long thick hair that he cut only once a year. People liked him, and he began to try to win their loyalty to himself and away from David.

Absalom went to Hebron and gathered a lot of followers. Some men blew trumpets and everyone shouted, "Absalom is king in Hebron."

WHEN David realized how popular Absalom had become, he thought, "I'd better get out of Jerusalem before he comes after me to kill me." David wasn't even sure he deserved God's help, because he remembered how his sin with Bath-sheba had displeased God.

David's friend Hushai wanted to go with him, but David said, "No, you stay here and keep an eye on what Absalom does. You can send me messages that may save my life." So Hushai stayed in Jerusalem, but David and his loyal soldiers went out and hid in the wilderness.

They had just gotten away, when Absalom and his army entered the city. His advisor said, "Let's take twelve thousand men and chase after David. We can easily kill him, and his people will make you king in his place."

Hushai pretended to be loyal to Absalom, so Absalom asked Hushai what he thought he should do.

Hushai said, "Oh, you had better wait and gather a much larger army than that." He said this so David would have more time to escape and hide. Then he sent a secret message to David, telling him what Absalom was planning.

The messengers were priests' sons named Jonathan and Ahima-az. Some of Absalom's spies saw them and chased them. A man hid Jonathan and Ahima-az in his well until the enemy gave up looking for them. Then they went on and warned David to get ready for war.

DAVID prepared for battle by dividing his army into three groups, each under one of his generals. He planned to march out with his troops, but the leaders said, "No, you stay here and send us support as we need it."

So David agreed to do this. As the soldiers marched out to battle, David said to the three generals—Joab, Abishai, and Ittai—"Please, for my sake, be gentle with my son Absalom." And all the soldiers heard what David said to the generals.

The two armies fought the war in a forest, and David's forces won. Twenty thousand men were killed. As Absalom was riding his donkey away from the battlefield, his long hair got caught in the branches of an oak tree. The donkey ran on and left him hanging there by his hair. One of David's soldiers saw him there and rode on and told Joab about it.

Joab said, "Well, why didn't you kill him when you had the chance? I would have rewarded you!"

The soldier said, "I should say not! I heard what King David said to you and the other generals about being merciful to Absalom. I certainly wouldn't do the king's son any harm after that, not for any amount of reward!"

Joab said, "Well, I don't mind doing it." He rode back to the tree where Absalom was hanging and stabbed him with darts. And that was the end of the rebellion against King David.

EVEN though Absalom had been rebellious, David loved him and was sad when he got killed. He cried, "Oh, Absalom, my son, my son!" This began to make everyone else feel sad instead of joyful about their victory.

Joab said to David, "Look, your people have fought bravely to save you from that traitor Absalom. Now you are behaving as if they had done something wrong. If you want them to be loyal to you, you had better stop this and congratulate them." So David stopped mourning and went out to thank his army.

Then everyone was happy, and for awhile it looked as if the country would be united and peaceful. But then Sheba, another rebel, came along and got Israel to follow him. But the people of Judah were still loyal to David. After more fighting, Sheba was killed and his rebellion stopped.

At last the nation was united. David had many strong, faithful warriors who helped defeat Israel's enemies. When David grew too old to fight, his warriors protected him. One of them killed the brother of Goliath, a giant almost as large as Goliath had been. And three other giants were killed—one of them had six fingers on each hand and six toes on each foot!

In his old age David made up songs of praise to God, just as he had done when he was a young shepherd boy. Many of David's songs are in the Bible, in the book of Psalms.

JUNE

16

King David Praises God

2 SAMUEL 18–24

E VEN after Amnon and Absalom had died, David still had several sons. He knew he was going to die soon, so he had to decide who would be king after him. One of the sons, Adonijah, tried to force the people to accept him as king.

When Bath-sheba heard that, she went to David and said, "Didn't you tell me that my son, Solomon, is to be the king after you die? Well, Adonijah has persuaded the people to crown him without your knowing about it. What are you going to do about this?"

The prophet Nathan came to see David too, and he urged David to make Solomon king right away. So David said to Bath-sheba, "I give you my word, just as I did before: your son, Solomon, shall be king."

Then he told Nathan and the priests to anoint Solomon and to announce to all the country that he was the new king.

When Adonijah heard the news, he was afraid Solomon would kill him as punishment for trying to get the kingdom. He went to the Tabernacle and took hold of the horns of the altar for protection. Solomon said, "Tell Adonijah that if he will be a good man, I won't harm him. But if he gets into trouble, he shall die."

David talked with Solomon and told him many things he needed to know to be a good king. He told him which men would be loyal to him and which ones could not be trusted.

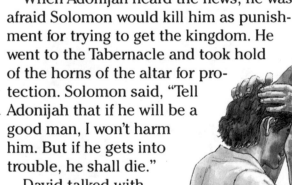

SOON after this, King David died. He had been king for a total of forty years—seven years in Hebron and thirty-three years in Jerusalem. His children buried him in Jerusalem, the City of David. Now Solomon was the king, and he tried to rule wisely.

During the last years of David's life, he had had a nurse named Abishag. After Solomon became king, Adonijah wanted to marry Abishag. He asked Bath-sheba to get Solomon's permission.

When Solomon heard the message, he said, "Don't even ask such a thing. I certainly won't say yes. And I vow that even today I will see that Adonijah is killed!" And he ordered Benaiah to kill Adonijah.

Solomon didn't trust Abiathar the priest, but he didn't want to kill him because of Abiathar's faithfulness to King David. So he told him he could no longer be a priest, and he had to return to his boyhood home. This made the prophecy come true that God had spoken when he told the boy Samuel that Eli's family would not continue to be priests, because of their disobedience.

Joab had helped Adonijah try to become king, so when he heard about Adonijah's death and Abiathar's exile, he thought he would probably be next. He went to the Tabernacle and held the horns of the altar for safety, but Solomon had him killed anyway, because of his rebellion. Then no one was left who wanted to rebel against Solomon.

JUNE

19

*Solomon
Makes
a Wise
Decision*

1 KINGS 3

SOLOMON longed to be wise enough to rule well. One night he had a dream in which he told God he wanted wisdom more than anything else in the world.

Then God said, "That was such a good request that I am going to give you the wisdom you asked for, and I am going to give you riches and honor too, even though you didn't ask for them."

One day two women who lived in the same house came to ask Solomon to settle a quarrel. One of them said, "This other woman and I each had a baby. Her baby died, but in the night she took my baby and left her dead baby in my bed. In the morning I could see that the dead child was not mine, but she won't give back my own baby."

The other woman said, "That's not true! The dead baby is hers, and the living baby is mine."

Solomon decided to test them. He took a sword and held up the living baby and said, "We'll settle this by cutting the baby in two and giving half to each woman."

One of the women agreed, but the woman who was really the baby's mother cried out, "Oh, no! Give him to her! I'd rather give him up than let him be killed."

Then Solomon said, "Give the baby to the one who wants his life spared. She is the real mother."

And everyone in the kingdom could see how wise God had made Solomon.

K ING David had always wanted to build a Temple as a permanent house for God, but God said he wanted Solomon to do that. So Solomon was eager to start the work.

King Hiram of Tyre offered to help. He cut beautiful cedar and cypress logs in Lebanon, and floated them down to Israel on the Mediterranean Sea. Solomon paid him by providing food for Hiram's workmen. Solomon sent men to help with the logging and also used some men to cut big blocks of stone from quarries.

After they had prepared all the materials, the building began. The main part of the Temple was ninety feet long, thirty feet wide, and forty-five feet high. Because all the stone had been cut to the right size at the quarry, the building was put together without the sound of hammers and chisels. The inside of the walls was lined with the cedar boards, then everything was covered with gold—even the ceiling and the cypress floors were bright gold.

Like the Tabernacle, the Temple had a special inner room called the Most Holy Place. That room was thirty feet square, and everything was covered with pure gold. There the Ark was kept, and the gold-covered altar. Beside the Ark were two very large carved figures of cherubs.

The whole Temple was a beautiful house for God. The Lord said to Solomon, "As long as you obey me and live as you should, I will live here among your people and will never abandon you."

20

Solomon Builds God's Temple
1 KINGS 6–7

THE NEXT job was to make all the furnishings for the Temple. Skillful craftsmen made basins, pots, shovels, tanks, latticework, and pillars. They did beautiful carving in the wood paneling, then overlaid it with gold. Everything was made as perfectly as possible, because it was for the house of God.

After seven years of work, everything was finished. Then Solomon called all the people together in October for a big celebration. The priests carried the Ark from the Tabernacle and placed it in the Most Holy Place, with the wings of the two large cherubs shadowing its cover. Inside the Ark were the tablets of stone on which the Ten Commandments were written.

As the priests came out of the Most Holy Place after setting the Ark in its place, the glory of God came and filled the Temple like a huge cloud. What an exciting and holy moment!

King Solomon blessed the people of Israel, and then he prayed a long prayer to God. He dedicated the Temple to God's service and promised that he and his people would always worship God faithfully.

Then he sacrificed thousands of cattle, sheep, and goats as a peace offering. He and the people celebrated for fourteen days. After that they went to their homes with their hearts full of joy and thanksgiving for God's blessings to them.

GOD had said he would make King Solomon rich and powerful, and he certainly kept his word. Solomon's riches and the beauty of his palace were famous all over the world. Much of his wealth came from taxes paid to him as well as money earned from trade with other countries. He received gold worth millions of dollars. He had so much gold that he ate his food off of solid gold dishes and covered many of his furnishings with gold.

He had the most unusual throne in the world. It was made of ivory, all covered with gold, and six steps led up to it. A lion stood by each arm of the throne and a lion at each end of the six steps. He owned many thousands of horses, with 1,400 chariots and twelve thousand cavalrymen. Many of his horses were imported from Egypt and Turkey.

Because God had given him great wisdom, people came to him from all over the world to ask his advice about their problems. They brought him expensive gifts in appreciation for his help.

The queen of Sheba came to visit him because she was curious about all the reports of his wealth and his wisdom. She brought him many gifts, and he gave her a tour of his palace and all his possessions.

She asked him hard questions, and he was able to answer them all. She was amazed at everything she saw, as well as by his God-given wisdom.

JUNE
23

King Solomon Breaks God's Law

1 KINGS 11

EVEN wise people can make mistakes, and that is what happened to King Solomon. The mistake he made was that he married the wrong kind of women, and too many of them. His first wife was the daughter of Pharaoh, the king of Egypt.

But that was only the beginning. After that he married hundreds of women, and most of them came from countries and tribes where the people worshiped idols. His wives were idol-worshipers; so Solomon built places for them to worship their false gods. After awhile he himself began to believe in those gods and worship them too.

This was a great sin, breaking the first two commandments, which warned about having other gods besides the one true God and also about making idols and worshiping them. Of course God was disappointed in Solomon and became angry with him.

Finally God spoke sternly to Solomon: "You told me you would always obey me and keep my commandments. You said you would lead the people to worship only me. Now you have broken your word. I will punish you by taking away most of the kingdom from your family. Because I loved your father, David, I will let you go on being king as long as you live. But after you die, all but one tribe will rebel against your son."

And that was the end of Solomon's peaceful years. Enemies began to attack him, and the rest of his life was full of trouble and warfare.

ONE day a prophet named Ahijah met Jeroboam, one of Solomon's government officials. Ahijah was wearing a new coat. He took it off and tore it into twelve pieces.

He handed ten pieces to Jeroboam and said, "Here, the Lord is going to make you the king of ten tribes of Israel. He will let only the tribes of Judah and Benjamin stay in Solomon's family after his death."

Solomon heard about this and tried to kill Jeroboam. But the young man ran away and hid in Egypt.

After Solomon had been king for forty years, he died and was buried in the City of David. Then his son Rehoboam was crowned as king. All the people gathered in Jerusalem for the coronation.

Jeroboam heard about Solomon's death and returned for the ceremony. He stirred up trouble for Rehoboam by getting some of the citizens to ask the new king, "Are you going to be as hard on us as your father was, or will you be more kind?"

Rehoboam wasn't sure how to answer, so he asked advice. Older people told him to answer gently and pleasantly, but young men advised him to get tough with the people. He took the young men's advice, and this made the people angry.

They said, "We don't want this mean fellow to be our king. Down with the family of David! Let Rehoboam rule his own little family tribe, and we'll get Jeroboam to rule the rest of the country." This was just what God had planned.

NOW God's people were divided into two different nations. Jeroboam's part was called Israel, and Rehoboam's was called Judah—named for the larger of the two tribes that formed it. Rehoboam thought he should fight to reunite the kingdom, but God said, "No, this is the way I want it."

Jeroboam set up his capital at Shechem. He got to thinking, "If my people go to the Temple in Jerusalem to make sacrifices, they may begin to want to be part of Judah and give their loyalty to Rehoboam. I'd better make them a place to worship here in Israel."

Then he committed a great sin. He formed two golden calves and set up one in Dan and the other in Bethel.

He said to the people, "Here are your gods who brought you out of Egypt and gave you the Land of Promise." Then he made shrines all over the countryside and appointed new priests who were not Levites. He also set new times for feasts and festivals, entirely ignoring the rules God had given the people for proper worship.

God sent a prophet from Judah to an altar where Jeroboam was making an offering. The prophet said, "Someday one of the kings of Judah will kill these false priests. To prove that what I say is true, God will split the altar in two."

This made Jeroboam angry. He pointed to the prophet and yelled, "Grab him!" Instantly the king's arm was paralyzed, and the altar split in two, spilling all the ashes.

WHEN Jeroboam found he couldn't move his arm, he begged the prophet to pray for him. The prophet asked God to heal him, and immediately the arm was all right.

Jeroboam invited the prophet to come and eat at his home and receive a reward. The prophet said, "No, God told me I must not eat or drink anything here, and that I must go home by a different way than I came." So he started back to Judah.

Another old prophet lived in Bethel. His sons told him about the prophet who had come from Judah and about what had happened to Jeroboam. The father got on his donkey and rode after him. When he found him, he said, "Do come home with me and have a meal."

"No," said the prophet from Judah, "God has forbidden me to eat or drink anything in Israel."

Then the older prophet told him a lie. He said, "Well, I am a prophet too, and God told me it would be all right."

The prophet believed him. He went to his home, where he ate and drank. Then the Lord gave the old prophet this message for the prophet from Judah: "You have disobeyed me. Therefore your body will not be buried with your ancestors."

The prophet hurried away and started home again. But a lion attacked him on the road and killed him. His body was taken back to Bethel and buried, far away from his family burial place.

27

Jeroboam's Son Dies

1 KINGS 14

JEROBOAM had a little boy named Abijah, who became very sick. His father was worried about him, so he said to his wife, "Put on old clothes so no one will know you are the queen. Go and visit that old prophet, Ahijah, who told me I would be king. Ask him what will happen to our son."

His wife obeyed. She took gifts of bread, figs, and honey and went to find Ahijah, who by this time was very old and blind.

Before she got there, the Lord told Ahijah she was coming. And he told Ahijah how to answer her. When the old man heard her footsteps at his door, he called, "Come on in, wife of Jeroboam! Why are you trying to fool me?"

Then he gave her a long message for her husband. "Tell Jeroboam that the Lord took the kingdom away from David's family and made him king. But he has disobeyed the Lord all along the way by making idols for the people to worship. As his punishment, I am going to let your little boy die. He is the only one who will be buried, because when the other members of your family die, the dogs and the birds will eat their bodies."

Ahijah then told the queen, "Go on home. As soon as you get there, your little son will die." And that is just what happened.

Jeroboam ruled for twenty-two years. Then he died, and his son Nadab became king of Israel.

DURING the next forty years, Israel had one king after another, and they did many things that displeased God.

Nadab ruled Israel for only two years. During that time he led the people in worshiping the golden calves his father, Jeroboam, had made. Then a man named Baasha wanted the throne, so he killed Nadab and became king. As soon as he began his reign, he killed every one of Jeroboam's family members.

Baasha was an idol-worshiper too, and he bowed down to the golden calves, thus disobeying the Ten Commandments. After he had been king for twenty-two years, he died and his son Elah became king.

Elah was a bad king too, but he ruled for only two years. A man named Zimri assassinated him and took the throne. He did this while many of the men of Israel were away fighting the Philistines. When they heard the news, they said, "We don't want that fellow to be our king. We want Omri. Let's get rid of Zimri right away!"

They marched up to the city where Zimri had his palace. He saw that he would be captured for sure. He shut himself into his palace and set fire to it, committing suicide before the soldiers could kill him. He really had a short reign—only a week!

Omri established the capital of Israel at Samaria, and there it stayed for many years. Omri wasn't a good king, either. He worshiped the golden calves and turned his back on the Lord God. He ruled for twelve years, and after his death his son Ahab was crowned king.

FROM Jeroboam to Omri, Israel had six kings, and not one of them loved and obeyed God. All of them bowed down to idols and worshiped false gods.

Some of the people must have been hoping for a godly king, but when they got Ahab, they got the worst one of all! He did all the bad things the other kings had done—and even more.

He married Jezebel, the daughter of a heathen king. She worshiped the false god Baal, and soon Ahab began to worship him too. He even built a temple to Baal and set up other altars for idol worship.

No other king had ever made God as angry as Ahab did, so God sent a messenger to tell him about the punishment God would send.

The messenger was the prophet Elijah, and the message was this: "My God says that for the next few years, no rain will fall—not even a drop of dew will moisten the earth—unless I give my permission."

Of course Ahab was furious with Elijah, so God told Elijah to hurry away and hide near Cherith Brook. "You can drink the water from the brook, and I will send ravens to bring you food."

For a long time Elijah ate the bread and meat the ravens brought, and he had water to drink from the brook. But without rain, the brook finally dried up, so God said, "Now go to the village of Zarephath. I have told a widow there to take care of you."

JUNE

30

*Elijah
Raises a
Dead Boy
to Life*
1 KINGS 17

AS ELIJAH entered Zarephath, he saw a woman picking up sticks. He said, "May I please have a drink of water?" She turned to get the water, and he called, "May I have some bread, too?"

She shook her head sadly. "I don't have a bit of bread in the house—just a handful of flour and a few drops of oil. These sticks are for a fire, so I can bake a last loaf for my son and myself. After that we will starve to death."

Elijah said, "Don't worry about food! You go home and bake bread with the flour you have, but give me the first small loaf. God has promised you will never run out of flour and oil."

She baked bread and gave Elijah the first piece. And from then on, until the rains came and crops could grow again, she always had enough food for herself, her little boy, and the prophet.

One day her son got sick and died very suddenly. She was heartbroken. Elijah took the boy to his room and laid him on the bed. He prayed, "O Lord, this woman has helped me. Why have you let her boy die?"

Then three times Elijah cried out to God, "Please give back this child's life!" And the boy came back to life!

Elijah took him to his mother and said, "Look! He's alive again!"

The woman said, "Now I realize you are a man of God, and everything he tells you to say is true."

1

Drought and Famine

1 KINGS 18

THREE years went by and still it didn't rain. Finally, God told Elijah to go to King Ahab and tell him God was going to end the drought.

While Elijah was on the way, the king and Obadiah, one of his palace staff members, went out to look for some grass for their horses and mules. The king said, "Obadiah, you go one way and I'll go the other. We must find food to save these animals from starvation."

Obadiah met Elijah, who was walking toward the palace. He said, "Aren't you Elijah, the prophet?"

"Yes," Elijah said, "and I'm on my way to the palace to see Ahab. Please tell him I am coming."

"If I do that," Obadiah groaned, "I'll be in big trouble. The king has been looking for you and asking about you everywhere. If I tell him you are coming, and then the Lord takes you away somewhere else, he will be furious. He'll probably kill me!"

Elijah said, "Don't worry. I give you my word that I won't disappear again but will really come before Ahab."

When Ahab heard Elijah was coming, he went out to meet him. He yelled, "So, there you are! You're the one who has brought so much trouble to Israel!"

Elijah answered, "Not I! You are the one who has caused all the trouble, because you turned your back on the Lord God and worshiped Baal and other false gods."

ELIJAH decided to prove to the people of Israel who their true God really was. He said to King Ahab, "Call all the people to Mount Carmel. Bring the 450 prophets of Baal and the 400 prophets of Asherah who eat their meals at the queen's table."

Ahab got all the people and the prophets together, and then Elijah spoke to the people of Israel: "How long are you going to go on like this, saying you are God's people but actually worshiping Baal? If God is the true God, then worship him. But if Baal is really God, then follow him." The people didn't know what to say.

Then Elijah said, "I'm the only one of God's prophets left alive. Baal has 450 prophets. Let them take a bull for sacrifice and cut it up and put it on their altar, but don't light the fire. Then let Baal's prophets pray to him, and if he is really God, he will send fire to burn up the sacrifice."

The people all said, "Yes! That's a good idea."

So the 450 prophets began to pray to Baal, but nothing happened. They jumped and danced around; they even cut themselves with knives. This went on all day, but of course Baal didn't answer them, because he was just an idol. Elijah made fun of them and yelled, "Maybe your god is asleep or taking a trip or something!" But still nothing happened, no matter what the prophets did.

THEN it was Elijah's turn. He called the people to gather around him. He chose twelve large stones to represent the twelve tribes of Israel, whom God had chosen to be his special people. Using those stones, Elijah repaired the altar of the Lord that had been broken down. Then he dug a ditch around it.

He killed a bull, cut it in pieces, and put the pieces on the altar. Once—twice—three times he poured water over the altar, so much water that it covered the sacrifice and then ran down and filled the ditch around the altar.

At last everything was ready. He stood quietly before the altar and prayed, "O Lord, you have been the faithful God of Abraham, Isaac, and Jacob. Now prove to these people that you are indeed the one true God, so they will worship you again."

Instantly, fire swooped down from heaven and burned up the sacrifice, the wood, and the stones. It even dried up all the water in the ditch. The people all fell down on their faces and cried out, "Almighty God is the true God! Almighty God is the true God!"

Elijah told the people to grab the prophets of Baal before they could escape. They captured them all and took them to the Kishon Brook. There Elijah killed all those false prophets so they could not lead God's people in idol worship anymore.

WHEN Elijah had finished getting rid of the prophets of Baal, he said to King Ahab, "Go and enjoy your dinner, because I can tell that rain is on the way."

While Ahab was eating and drinking, Elijah climbed to the top of Mount Carmel and got down on his knees. He said to his servant, "Go and look out toward the sea, then tell me what you see."

The servant came back and said, "I don't see anything."

Elijah said, "Go again." And he said this to his servant over and over, seven times.

Finally the servant returned and reported, "Well, I do see a very small cloud on the horizon, far across the sea. It isn't any larger than a man's hand."

"Good!" said Elijah. "Now go and tell Ahab that he'd better get into his chariot and drive quickly down the mountain. Soon the rain will be so heavy he can't make the trip."

Even as he said this, that little cloud grew larger and moved toward them. In just moments the sky became black with storm clouds. The wind blew fiercely, and then the rain came. It just poured! King Ahab was riding in his open chariot, on his way to the city. After three years without rain, it must have felt good to get soaked to the skin! God gave Elijah strength to run along the road even faster than Ahab's chariot horses. He passed them up and got to the city first!

A S SOON as Ahab got home, he told Queen Jezebel everything that had happened on Mount Carmel—how her Baal prophets had failed in the contest with Elijah and how the Lord God had proved himself. She got more and more upset, but when he got to the part about how Elijah had actually killed all the Baal prophets, she became terribly angry. She sent this message to Elijah: "By this time tomorrow, I will see to it that you are as

dead as those prophets!"

Elijah was really afraid she would kill him, so he fled from the city. He left his servant in Beer-sheba, then he traveled all day out into the desert where, he hoped, Jezebel couldn't find him.

By night he was tired out from everything he had been through that day. He sat under a tree and told God how discouraged he was. "You might as well take my life," he said. Then he stretched out and fell asleep.

Pretty soon an angel came and touched him, waking him up. "Get up and eat," the angel said. Elijah looked around and was surprised to see some fresh bread and a jar of water on a rock nearby. He ate and drank, then went back to sleep. Again the angel came. "Come and eat some more. You need strength for a long journey."

Again Elijah ate, and then he started a trip that lasted forty days and nights. He went to Mount Horeb, where he camped in a cave.

GOD spoke to Elijah on Mount Horeb. "What are you doing here, Elijah?"

Elijah said, "I've been trying to serve you well. Your people have broken their promises to you and have been worshiping idols. In fact, I'm the only true believer left, and now they want to kill me, too."

God answered, "Step outside the cave, Elijah, and stand before me as I pass by." Elijah stood on the mountain, and a strong wind blew by, but that wasn't the Lord.

Then an earthquake shook the land and the rocks, but God wasn't in the earthquake. A fire came, but still God didn't pass by.

Finally Elijah heard a small, quiet voice, and he knew God had come.

The voice said, "Elijah, why are you here?"

Again Elijah told God he was the only faithful believer left in Israel. God replied, "Listen here, Elijah. You are not alone! I still have seven thousand loyal followers who have never worshiped Baal. Now I want you to anoint a new king for Syria and a new king for Israel. Then I want you to find a man named Elisha. He will be your assistant, and later he will take your place."

Elijah found Elisha plowing in a field. He threw his cloak around Elisha's shoulders. Elisha knew this meant he was to be his successor. He went home and celebrated with his family, then he joined Elijah and worked with him.

JULY

6

God Chooses a New Prophet

1 KINGS 19

JULY

7

*A Victory
for
Israel*

1 KINGS 20

KING Ben-hadad of Syria gathered a huge army, planning to attack Samaria, the Israeli capital. First he sent this message to King Ahab: "You must give me your wives and children, plus a lot of silver and gold!" Ahab was afraid of Ben-hadad, so he agreed.

Then Ben-hadad sent another message: "My men will search your palace and your people's homes and take whatever they want."

This time Ahab's advisors said, "Don't let him do that to you! Stand up to him!" So Ahab refused Ben-hadad's second demand.

When Ben-hadad heard that, he was angry. He sent this message to Ahab: "By this time tomorrow, Samaria will be just a pile of trash."

Ahab was getting braver now, so he replied, "Don't brag about it until you've done it!"

The Syrian army got ready to attack. Meanwhile, a prophet told Ahab, "The Lord will help you win. Then you will know he is the true God. Take part of your army and go out to meet the Syrians."

When the Syrians started the battle, the Israelis killed a great many of them. The rest panicked and ran away.

The next spring the Syrians tried again to make war with Ahab, but again they were defeated. Ben-hadad made a deal with Ahab not to kill him, and Ahab agreed.

The prophet told Ahab that God would punish him because he had not killed Ben-hadad, the way God had told him to.

A MAN named Naboth owned a vineyard near King Ahab's palace. Ahab wanted that vineyard so he could plant a vegetable garden, so he offered to buy it. Naboth said, "No, thanks. It has been in my family for generations. I wouldn't think of selling it."

Ahab said, "I'll trade you a better piece of land for it." But Naboth still would not part with his land.

Ahab was so disappointed that he went back to the palace and pouted. He went to bed without his dinner and lay there sulking.

Jezebel asked, "What in the world is the matter with you?"

When Ahab told her, she was disgusted. "Are you the king or aren't you? You can have anything you want. Listen, I'll get Naboth's vineyard for you!"

She hired some men to say they had heard Naboth saying bad things about God and about the king. The law said a person who did that had to be punished. Naboth was dragged outside the city walls, and people threw stones at him until he was dead, then stray dogs came and licked up his blood.

When Jezebel heard he was dead, she said to Ahab, "All right, now you can have Naboth's vineyard."

But Elijah came to Ahab and scolded him for causing Naboth's death and stealing his property. "Now you too will die, and in the very place where the dogs licked Naboth's blood, they will someday lick yours!"

JULY

8

Ahab and Jezebel's Sin
1 KINGS 21

FOR three years Israel and Syria did not fight. But the Syrians still held an Israeli city, and Ahab wanted it back. He asked Jehoshaphat, king of Judah, to help him recapture Ramoth-gilead.

Jehoshaphat said, "I'm willing, but first let's ask the Lord's advice."

So Ahab gathered four hundred of his heathen prophets and asked them if he should go to war. They all said, "Yes, God will let you win."

Jehoshaphat didn't trust them, and he asked, "Isn't there a real prophet of the Lord here?"

Ahab said, "Well, there's Micaiah, but I don't like him. He always prophesies bad things about me."

But they asked Micaiah anyway, and he said, "Sure, go on to war."

Ahab said, "Now listen, I want you to tell me the truth."

Then Micaiah said, "I can see Israel's soldiers scattered like sheep without a shepherd."

Ahab knew the vision meant he would be killed. He said to Jehoshaphat, "You see what I mean? He always says bad things about me!" Then he threw Micaiah into prison. "Stay there until I get back from the war."

Micaiah said, "If I'm right, you won't be coming back!"

Ahab and Jehoshaphat went out to the battle. During the fighting, a stray arrow hit Ahab between the pieces of his armor. He bled to death in his chariot. When his chariot was washed, dogs came and licked up the blood, just as Elijah had predicted.

A HAB'S son Ahaziah became the next king of Israel. He was just as bad as his parents. He worshiped Baal and made God very angry. One day Ahaziah was hurt in a bad fall in the palace. He sent someone to ask an idol whether he would get well.

When Elijah heard this, he met Ahaziah's messenger and said, "Why ask advice of an idol? Isn't there a real God you could ask? Go tell Ahaziah he will die!"

The messenger delivered the message, and Ahaziah sent an army captain with fifty men to capture Elijah. The captain said, "Man of God, come with me."

Elijah answered, "If I am a man of God, fire will come from heaven and destroy you and your men!" Instantly fire fell on them and killed them.

Then the king sent another captain and fifty more men. This captain said, "Man of God, you must come with me." Elijah answered him the same way, and fire from God burned up that group too.

Ahaziah tried once more, sending another captain and fifty men. But this captain knelt and begged Elijah for mercy. "Please don't destroy us, as you did the others." God told Elijah not to be afraid of the king but to go with the soldiers.

He went to Ahaziah and said, "You will die because you asked advice of a false god instead of the true God." Ahaziah did die, and his brother Jehoram became the new king.

GOD planned that Elijah should not die but be taken to heaven in a fiery chariot. As the time came near, Elijah said to Elisha, "Stay here while I go to Bethel."

Elisha said, "No, I will go with you." And he followed Elijah to Bethel.

Then Elijah said, "Elisha, stay here while I go to Jericho." But again Elisha said, "No, I will go with you."

Prophets at Jericho said, "Elisha, did you know God is going to take Elijah away?"

And Elisha said, "Hush! Of course I know."

Then Elijah said, "Stay here while I go to the Jordan."

But Elisha went with him to the river. Elijah rolled up his cloak and hit the water with it. The water parted and they walked across on dry land. Elijah asked Elisha, "Before I go, what do you want me to do for you?"

Elisha asked for twice as much power as Elijah had. Elijah said, "That's not easy, but if you see me when I go, you shall have it."

As they were talking, suddenly a chariot of fire, with horses of fire came from heaven and Elijah rode right up to heaven. Elisha cried out, "Oh, I see the chariot and the horsemen of Israel!" Then he struck the water with Elijah's cloak. Again it opened up and he walked across on dry land.

WHEN Elisha got back across the river, about fifty prophets, who had been waiting for him and watching what was going on, said, "We can see that the spirit of Elijah now rests upon you! Now, shouldn't we go and look for Elijah? Maybe the Lord just took him away for a little while."

Elisha said, "No, don't look for him."

The prophets kept insisting, so Elisha said, "Oh, all right. You may look for him." But of course they didn't find him.

After three days they finally gave up. Elisha said, "I told you he wasn't around here."

Some men came to see Elisha and said, "We are from Jericho, which is a nice place to live except for one thing. The drinking water makes us sick, and it seems to keep the land from producing good crops."

Elisha answered, "Bring me a bowl of salt."

When they handed it to him, he threw the salt into the village spring and said, "The Lord says he will heal the water. Now the land will produce abundantly again."

As he walked back through Bethel on his way home, some young fellows laughed at him and teased him, calling him an "old baldhead." He turned and shouted a curse at them in the name of the Lord. Just then two mother bears came out of the woods and attacked the gang of young men, seriously injuring forty-two of them. Then Elisha returned to Samaria.

THE PEOPLE of Moab were supposed to provide Israel with lambs and wool each year. One year they refused to do it anymore. Jehoram, the new king of Israel, was angry. He asked Jehoshaphat to help him fight against Moab. Some Edomite soldiers helped too. After they had marched for several days, their water was all gone, and they couldn't find any wells.

A soldier suggested that they ask Elisha for advice. Elisha said, "I wouldn't do it for that idol-worshiping Jehoram, but for the sake of King Jehoshaphat of Judah, who honors the true God, I'll help you.

"Go out and dig many ditches, and the Lord will send plenty of water to fill them. Besides that, he will give you victory over Moab, and you will really wipe out their cities, fields, trees, and water supply."

The men got busy and dug ditches. The next morning water flowed into the land from Edom and filled all the ditches. The soldiers and their animals had plenty of water.

The soldiers of Moab were lined up, ready to defend their border against Israel. When they saw the water on the ground, the morning sun made it look like blood. They thought the enemy soldiers had been killing each other. They said, "Now we'll march in and finish them off and steal everything we want."

But the armies of Israel, Judah, and Edom completely defeated them and destroyed their land, just as Elisha had said.

A MAN from the school of the prophets died, leaving his widow with two sons. The widow came to tell Elisha her troubles. "My husband loved the Lord, as you know. But at the time of his death, he owed another man a lot of money. If I can't repay the debt, that man will take my boys away from me and make them his slaves. What can I do?"

Elisha said, "Don't you have something you can sell to raise the money?"

"All I have," she replied, "is a jar with some oil in it."

"Good!" Elijah said. "Go to all your neighbors and friends and borrow every jar and bottle they can spare. Don't be satisfied with a few. Get a lot of them."

She asked everyone for extra jars and bottles, then she took them to her home and she and her sons closed the door. She poured oil from her jar into the first borrowed jar and filled it up. Then she filled another one, and another. She still had plenty of oil in her first jar. One after another, all the borrowed bottles and jars were filled up.

She said to her son, "Hand me another jar."

He said, "That was the last one, mother."

At that very moment, the oil stopped coming into her original jar.

She took all the oil to a merchant, and he bought every bit. She used the money to pay her husband's debt, and she had enough left to support herself and her sons.

15

A Special Room for Elisha

2 KINGS 4

A RICH woman in the town of Shunem once invited Elisha to her home for a meal. After that, he often stopped for dinner when he was in town.

She said to her husband, "That prophet is really a man of God. Let's build and furnish a small guest room for him on the roof of our house. Then he will always have a comfortable place to stay when he is in Shunem."

On one of his visits Elisha and his servant, Gehazi, were in his rooftop room. Elisha sent Gehazi to bring the woman to his room.

He had Gehazi speak to her for him. "You have done so many kind things for me. I really appreciate your fixing up this room for me. I want to do something for you in return. Shall I ask the king or the general of the army for some favor for you?"

"No, thank you," she replied. "I don't need a thing."

After she had left, Elisha asked his servant, "Can you think of anything we could do for her?"

Gehazi said, "Well, as you see, she has no children. She will have no one to take care of her when she is old."

"Ah, that's it!" said Elisha. "Ask her to come back."

When she came to his doorway, Elisha said, "I promise that by this time next year, you will have a son."

She could hardly believe him, but the next year, she and her husband did have a baby boy.

THE WOMAN of Shunem was very happy to have a little son. He grew rapidly, and when he was big enough, he liked to run out and watch his father work on the farm.

One day when he was with his father in the field, he began to feel sick. He said, "Oh, daddy, my head hurts. It really hurts a lot!"

His father said to one of the servants, "Carry him home. His mother will take care of him."

She held him in her arms, but soon he died. She took him to Elisha's room and laid him on the bed. Then she borrowed one of her husband's donkeys to ride, so she could go find the prophet.

She found Elisha at Mount Carmel. She knelt at his feet and cried out, "Was it *my* idea that God give me a baby? You raised my hopes for nothing!" When she said that, Elisha realized that the boy was dead. He sent Gehazi to run on ahead and put Elisha's walking stick on the boy's face. But that didn't do any good.

When Elisha got there, he prayed that God would bring the child to life. Then he lay down on top of the body, and the flesh began to get warmer. Elisha got up and prayed then lay down again. Suddenly the child sneezed several times—and came back to life!

What joy there was in that home when Elisha gave the mother her little boy, alive again!

JULY

16

A Dead Boy Lives Again

2 KINGS 4

17

The Poisonous Food

2 KINGS 4

ELISHA traveled to Gilgal, where a famine was causing much suffering. He taught classes of young prophets, and one day they all got hungry. Elisha told the servants to prepare some stew. They went out into the fields to find vegetables and herbs. One of them found some wild gourds on a vine—something like squash.

No one knew for sure whether those gourds were good to eat, but they were all so hungry that they chopped them up and added them to the stew.

When it was done, one of the cooks served it to all the prophets. When they began to eat, one of them shouted, "Stop! I think something in it is poisonous!"

Elisha said, "Bring me some flour." He put a handful of flour into the pot and stirred it up. "Now you can eat it. It's perfectly safe." And the stew didn't poison them at all.

A few days later Elisha did another miracle for the school of the prophets. Someone had given them some corn and several small loaves of barley bread. Elisha told Gehazi to serve it to the prophets.

Gehazi asked, "What will they do with this little bit of food? It's not enough to feed a hundred hungry men."

Elisha said, "Just do it. God will provide enough for everyone, and some food will even be left over!"

When all the prophets had had plenty to eat, there was extra food left over, just as Elisha had said.

DURING one of the wars Syria had with Israel, the Syrian army took some prisoners to be their slaves. One of them was a little girl, who became the maid of the wife of Naaman, the commander of the Syrian army.

Naaman and his wife were kind to her, and she liked them very much. She felt sorry for Naaman, because he had leprosy, a disease that made the skin turn white and lumpy and sometimes even destroyed parts of the patient's body.

The little maid said, "I know a prophet back home in Samaria who can do miracles. I know he could cure Naaman's leprosy."

Naaman told the king what the girl had said, and the king sent him to Samaria with a letter of introduction to the Israeli king. Naaman took gifts of money and clothing and went to the king.

The king read the letter and was very upset. "What do they think I can do about this man's leprosy? The king of Syria is just trying to start another war with us."

Elisha heard about it and offered to help Naaman, which is what the little girl had intended all along! Naaman went to Elisha's home, and Elisha sent out a message, telling him to go to the Jordan River and wash himself seven times.

Naaman was insulted. "We have better rivers in Syria than they have here in Israel. Why didn't the prophet come out and wave his hands over me and call on his God? I'm going home!"

JULY

18

A Servant Girl's Advice
2 KINGS 5

*Naaman
Is
Healed*

2 KINGS 5

SOME of the soldiers in Naaman's army had gone with him to Israel, and they were worried when he got angry at Elisha. They said, "Oh, sir, don't give up. If the prophet had told you to do something hard, you would do it, wouldn't you? Well, he's told you to do something very easy—just to wash in the river. What harm could there be in trying this simple cure?"

So Naaman washed himself in the Jordan River over and over, until he had done it seven times. When he came out the seventh time, his skin was completely clear; the disease was all gone!

Naaman was excited and happy. He and his men went back to Elisha's house and Naaman apologized. He said, "Now I realize that the God of Israel is the one true God in all the world. Here, please take these gifts of gold and silver and the clothing I brought."

Elisha said, "Oh, no. I would never accept payment for what I did. God would not want me to do that."

Naaman kept urging him, but Elisha still refused the gifts.

Naaman said, "All right, then; I will leave. But I want to take some of the dirt from the ground, because when I get home I will always make sacrifices on an altar to the true God. I'll never worship false gods again."

He told Elisha and Gehazi good-bye and started back to Syria, thankful to be healed of his terrible disease.

GEHAZI had heard his master refuse Naaman's gifts. After Naaman had left, Gehazi said to himself, "I don't understand why Elisha didn't take some of those valuable things. What a waste! I think I'll go get some for myself!"

Gehazi hurried to catch up to Naaman and his group of soldiers.

Naaman asked, "Is something the matter?"

Gehazi answered, "No, but Elisha has sent me to tell you that two of the prophets from the hills of Ephraim have come to visit him, and he would like to have a bar of silver and two of the sets of clothing to give them."

Naaman believed Gehazi's lie and said, "Why, of course. I will give you twice as much as you asked for." And he had his servants put the silver and clothes in bags and carry them home for Gehazi.

When they got there, Gehazi took the bags from the servants and hid them in his own house. Then he went back to Elisha, who asked, "Where have you been, Gehazi?"

"I didn't go anywhere," Gehazi said.

"Listen, don't you think I knew when you followed Naaman and he talked to you? This is no time to be accepting money or other rich gifts for the work we do for God. Now, because of your greed and your lies and trickery, you and all your descendants are going to have leprosy instead of Naaman."

Immediately Gehazi's skin became white with the terrible disease of leprosy.

THE SCHOOL of the prophets was growing, and their
building wasn't large enough. They said to Elisha, "Let's
use logs from the banks of the Jordan and build a new school
building."

Elisha agreed, so they all went to the river bank to cut logs. As
one of the student prophets was chopping down a tree, the iron
head of his ax became loose and fell off the handle into the river.
It sank out of sight. The fellow was very upset, because he had
borrowed the ax, and now he had lost it.

Elisha cut a stick and threw it into the water. The ax head
floated to the surface, and the young man could get it back.

Later, when Syria was at war with Israel, the king told some
battle plans to one of his generals. Elisha warned the king of
Israel about the plans. The Syrian king wondered how his secret
had leaked out. He thought there was a spy in his troops. But
one of his soldiers said, "No, it's that prophet, Elisha. God reveals
secrets to him."

"Well, then, we'll kill him," the king said. He sent soldiers to
capture Elisha, but God protected Elisha by blinding the soldiers. Elisha led them right into Israel's capital city and
then let them see again!

The Israeli king wanted to kill them, but Elisha said no. They
fed the soldiers and let them go home. And that was the end of
the Syrian raids against Israel.

LATER King Ben-hadad got his whole army together and attacked Samaria. They surrounded the city and kept any food from being brought in. The people in Samaria got extremely hungry and did terrible things to get something to eat. Some even killed and ate other people.

King Jehoram decided that all this trouble was Elisha's fault. He said, "When I find that prophet, I'm going to kill him." Jehoram wouldn't admit that the real cause of the fighting and the hunger was his own wickedness. He had forgotten Israel's true God and worshiped idols.

But although he was not a good man, he was sad about the suffering of his people. He wore a rough garment next to his skin to remind himself of their needs.

Elisha heard about the king's threats, so he stayed inside his house. He said to his friends, "Guard the door. Keep the king's messenger outside. Soon the king will come after me himself."

He was right. When Jehoram came, Elisha told him that God had promised to end the food shortage the next day. "In fact," he said, "food will be so plentiful that you'll be able to buy flour and grain for a very low price."

One of the king's helpers said, "I don't believe that!"

Elisha said, "Because you doubt the message of the Lord, you won't get to enjoy any of the food when it is available tomorrow."

FOUR lepers lived just outside the gate of Samaria. They thought, "If we stay here, we're going to starve to death. Let's go over to the Syrian camp and surrender. They may kill us, but if they don't, they might give us a little food."

When they arrived, not a single soldier was there. God had made the Syrians think they heard a lot of soldiers coming to attack them. So they had run away in the night, leaving everything in their camp!

The lepers went into one tent and found a lot of food, so they sat down and ate all they wanted. Then they looked around and found clothing and gold and silver. They grabbed everything they could carry and took it out and hid it. Then they started back for more.

Suddenly they said, "We shouldn't be taking all this stuff for ourselves. We should share it with the suffering people in the city."

They hurried back to the gate of Samaria and called to the guards, "We've found a lot of food in the Syrian camp. The soldiers have left; we can take all we want."

When they were sure it wasn't a trap, all the people of the city rushed over to the camp and helped themselves.

Remember the man who didn't believe Elisha about the end of the food shortage? Well, he was trampled to death by the crowds, so he really didn't get any of the food!

DO YOU remember the woman whose little boy Elisha brought back to life? Elisha had warned the woman about the famine that was coming in Israel. He said, "I advise you and your family to leave Israel and live somewhere else until the famine is over." So they moved to the country of the Philistines for several years.

One day, after the famine had ended, Gehazi, Elisha's servant, was talking to the king.

The king said, "I want to know more about Elisha. Tell me some of the wonderful miracles he has done."

The servant told him about the woman with the little boy. Just as he was talking about her, she and her son walked into the palace. She had come to see the king about getting her land and home back.

Gehazi said, "Why, here she is now, Your Majesty. This is the woman I was telling you about. And this is the boy who was dead."

The king asked her, "Did all those things really happen to you? Did you build a room for Elisha, and did he pray that you would have a son? And is it really true that he raised your son from the dead?"

"Yes," she said. "That's exactly what happened."

So the king arranged for her to get back her house and all the family land. He even gave her money to pay for the crops that had been harvested from her land during the seven years she had been gone.

JULY

25

Hazael Commits Murder

2 KINGS 8

ELISHA went to Syria and stayed for awhile in Damascus, the capital city. While he was there, King Ben-hadad got sick. Ben-hadad sent a messenger named Hazael to Elisha. "Take gifts to him and ask him to find out from God whether I will ever get well."

Hazael loaded forty donkeys with beautiful and precious things. He went to find Elisha and asked him the king's question. "Will my king recover from this illness?"

Elisha replied, "Tell him I said he will get well. But that is not really true, because God has told me that he will die." He looked very hard at Hazael, and finally he started to cry.

"Why are you crying, sir?" Hazael asked.

"Because I know you are going to do a lot of cruel things to my people, the Israelis. You are going to burn down buildings. You will kill not only the young men, but even little children and mothers who are expecting babies."

Hazael was amazed to hear this. "Do you think I'm some kind of animal, that I would do such things?" he asked.

Elisha replied, "God has revealed to me that you will be the king of Syria."

When Hazael went back to the king, he told him that Elisha had said he would get well. But then he held a wet blanket over the king's face. Ben-hadad couldn't breathe, so he died, and Hazael became the king in his place, just as Elisha had predicted.

ONE day Elisha called one of the young men from the school of the prophets. He gave him a little bottle of oil and told him to go and find Jehu, the son of Jehoshaphat.

Elisha said, "If he is with friends, call him out of the room and speak with him privately. Tell him that he is to be king, and pour the oil over his head to anoint him. Then get out of there fast."

The prophet found Jehu with a group of other army officers. "Sir," he said, "I wish to speak to you alone."

Jehu followed him out to a private place, and there the prophet poured the oil over Jehu's head. "Sir, you are to be the next king," he said. "The Lord God wants you to destroy all the household of Ahab and avenge the death of God's prophets. And Jezebel the queen shall die a violent death. She won't be buried, because dogs will eat her body."

Jehu Will Be King

2 KINGS 9

When the prophet had gone, Jehu went back to his friends. They asked him who that strange man was who had come to see him.

Jehu said, "Oh, you know who that is."

"No," they said, "we don't know him. What did he want?"

Jehu told them what the prophet had said about his becoming king. His friends were glad to hear the news, and they rolled out the red carpet for him and blew a trumpet.

Then they shouted, "Jehu is the king! Long live the king!"

J EHU said to his friends, "If you are really so glad to have me be king, you had better be sure no one gets to Jezreel. King Joram is there, resting while his battle injuries heal."

Jehu wanted to get there first, before anyone else could tell Joram that there was going to be a new king.

He got into his chariot and rode very fast to Jezreel. King Joram got into his chariot— with King Ahaziah of Judah, who was visiting him—and rode out to meet Jehu.

Joram asked, "Are you coming as a friend?"

Jehu answered, "How can we be friends when you do so many evil things, just like your mother, Jezebel?"

Then Joram was afraid. He tried to escape, but Jehu shot an arrow into his back, killing him. Then he killed King Ahaziah also.

When Jezebel heard that Jehu was riding into the city, she waited for him at an upstairs window. When he arrived, she shouted, "You murderer!"

Then Jehu called out, "Is anyone up there on my side? If so, throw her down!"

Several men pushed her out of the window and the fall killed her. Her blood was all over the street and wall, and she was trampled by horses.

Later Jehu said, "I suppose we ought to bury her. After all, she is a king's daughter." But when they went to get her body, not much was left, because dogs had eaten it.

That is just what Elijah had said would happen to that wicked, idol-worshiping queen.

JULY

28

*The Death
of a
Powerful
Prophet*
2 KINGS 13

KING Jehu killed every single one of King Ahab's family. Jehu was not a good king, but when he destroyed Ahab's family, he was doing exactly what the prophet Elijah had predicted. Years later his grandson, Jehoash, became king.

While Jehoash was king, the prophet Elisha got sick. He could tell he was going to die. Feeling very sad, the king visited him.

Elisha said to the king, "Put an arrow into your bow." Jehoash did as Elisha said, and Elisha put his hands over the king's hands. Together they pulled back the bowstring and shot the arrow through the open window.

Elisha said, "This is a sign to you that Israel is going to be free of the Syrians."

Then the prophet told the king to hold a bundle of arrows in his hand and hit the floor with them. The king struck the floor—once, twice, three times. Then he stopped.

Elisha spoke angrily to him. "You stopped too soon. This means that you will defeat Syria only three times. If you had hit more times, you would keep on defeating the Syrians until they were completely destroyed."

Then Elisha died and was buried. One day some men were taking a dead body to be buried. They saw some robbers coming, so they quickly put the dead man in Elisha's tomb so they could run away faster. As soon as the dead body touched Elisha's bones, the man came back to life again.

So even in death, Elisha could do miracles!

AS ELISHA predicted, Israel did fight with Syria and defeat it three times. After Jehoash died, his son, Jeroboam II, became king.

He, too, was an idol-worshiping king. We wonder how he could turn his back on God after God was so kind to Israel. God now chose new prophets. One of these was Amos, a shepherd. God gave Amos very harsh words of warning for the people of Israel.

For instance, God said, "The cities of Israel have sinned again and again, and I will not forget it. We cannot walk together because their sins keep getting between us. Now, prepare yourselves for the punishment I will send."

To be sure they understood, God gave them object lessons. He said, "A carpenter uses a plumb line to check how straight a wall is. I have checked you against my plumb line, and you are crooked with sin!"

Then he said they were like ripe fruit, ready to be picked. That meant they were ready to receive his punishment.

Hosea scolded the people too, saying, "You are like a wife who isn't loving and faithful to her husband. You have left God and loved idols instead."

Hosea said they were like people who chased the wind. In worshiping idols they were running after something they couldn't even touch, because the false gods weren't real.

These prophets' words are in the Bible so we can check up on ourselves today and be sure we are "straight" with God and not "ripe" for punishment.

JULY

29

God's Prophets Warn Israel

2 KINGS 14–15;
AMOS; HOSEA

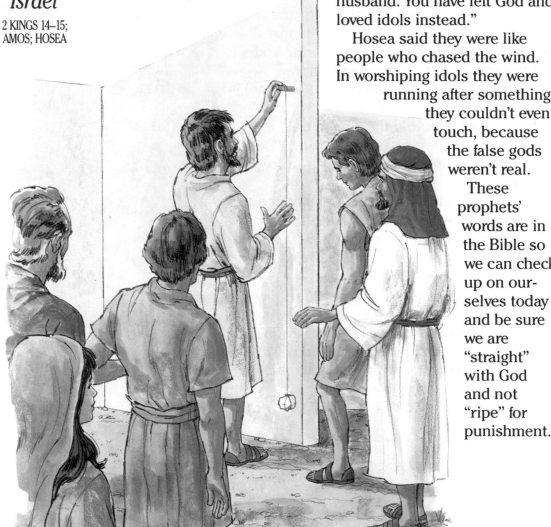

*The Death
of a
Nation*
2 KINGS 15–17

JEROBOAM II was king for a few years, then he was followed by several other kings, all of them idol worshipers. Not one of the kings of Israel was faithful to God, and they all did everything they could to lead the people farther away from true worship.

Remember what God had promised Israel when he first took them to the Land of Promise? "If you are faithful to me, I will bless you and protect you." But for more than two hundred years they had not been faithful, so finally God took away his protection.

The king of Assyria, a large enemy country nearby, attacked Israel and forced King Hoshea to pay taxes to Assyria. After awhile Hoshea thought of a way to get rid of that burden. He secretly asked the king of Egypt to help free him from Assyria 's rule, and he stopped paying the tax money.

The Assyrian king, Shalmaneser, heard about Hoshea's deal with Egypt, and it made him angry.

Shalmaneser grabbed Hoshea and put him in prison. Then he brought a big army and for three years attacked Samaria, the capital of Israel.

Finally the city could not defend itself anymore and surrendered. All the citizens of Israel became prisoners of war and were shipped off to live in Assyria.

Then Shalmaneser filled up Samaria with people from foreign cities. These people were all idol worshipers and cared nothing about the Lord God. What a sad thing to happen in the land God had prepared for his own people!

JULY

31

*Meanwhile,
Back in
Judah...*

1 KINGS 14–15

FOR a long time now our stories have been about all the things that happened to Israel after the great King Solomon died. His kingdom was divided into two groups of tribes. Israel, the larger group, was ruled by many ungodly kings and was finally captured by Assyria.

The other kingdom was the much smaller group, called Judah. Our next few stories will be about what was happening to Judah during the same years that Israel was getting into so much trouble.

The division into two kingdoms was bad enough, but it was even worse that the two kingdoms sometimes fought against each other.

During one of those fights, the king of Judah scolded Israel for having a king who wasn't from King David's family. He said, "You have a much bigger army than we do, but because you worship the gold calf idols your king made for you, the Lord our God will help us defeat you." And that's just what happened.

One of the kings of Judah was Asa. As long as he trusted God, he could defeat his enemies. But later he forgot to ask God for help and hired the Syrian army to defend him. This plan worked, but God wasn't pleased and sent a prophet to scold Asa.

The prophet said, "You should have trusted the Lord. From now on, he will let your enemies defeat you."

Asa was disgusted with the prophet and put him in jail. Then the king became ill and died. Jehoshaphat became the next king of Judah.

AFTER reading about so many unfaithful kings, we can enjoy hearing about King Jehoshaphat of Judah. He tried to please God all his life. His people all respected and loved him.

He chose teachers of the Law and sent them out to teach the people how to obey God. Even heathen people liked Jehoshaphat, and they sent him gifts of money and animals. Not since Solomon had there been such a popular and rich king.

Jehoshaphat let his son marry the daughter of King Ahab of Israel. (We'll see later what a big mistake that was.) Because of that marriage, Jehoshaphat went to Israel to visit Ahab. He was there to help when Ahab was at war with Syria. God wasn't so pleased about that, but most of the time Jehoshaphat was a faithful king.

He appointed honest judges to punish criminals and protect the innocent. He told the judges, "You must see that justice is done. You are responsible to God. He sees everything you do."

An unwise thing Jehoshaphat did was to go into partnership with one of the wicked Israeli kings. They formed a shipping company.

A prophet said to Jehoshaphat, "God doesn't want you to have this business arrangement with an ungodly king. So the Lord is going to destroy your business."

Soon a storm at sea wrecked all the ships, and that was the end of the partnership.

JUDAH was a small country with a very small army, so Jehoshaphat was worried when he heard that the armies of Moab, Ammon, and Edom were joining to attack them.

His first thought was to ask for God's help. He told all his people to fast and pray. (To fast means to go without food for awhile and concentrate on talking to God.) Many of the people of Judah came to Jerusalem and stood around the Temple while they prayed.

God's Spirit filled a man named Jahaziel, who gave them a message from God: "Don't worry about that big army! The battle is not yours but God's. You won't even have to fight. Just go out as if you were going to attack. Then stand still and see how God helps you."

The next morning Jehoshaphat led his army out, with a big choir in front singing a hymn about God's lovingkindness.

While Jehoshaphat's choir was singing songs of praise, the enemy troops started to fight among themselves. By the time Judah's army got there, the ground was covered with the dead bodies of their enemies. They didn't even have to lift a finger to defeat them!

Back home they went, singing and shouting for joy. An orchestra played as they marched into Jerusalem, praising God for the great victory he had given them.

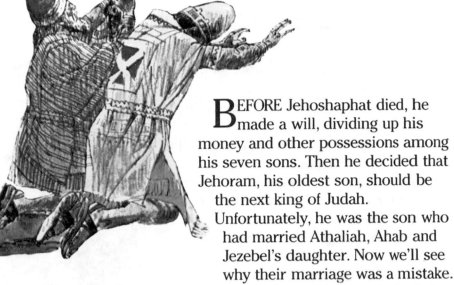

BEFORE Jehoshaphat died, he made a will, dividing up his money and other possessions among his seven sons. Then he decided that Jehoram, his oldest son, should be the next king of Judah. Unfortunately, he was the son who had married Athaliah, Ahab and Jezebel's daughter. Now we'll see why their marriage was a mistake.

Like her parents, Athaliah was an idol worshiper, and she led Jehoram away from the true God. When he became king, he put up idols for the people of Judah to worship, and soon many of them were unfaithful to the Lord.

Jehoram was afraid his six brothers would try to take the kingdom away from him, so he murdered them—his very own brothers! Of course God was displeased with him. When Jehoram went to war, God did not help him, and he lost his control over the Edomites.

The prophet Elijah sent him a letter with a message from God. It said, "You are more like a wicked king of Israel than you are like your father, Jehoshaphat. You are a murderer and an idol worshiper, and you have led my people away from me. I am going to send you a terrible sickness, and after you have suffered much pain, you will die."

But before Jehoram died, God sent some enemy troops to attack Judah. They looted the palace and captured the king's wives and all but one of his sons. Only his youngest son, Ahaziah, was left. Then Jehoram died of the painful disease God had sent.

AHAZIAH was the only royal son left to become king, but he wasn't a good man. His mother, Athaliah, had taught him to worship idols, and he cared nothing for God.

He ruled for only a year, because he happened to be visiting in Israel when Jehu assassinated Israel's king and took over the throne. Ahaziah got caught in that rebellion and was killed also.

Athaliah saw her chance to become the ruler of Judah. She had to get rid of Ahaziah's sons so they couldn't succeed their father. So although they were her own grandsons, she killed them.

But one of her grandsons had disappeared—a one-year-old baby boy named Joash. Ahaziah's sister was married to the High Priest, Jehoiada, and they had hidden the baby in the Temple to protect him from Athaliah.

For six years wicked Queen Athaliah ruled Judah. And for six years Jehoiada and his wife kept little Joash hidden in the Temple. He grew from a baby to a toddler, then to a seven-year-old boy.

Finally Jehoiada decided it was time to reveal his secret. He told the Levites, who were the ministers in the Temple, and they worked out a plan. Very quietly, priests and other leaders from all over Judah gathered at the Temple.

Then Jehoiada brought Joash out of his hiding place. He poured oil over the boy's head and crowned him king. The people in the Temple all shouted, "Long live the king!"

So Joash was crowned and the happy people shouted, "Long live the king!" Trumpeters blew their horns and choirs sang. Then an orchestra played and all the people joined in singing a hymn of praise!

Soon Athaliah heard the noise and came to see what was going on. She was shocked to see Joash standing there as the new king. In great anger she tore her robe and screamed, "This is treason!"

Jehoiada said to the soldiers who were guarding the Temple, "Take her out to the stable and kill her. And get rid of anyone who tries to help her." And that was the end of the wicked queen.

Then Jehoiada made a promise before God that he and the young king, and all the people too, would love and worship only the true God.

Everyone rushed out and started destroying idols and heathen altars. They tore down the temple of Baal and killed its priest. The High Priest put the Levites in charge of worship in the Temple, just as the Lord had instructed King David.

Finally, they took Joash from the Temple and seated him on the throne in the palace. And the country was peaceful at last.

Because Joash had been brought up by a godly priest, instead of by idol-worshiping parents, he grew up loving God and wanting to please him. Jehoiada continued to give him good advice after he became king.

When Joash was old enough to be married, Jehoiada chose good wives for him, and he had several children.

AUGUST

6

Joash
Repairs the
Temple

2 CHRONICLES 24

DURING the time Judah was ruled by idol-worshipers, most of the people had stopped going to the Temple of the Lord. The building was neglected and in disrepair. Some of Queen Athaliah's sons had even broken in and stolen dedicated items of worship and had taken them to the Baal temple.

King Joash was upset to see God's house in such condition. He asked Jehoiada, "Shouldn't we be collecting the Temple tax and taking better care of the Temple?"

He set a chest at the gate of the Temple for people to put their money in. Then he sent word all over the country that everyone should pay the Temple tax Moses had established many years before. The officials of the land and all the other people were happy to do this, and soon the chest was full of money.

The priests would bring it in and empty it and then return it to its place. Again and again the chest was filled with the people's taxes and gifts. Soon there was enough to pay for the repairs. Workmen replaced everything that had been damaged or stolen.

Carpenters and other craftsmen worked hard to bring the Temple back to its original beauty and usefulness. Some of the money was used to manufacture new incense bowls and spoons and other things that had been taken to the Baal temple.

As long as Jehoiada lived, Joash and the people worshiped God faithfully.

AFTER Jehoiada died, some of the leaders in Judah persuaded Joash to put up altars to false gods. Bit by bit, the king and many of his people grew cold toward the Lord God and stopped going to the Temple for worship. God was angry with them and sent prophets to warn them, but they wouldn't listen.

Jehoiada's son, Zechariah, called all the people together and made a speech. He said, "God is asking why you are turning away from him and disobeying his commandments. If you desert God, he will desert you and will not help you when you need him."

Just think of all the good things Jehoiada had done for Joash. He had taken care of him when he was a baby and had protected him from his wicked grandmother, Athaliah. He had made him king of Judah and had given him good advice for many years. He had taught him to love God and worship him properly.

But in spite of all that, Joash murdered Jehoiada's son, Zechariah. As Zechariah died, his last words were, "May God make you pay for what you are doing."

Later the Syrians brought an army against Judah. As Zechariah had predicted, God didn't help Judah. The Syrian army won the battle and left Joash badly wounded.

Some of Joash's men turned against him for killing Zechariah, and they killed him as he lay in his bed. What a sad end for a king who had started out so well!

AUGUST

8

A New King for Judah

2 CHRONICLES 25

JOASH'S son Amaziah was the next king. The first thing he did was to execute the men who had killed his father. He didn't kill their children, however, because he remembered God's warning that no one should punish children for the wrong things their parents do.

Most of the time King Amaziah did good things, but his heart really wasn't in it. He brought together a very large army—300,000 soldiers from Judah—then he hired another 100,000 soldiers from Israel to help him fight the Edomites.

A prophet came to Amaziah and said, "Your Majesty, you must not hire soldiers from Israel to fight in your army, because the Lord isn't blessing them. If you use them along with your soldiers, God will let you be defeated in battle."

Amaziah replied, "Oh, no! I've already paid them a lot of money. I'll lose all that money if I send them home."

The prophet said, "Don't worry about that. Obeying God is more important than the $200,000 you spent. God can see that you get your money back if you will just do as he says."

So Amaziah sent the paid soldiers back home, but they were really angry with him for changing his mind.

Amaziah took his own 300,000 soldiers out to battle against the Edomites, and God helped him win a great victory.

But then he did the wrong thing. He brought back a lot of the Edomites' idols and set them up to be worshiped in Judah—and that could only lead to trouble.

*King
Uzziah
Becomes
a Leper*
2 CHRONICLES 25–26

THE LORD was displeased with Amaziah for bringing idols to Judah, so he sent the prophet again to scold him. "Did these false gods help you fight Edom?"

"When I want your advice, I'll ask for it!" Amaziah roared. "Mind your own business, or I'll kill you!"

The prophet answered bravely, "God is going to destroy you because you worship idols and don't listen to my warning."

Amaziah foolishly declared war on Israel. His army was badly defeated, and he was taken prisoner. His own people were angry with him for getting them into trouble, so they killed him as he was trying to escape. Then his son Uzziah became the king.

Uzziah was only sixteen years old. He wanted to be a good king, and he had a wise counselor named Zechariah. God helped Uzziah build Judah into a powerful nation with a strong army.

Later Uzziah's success and power began to change him. He forgot to be grateful to God. One day he did something that only the priests should do. He entered the Most Holy Place in the Temple and burned incense at the altar. The High Priest and other priests scolded him, saying, "Get out, or the Lord will punish you."

But Uzziah refused to put down the incense burner or move out of the Most Holy Place. Suddenly the skin on his forehead became white and lumpy with the disease called leprosy. He was a leper all the rest of his life, and his son Jotham had to rule in his place.

10

Isaiah Says a Savior Will Come

2 CHRONICLES 27;
ISAIAH

JOTHAM was twenty-five when he was crowned king. He did a good job of ruling Judah. He obeyed God and tried to lead the people in the right way. He repaired the city walls that King Joash had broken down.

Like his father, he successfully made war against the Ammonites and forced them to pay $200,000 each year, plus 10,000 sacks of wheat and 10,000 sacks of barley.

Even though Jotham obeyed the Lord, most of his people were not living right. God sent one of his greatest prophets, Isaiah, to advise them and warn them about their sins.

Through Isaiah, God repeated what he had told his people when Moses first led them out of Egypt: "If you obey me, I will bless you. If you turn away from me and worship idols, I will stop hearing your prayers and will leave you alone. You will have much trouble and sorrow."

God said, "Don't bring me your offerings and then turn around and sacrifice to idols." And God warned them that if they went on disobeying him, enemy tribes would capture them and seize their country—the precious Land of Promise.

Some of Isaiah's prophecy was about Jesus, God's Son, who would come from the family of King David and would become the Savior of the world. Seven hundred years later these words came true.

How could Isaiah know what would happen long after he lived? He knew because he was God's prophet and God revealed the future to him.

JOTHAM died after ruling Judah for sixteen good years. He had been faithful to God, but his son Ahaz wasn't like him.

When Ahaz became king, he was like the kings of Israel—he worshiped the false god Baal. But even worse than that, he imitated the wicked tribes that made human sacrifice. He actually offered his own children on a heathen altar.

To punish him, God let the Syrian and Israeli armies defeat him in war. Many of his people were taken captive to Syria, and the army of Israel killed thousands of Judah's best soldiers, including the king's son.

The Israelis also took away 200,000 women and children from Judah. A prophet rebuked them for doing these things. He said, "It's true that God wants to use you to punish Judah, but you are going too far. Remember, you have many sins too." Then they let some of the captives go back home.

Ahaz needed help against his enemies, so he hired troops from King Tiglath-pilneser of Assyria. Tiglath-pilneser helped him defeat Syria and captured Damascus, but then he turned against Ahaz.

Ahaz became worse and worse. He destroyed some of the beautiful and sacred things in the Temple. Finally he nailed the Temple doors shut. No one could go there to worship the Lord.

Everywhere the people looked, they saw idols that their king had put up. And God was terribly disappointed in Judah and angry with King Ahaz.

AUGUST

11

*King Ahaz
Nails the
Temple
Shut*
2 CHRONICLES 28

HERE is some good news: Though Ahaz had been a very bad king, his son Hezekiah loved God and worshiped him faithfully. Hezekiah was king of Judah for twenty-nine years, and he brought the country back to the Lord.

In the very first month he was king, he opened up the Temple. He called in the Levites and priests, who hadn't had anything to do while the Temple was closed. He said to them, "Purify yourselves according to the law, and then clean up God's house of worship. From now on you must not neglect your Temple duties."

Each branch of the Levite tribe appointed certain men to work on the cleanup committee. They went through the Temple and cleaned out all the trash that had accumulated there in Ahaz's day.

It took them sixteen days to prepare the Temple for worship. Then they reported to Hezekiah, "Everything is clean and ready for use."

The next day Hezekiah went to the Temple with the leaders of the city. He took many animals for sacrifice. The priests made burnt offerings and sin offerings for all the people.

The king appointed some Levites to be in an orchestra and others to play trumpets, just as it had been in King David's time. Then they all joined in the worship of God. How happy King Hezekiah and all his people were to be obeying God once again in his holy Temple!

FOR many years the people in Judah had not celebrated the Passover. The Passover was the feast that reminded them of the time when God got them out of Egypt. God had punished Egypt because of Pharaoh's stubbornness, but Pharaoh wouldn't change his mind. Then came the last and worst punishment. The angel of death killed the firstborn in every home.

Do you remember what made the angel "pass over" the homes of the Israelis? Yes, they killed lambs or young goats and painted some of the animals' blood on their front doors. The angel didn't hurt the firstborn in homes that had blood on the door.

Now Hezekiah was trying to obey all of God's commands, and he wanted the people to celebrate the Passover again. He invited everyone to come to Jerusalem and join in the celebration.

Of course, he wanted all the priests and Levites to get ready for it too. Usually the Passover was in April, but because there wasn't enough time to get ready that early, the king decided to have it in May.

What a great time they had! The festival lasted for seven days and was filled with praise and music and reading of God's Word. The people were so happy that they stayed for another week, enjoying the celebration.

When they went back to their homes in different parts of the country, they got busy tearing down idols and heathen altars. They wanted their country to be a place where only the true God was worshiped.

Passover— a Happy Time Again
2 CHRONICLES 30

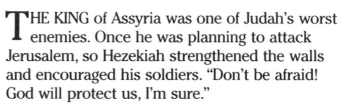

14

*An Angel
Fights for
Judah*

2 CHRONICLES 32

THE KING of Assyria was one of Judah's worst enemies. Once he was planning to attack Jerusalem, so Hezekiah strengthened the walls and encouraged his soldiers. "Don't be afraid! God will protect us, I'm sure."

But in his heart, Hezekiah was afraid of the Assyrians' big army. He sent their king some gifts, hoping to get them to call off their attack.

They went away for awhile, but later their king sent some soldiers to boast about what he was going to do. They called to the watchmen on the wall, "Don't believe what Hezekiah says about God's protection. You might as well surrender right now and be our slaves."

Hezekiah prayed, and he asked the prophet Isaiah to pray too. Isaiah sent the king these encouraging words: "The Lord says not to be afraid of the king of Assyria. God will punish him and turn him back home. There he will be killed."

The Assyrian king sent a threatening letter, but Hezekiah took the letter to the Temple and had a prayer meeting. God sent him an answer through Isaiah: "I will do as you have asked. The Assyrian army shall not even get close to Jerusalem. I will save your çity!"

That very night God sent his angel of death to the Assyrian camp, and the angel killed thousands of the soldiers. Then the Assyrian king hurried back home. But he wasn't safe even there, because two of his own sons assassinated him while he was worshiping his idol.

SOON after God saved Judah from Assyria, King Hezekiah became very sick. Isaiah said, "You must prepare yourself, because God has said you are going to die."

Hezekiah turned his face toward the wall and cried, "Oh, Lord! Please, please remember me."

As Isaiah left the court, the Lord said to him, "Go back and tell Hezekiah that I have heard his prayer and have seen his tears."

Isaiah hurried back to Hezekiah's bedside. He said, "O king, the Lord is going to heal you! In three days you will be well enough to worship at the Temple. And God will let you live another fifteen years." In exactly three days the king was healthy again.

King Hezekiah became a very rich and powerful king. Everything he had was because of God's kindness, but he forgot to give God the credit. He acted as if he had done it all himself.

Once Hezekiah foolishly showed some Babylonian men all his valuable things. Isaiah said, "Someday they will come back and steal all your treasures."

Hezekiah replied, "Well, just as long as it doesn't happen during my lifetime!"

So we see that Hezekiah didn't use his extra fifteen years very wisely. He was selfish and proud, and his people slipped back into idol worship. Isaiah and another prophet, Micah, tried to warn them, but they wouldn't listen.

AUGUST

15

Hezekiah's Life Is Lengthened

2 KINGS 20;
2 CHRONICLES 32

16

King Manasseh's Heart Is Changed

2 CHRONICLES 33

A FTER Hezekiah died, his son Manasseh became king at age twelve. He was king for a very long time—fifty-five years! But he didn't use that time to help his country. Instead, he turned all the people of Judah back to the worship of idols.

He even put up false gods in the Temple, God's house! He sacrificed his own children on altars, and he got advice from fortune-tellers and magicians instead of from God. It seems as if he did every bad thing he could think of.

God's prophets warned him, but the king didn't listen. Finally the Lord let the Assyrian troops come and take Manasseh captive. They put a ring in his nose, just as if he were an animal. They led him away to Babylon as their prisoner.

There he had time to think about all his mistakes. He became really sorry for his foolishness and his sin. He cried out to God and asked for help. God knew that Manasseh was truly sorry, so he forgave him.

He put it into the hearts of Manasseh's captors to take him back to Jerusalem. Then the king could be sure that the Lord was the only true God.

He tore down the idols he had built, and he repaired the city wall to protect Jerusalem. He also removed the false gods from the Temple and got it ready for the true worship of God.

Manasseh's life shows us that a person can come back to God late in life.

MANASSEH'S son Amon ruled only two years, then he was assassinated. His little son Josiah—only eight years old— became the next king. Right from the start, Josiah loved God and wanted to please him.

By the time he was a teenager he began to try to learn all he could about the Lord. He finished getting rid of the heathen altars and idols his grandfather, Manasseh, had built.

Josiah even went around to neighboring tribes and destroyed idols there, too. In his twenties he went to work on the Temple, repairing parts that had been neglected. His helpers, Shaphan and Ma-aseiah, worked out a system to collect gifts from the people with which they would repair and refurnish the Temple.

Some of the Levites stayed by the Temple gates and guarded the offering boxes into which the people of Judah and some of the other tribes put their gifts of money.

The money was used to pay carpenters and stone-masons and to buy building stone, timber, and beams. While the workmen were building and repairing, some of the Levites played and sang music to entertain and encourage them.

Others of the Levites were the bosses who told the workmen what they should do. It was a busy place, and everyone worked joyfully because they really wanted God's house to be a beautiful place of worship. They were glad their king's heart was warm and loving toward the Lord.

ONE day the High Priest, Hilkiah, was working in the Temple. He found an old scroll. It was a copy of the law God had given to Moses. Hilkiah showed it to Shaphan, the king's assistant. "Just see what I found in the Temple!" he said. "These are God's rules for his people."

Shaphan took it to King Josiah and said, "Everything is going very well at the Temple. The money is coming in well, and all the workmen are being paid. Oh, yes . . . and here is an old scroll that Hilkiah found. It is the law of Moses. Here, I'll read it to you."

When Josiah heard what the scroll said, he realized that his people had not always kept the rules. He felt terrible about it and said to the priests, "No wonder we've had so much trouble. Go to the Temple and pray for our country and for Israel."

The priests talked to Huldah, one of God's prophets. She said, "Yes, it is true that God has been punishing his people for not obeying his law. Tell the king how to make it right, and the Lord will forgive the nation."

Josiah did everything he could to make up for the sins of the nation. He arranged for the Passover to be celebrated again on April 1. Everyone turned out for the celebration, and it was the best Passover since the days of Samuel.

Later King Josiah was killed in a battle with the king of Egypt, and all his people were sad.

JOSIAH'S son Jehoahaz ruled for awhile, but he was a weak king. Soon the Pharaoh of Egypt captured him and appointed Jehoahaz's brother Jehoiakim to take care of things in Judah.

But soon a very powerful king named Nebuchadnezzar came from Babylon and took control of Judah.

The prophet Jeremiah tried to warn the people about the results of their sin, but they didn't pay much attention. Nebuchadnezzar stole things from the Temple and took them back to Babylon, where he put them in his heathen temple.

Jehoiakim died after a few years, and his son became king. But soon he was called to Babylon and his brother Zedekiah was named king. He ruled for about eleven years, but he didn't worship God. And he ignored all Jeremiah's good advice.

He was what we call a "puppet king." That means he was controlled by someone else and had no real power of his own. The person who controlled him was, of course, King Nebuchadnezzar.

Zedekiah had to pay a great deal of money to Nebuchadnezzar as taxes each year. Zedekiah wasn't very loyal or cooperative, and finally Nebuchadnezzar was so disgusted that he invaded Judah and began to attack Jerusalem.

When things got really bad, Zedekiah asked Jeremiah to pray that God would help them. But his request came too late. God sent this message through Jeremiah: "If you surrender and are obedient slaves, you will be all right. But if you are stubborn and rebellious, you will all die."

Then God told Jeremiah to do something like "show and tell." Not only should he tell the message, but he should act it out. He was to wear a heavy wooden yoke on his shoulders, showing how they should be Nebuchadnezzar's slaves.

AUGUST

20

*Jeremiah
Is Put into
a Well*

2 CHRONICLES 36;
JEREMIAH

A S JEREMIAH went
around wearing the yoke
and telling the message, the
leaders of the city were angry. They asked
the king to kill the prophet. "His gloomy
messages are bad for the people's morale. He sounds like a
traitor."

The king said they could punish Jeremiah, so they took him to
the city prison and let him down into a deep, dark well that was all
muddy on the bottom.

After awhile one of the king's men told him what the leaders
had done to Jeremiah. "I'm afraid he will starve down there. After
all, he is the Lord's prophet. What they have done is cruel."

The king sent some men to get Jeremiah out of the well. They
threw down some long strips of cloth. Jeremiah wrapped them
around himself and under his arms so the men could haul him up
to the surface. They didn't let him go but kept him in the prison.

SOME of the people of Judah were taken away to Babylon by Nebuchadnezzar, and one of them was Ezekiel, a priest. In those days people couldn't read the whole Bible, as we can, because only the first few books had been written. So God had to talk to people through his special messengers, called prophets.

Sometimes he talked to the prophets through dreams when they were asleep or visions when they were awake. One day Ezekiel had one of those visions. He saw God's throne and all the glory of heaven, and it made him bow and worship God.

Then God said, "I want you to warn all the captives. Use object lessons so they will really listen to you. First draw a picture of Jerusalem on a piece of clay and put a pan in front of it, like a wall. Then build a fort outside the wall. Next, you must lie down in front of it and pretend to be almost starving. The people will know it is because of Nebuchadnezzar's attack on Jerusalem."

Ezekiel's next object lesson was to cut off all his hair and beard and weigh the hair into three parts. He burned one part, cut up one part, and blew away the third part.

This showed that part of the people would starve when the city was burned up, one part would be killed away from the city, and one part scattered everywhere.

AUGUST

21

*Ezekiel
Teaches
Object
Lessons*
EZEKIEL

22

No One Believes Ezekiel

EZEKIEL

T HE NEXT thing that happened to Ezekiel was that he had another vision. This time he seemed to be picked up by the hair and whisked away to Jerusalem, where he used to live before being taken to Babylon. The Lord pointed out to him the idols his people had been worshiping, then he told him to look in an inner room of the Temple.

There he saw leaders of Judah bowing down to pictures of false gods. He also saw people worshiping the sun. Of course, people who did these things were disobeying the Commandments of God given to Moses on Mount Sinai many years before.

The Lord then told Ezekiel how he was going to punish his people for being so disobedient. "Their city will be destroyed, and many of them will be killed by the invading troops. Even though they cry out to me, it will be too late, and I will not listen or help them."

Then Ezekiel found himself being taken through the sky, back to Babylon. Immediately he started telling the other captured Jews what he had seen. But they chose not to believe him.

They preferred to believe the lies the false prophets were telling them—that the people of Jerusalem would not be punished for their sins and that Nebuchadnezzar would never burn up the city and the Temple.

EZEKIEL wrote down all of these things God told him to do. But while they were happening, the people around him had to learn just by noticing what he did and said.

The next object lesson Ezekiel did was to make a hole in the back wall of his house and pretend he was moving out in the dark night. He took his clothes and other things with him.

He told the people, "This is like a play on a stage. King Zedekiah will try to get away from Jerusalem, but he will be caught and brought here as a prisoner. He will be here, but he won't see the city."

Then Ezekiel acted like someone who was badly frightened—shaking and trembling as he tried to eat and drink. This showed how scared the people of Jerusalem would be when the attack came. God even revealed to Ezekiel exactly what day all these things would happen, even though he wasn't anywhere near Judah. God told him this secret because he was God's special messenger. When Jerusalem was finally conquered, three years later, Ezekiel's fellow captives realized he had been telling them the truth.

IN spite of all their sin and trouble, God still loved Israel and Judah. He gave Ezekiel more messages for the people, to encourage them and give them a promise for the future.

First God gave Ezekiel a vision of a big field covered with the dry bones of the skeletons of dead people. He could see arm bones and leg bones and some ribs, backbones, and skulls.

God told Ezekiel to say to the bones, "Listen to what God is going to do. He will put flesh on you and let you breathe and become alive!"

As Ezekiel watched in surprise, those words came true. Flesh grew on the bones, and the bones joined together and became human forms. But they still weren't breathing. Then Ezekiel called to the wind to blow on the bodies and put breath into them.

That's just what happened—and the bodies came to life and were like a huge army. God said, "Ezekiel, this shows what is going to happen to poor dead Israel and Judah. They will receive new life and strength and will become powerful again."

God told Ezekiel to pick up two sticks and name one of them "Israel" and the other one "Judah." As he held them in his hand, they grew together into one stick. This showed that the two countries would someday be together again, as they were in the days of David and Solomon. What good news!

ONE day, back in Jerusalem, King Zedekiah sent for the prophet Jeremiah to come for a secret conversation. "I want you to tell me the truth about what is going to happen," the king said.

Jeremiah answered, "If I do, you will probably kill me!"

"No, I promise not to kill you," the king said.

Then Jeremiah told him again what he had said before: "If you and your people will surrender peaceably and become his slaves, you will be kept from harm and the city will be saved from harm."

But Zedekiah was afraid to do that, so he held out against Nebuchadnezzar. The Babylonian army kept attacking Jerusalem time after time, for eighteen months. No supplies could get into the city, so the people began to be in danger of starvation.

Zedekiah panicked and tried to escape, but he was captured and taken to Nebuchadnezzar. As Zedekiah watched, Nebuchadnezzar killed his two sons and then blinded Zedekiah. (That's why he couldn't see the city.) He took him to Babylon and kept him in prison there until he died.

Then the Babylonian army looted Jerusalem and burned down the beautiful Temple and the palaces and homes. They smashed the walls of the city and killed many of the people. They took the rest of the citizens captive to be slaves in Babylon for many years.

So the history of the kingdom of Judah came to a sad end because of the people's sin and indifference to God.

AUGUST

26

Judah—
a Lonely,
Deserted
Country

2 KINGS 25;
JEREMIAH

NEBUCHADNEZZAR told his army general to be kind to Jeremiah. The general got Jeremiah out of prison and said, "You may go with me to Babylon, where you will be treated very well, or you may stay here, whichever you wish."

Jeremiah decided to stay, so the general gave him a supply of food and some money. Jeremiah stayed with Gedaliah, who was the governor Nebuchadnezzar appointed.

Some of the people of Judah had run away when they knew Nebuchadnezzar was going to capture the city. When they heard the war was over and Gedaliah was left in charge, they came back and asked him if they could stay.

He said, "Yes, indeed. Just be obedient to the king of Babylon, and everything will go well for you."

After awhile the Ammonites got one of the princes of Judah to kill Gedaliah, and then the rest of the people were afraid Nebuchadnezzar would punish them because of Gedaliah's death. They asked Jeremiah what they should do.

The Lord sent them this answer: "Stay here in Judah and you will be safe."

But the people didn't believe the Lord. They ran away to Egypt, and they made Jeremiah go with them. So Judah was deserted and lonely, lying in ruins.

If only the people had listened to God's prophets instead of insisting on their own way! Now both Judah and Israel were in captivity, and God's special people had lost their home in the Land of Promise.

DANIEL was a boy who lived in Jerusalem. He was a lot like boys you know. He loved his parents. He was a good student. And he obeyed everything his parents taught him about worshiping God and following the law, including what to eat and drink.

When Nebuchadnezzar destroyed Jerusalem, Daniel was one of the captives taken to Babylon.

The king chose some of the smartest and strongest boys from Judah to go to a special school. Teachers trained them in many important subjects. After three years they would be ready to get good jobs in the government. Daniel was one of the boys chosen, along with three of his best friends—Shadrach, Meshach, and Abednego.

Nebuchadnezzar didn't care about the true God. He expected the boys to do some things they knew were wrong. For instance, the food and wine they were given had been used in idol worship. The boys asked to be excused from eating it.

Their teacher said, "Oh, I wouldn't dare change the menu. If you became weak and sick, the king would punish me."

Daniel said, "Let's just try it. Give us plain vegetables and water for ten days. We'll be fine— you'll see."

They tried the experiment, and what do you think happened? Yes, at the end of ten days, they were the healthiest boys in the school! When they had their final tests, Daniel and his friends were the wisest students of all. And God gave Daniel the special gift of understanding dreams.

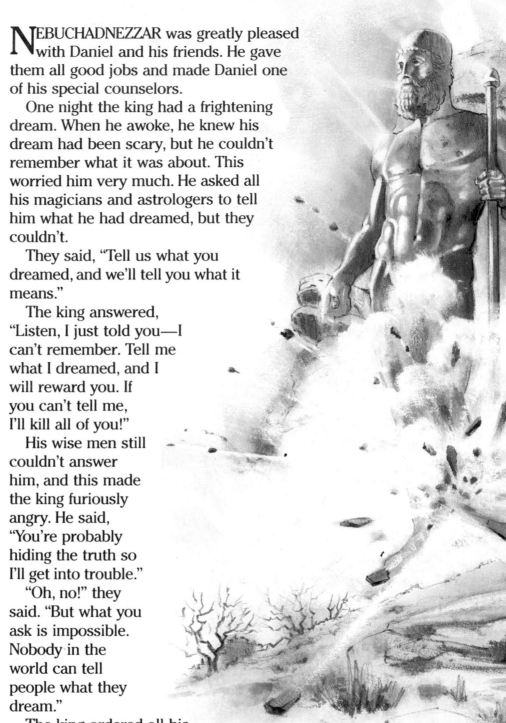

28

The King Has a Scary Dream

DANIEL 2

NEBUCHADNEZZAR was greatly pleased with Daniel and his friends. He gave them all good jobs and made Daniel one of his special counselors.

One night the king had a frightening dream. When he awoke, he knew his dream had been scary, but he couldn't remember what it was about. This worried him very much. He asked all his magicians and astrologers to tell him what he had dreamed, but they couldn't.

They said, "Tell us what you dreamed, and we'll tell you what it means."

The king answered, "Listen, I just told you—I can't remember. Tell me what I dreamed, and I will reward you. If you can't tell me, I'll kill all of you!"

His wise men still couldn't answer him, and this made the king furiously angry. He said, "You're probably hiding the truth so I'll get into trouble."

"Oh, no!" they said. "But what you ask is impossible. Nobody in the world can tell people what they dream."

The king ordered all his wise men killed. When the men were all brought before him, Daniel and his friends were in the group.

When Daniel heard why the king was so angry, he told him that he would be able to tell him about his dream and its meaning. But first he needed time to pray and get his friends to pray too. That night God gave him the answer in a vision.

In our next story we'll find out what Daniel told the king.

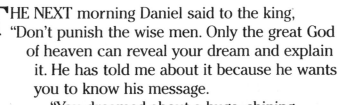

THE NEXT morning Daniel said to the king, "Don't punish the wise men. Only the great God of heaven can reveal your dream and explain it. He has told me about it because he wants you to know his message.

"You dreamed about a huge, shining statue. Each part of its body was made of a different material—the head was gold, its chest and arms were silver, the middle part was bronze, the legs were iron, and the feet were of iron and clay mixed together.

"You saw a rock miraculously cut from the mountain—not by human hands—roll down the mountainside and crash into the feet of the statue. The statue collapsed—gold, silver, bronze, iron, and clay all jumbled together. Then the rock grew bigger until it filled the whole earth."

The king asked what this strange dream meant. Daniel continued, "Sir, the statue is you, the great king. You are the head of gold. But after your kingdom is gone, another kingdom will take its place. It will be less powerful, just as silver is not as great as gold.

"Then the 'bronze' kingdom will rule the world. It will be followed by another, like the iron legs. Soon it will divide and be like the mixture of iron and clay.

"Finally, the stone stands for a great kingdom that will destroy all the others. It will be the strongest of all. It won't be manmade but will come from God."

The king was so grateful that he made Daniel a ruler, with his three friends as assistants.

NEBUCHADNEZZAR became very proud, so he built a big statue of himself, ninety feet high and nine feet wide. Then he sent this message to all the leaders in the country, "When you hear the band play, everyone must bow and worship the statue. Anyone who doesn't will be thrown into a hot furnace."

The band played, and everyone bowed to the statue. Daniel was out of town on business, but his friends, Shadrach, Meshach, and Abednego, didn't bow.

Can you guess why they didn't? If you said, "Because it would have been like worshiping an idol," you are right. They could never bow to anyone except the one true God.

Some of the government leaders came to the king and said, "You know those young men who came as captives from Judah? Well, they aren't paying any attention to your rule about falling down and bowing to your statue. Are you going to let them get away with that?"

As soon as the king heard this, he called the young men and yelled at them, "What's the matter with you? Don't you respect me? Don't you know I can throw you into the furnace?"

They answered quietly, "O king, if you put us into the furnace, our God will take care of us. But even if he should let us die, we would never, never worship anyone but our God. We will not bow to your statue."

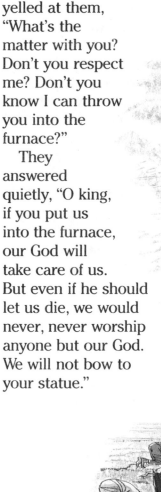

W HEN the three young men refused to bow to the statue, the
king became even more angry. He shouted, "Heat up that
furnace seven times hotter than before. Tie these men up and
throw them into the fire!"

The soldiers obeyed, but the fire was so hot that it burned them
when they got close enough to throw the three men in.

As King Nebuchadnezzar watched, he saw something very
strange. He jumped up and looked more closely. "Why, I thought
we put only three men into the furnace. Now I see *four* men
walking around in the flames. They don't even seem to be hurt by
the fire. And the fourth man looks like a god!"

The king came as close to the furnace as he could and called to
the men, "Shadrach! Meshach! Abednego! You servants of the
Most High God, come on out of the furnace."

When the men stepped out, everyone could see they were not
burned. Their hair wasn't even singed, and they didn't smell as if
they had been near smoke.

King Nebuchadnezzar was so amazed that he made a new
announcement to his citizens. "I bless the name of the God of
these men. And I command that from now on, if anyone in this
country says anything bad about that God, he shall be killed and
his house pulled down in ruins."

Then he promoted Shadrach, Meshach, and Abednego to higher
positions in his government.

1

Another Strange Dream

DANIEL 4

LATER King Nebuchadnezzar had another strange dream. This time he was able to remember it.

He told Daniel, "I saw a very tall tree, so high that everyone in the world could see it. It had beautiful leaves and fruit. An angel came and said, 'Cut down the tree, shake off the leaves, and scatter the fruit. Leave the stump in the ground where it will be soaked with rain. Let this "tree" eat grass like an animal and have a mind like an animal's instead of a man's. Then everyone will know how great God is.'"

Daniel knew right away what the dream meant, but he didn't want to tell the king.

The king begged him to tell, so finally he said, "O king, you are the great tree. But your kingdom will be taken away, and for seven years you will act like an animal—soaked with rain, living outdoors, and eating grass. Only when you admit how great God is will you be healed and get your kingdom back."

Nothing happened for a whole year, and the king kept getting more proud. He didn't give God credit for the good things that happened to him. He thought he had done it all himself! The angel said, "It's time for the dream to come true." And all the terrible things in his dream happened to him.

After seven years, he began to think straight, and he praised and worshiped God as he should. Then he got his throne back and told everyone how wonderful the Lord God is.

ONE of the kings after Nebuchadnezzar was Belshazzar. He just loved to have a good time. Once he had a big party—and how many guests do you think he invited? Well, it was one thousand! They were his government and army officers.

They got drunk and behaved foolishly. Belshazzar told his servants to bring in the silver and gold cups that had been taken from the Temple in Jerusalem. Even worse, the king and his guests drank wine from the sacred cups and used them in a ceremony honoring their idols!

All of a sudden, they saw a hand—just a hand, not attached to a body—writing some words on the wall. They were all frightened, Belshazzar most of all. None of his wise men could read or explain the strange words.

Then the queen came to see what was the matter. She said to the king, "Don't get so upset. Send for the man named Daniel. His God has given him special ability to explain things like this."

Belshazzar said to Daniel, "If you can explain these words, I'll make you a rich man."

Daniel replied, "I don't want your money, but I will tell you what the handwriting means. God is telling you that you are not fit to rule. He is going to let your enemies capture the city."

The king gave Daniel gifts and made him an important official. But that night the enemy army sneaked into Babylon and killed Belshazzar. Then Darius the Mede was the new king.

SEPTEMBER

2

The Mysterious Hand

DANIEL 5

THE NEW king, Darius, soon noticed what a wise official Daniel was. When he planned his government, he gave Daniel one of the most important jobs.

The more the king honored Daniel, the more angry and jealous the other governors became. They wished they could find something bad in Daniel's life so the king wouldn't like him so much. But Daniel was such an honest, hardworking man that no one could find any fault with him.

One reason Daniel was so successful was that he trusted God and obeyed him. Three times each day he knelt beside an open window in his room and prayed, worshiping God and asking him for wisdom.

Daniel's enemies said, "Hmm, maybe we can get him into trouble for praying."

They went to see the king and said, "We all think you are so wonderful that everyone should pray to you. In fact, we think that if a person in your kingdom prays to anyone else, he should be thrown into a pit full of wild lions. Now, we've written this down as a new law. All you have to do is sign it, right here on this line."

This made the king feel really powerful and proud. Wouldn't it be great to have everyone in the kingdom praying to him! Quickly he signed the law.

Daniel heard about the new law, but he still prayed to his God as usual. His enemies were spying on him. They saw him kneeling at his open window. "Aha!" they gloated. "Now we have him!"

WHEN Daniel's enemies saw him praying, they rushed to the king. "O king, didn't you make a law that anyone who prays to any god but you shall be thrown to the lions?"

The king said, "Yes, indeed. And no one can change a Persian king's law."

Then the men said, "Well, Daniel is breaking your law. He kneels and prays to his God every day."

The king felt terrible. He respected Daniel and had never intended that he should be punished for praying to the God of Israel. He tried to think of a way to get Daniel out of trouble, but his governors insisted, "You can't change the law just for him!"

So Daniel was arrested. King Darius said to him, "Daniel, I really believe your God can protect you."

Then the guards threw Daniel into the lion pit and blocked the opening. All that night the king was so concerned about Daniel that he couldn't eat or sleep.

In the morning he hurried to the pit and called, "Daniel! O servant of the living God, did your God keep you safe from the lions?"

How happy he was to hear Daniel answer, "I'm fine, sir. God sent an angel to keep the lions' mouths shut. I don't have even a scratch!"

The king shouted, "Wonderful! Now you rascals get him out of there!" He was so angry with the men who had made trouble for Daniel that he threw *them* into the pit with their families. And the lions killed them all!

5

*Daniel
Prays
for His
Country*

DANIEL 9

KING Darius had seen what God could do for his people, so he said everyone in his country should honor and worship the God of Daniel. And he kept promoting Daniel to higher and higher positions in the government. When Darius died, the next king, Cyrus, did the same.

Daniel himself had some dreams that showed him that kingdoms would rise and fall, but that God had good plans for his special people, the Israelis. Daniel read the book the prophet Jeremiah had written. He found out that the time of the Israelis' captivity in Babylon was almost over. Soon they would be able to return to the land of promise.

Remember how faithful Daniel was about praying? Well, now he began to pray that God would lead his people back to Jerusalem, where they could repair the damage and begin to live in their own land once more. Daniel wanted this so much that he even skipped some meals so he could spend more time in prayer.

Daniel admitted to God that his people had been disobedient. "We don't really deserve your kindness. Please be good to us just because you are a merciful God."

He had been praying this way for three weeks, when suddenly the angel Gabriel came to make some wonderful promises to him. Not only would the people of Israel get to go back home, Gabriel told him, but almost 500 years later, God would send a Savior to the world.

SEVENTY years had gone by since God's people were taken captive. The people remembered that Jeremiah had told them God would free them after seventy years.

The king who ruled them now was Cyrus. Here is an amazing fact about Cyrus: Almost 200 years before he became king, his name had been mentioned in Isaiah's messages from God! Yes, God knew Cyrus by name long before he was even born. God had said Cyrus would be a kindhearted ruler. He would help his captives get back to their own land and rebuild the ruined Temple.

Now Cyrus said, "Everyone who wants to go is free to leave." He gave them money and also sent back the gold and silver dishes that Nebuchadnezzar had stolen from the Temple. Almost 50,000 people decided to make the trip, and they took many animals. Those who couldn't or wouldn't leave gave gifts to help their friends.

Joshua, the High Priest, and Zerubbabel led the people and helped them get organized when they arrived in Judah. The first thing they did was to build an altar outside the ruins of the Temple. There they worshiped God and asked for his help as they settled down and rebuilt his house.

They laid the foundation stones, then they celebrated with songs of praise. "We're off to a good start," they said.

But the old men, who could remember seventy years back, cried. They shook their heads sadly and said, "It will never be as beautiful as the Temple Solomon built!"

SEPTEMBER

7

The Most Beautiful Queen

ESTHER 1–2

THOUGH thousands of the Jews returned to Judah, many stayed in Babylonia, which was now ruled by Persian kings. One of the great kings of Persia at that time was Ahasuerus.

Once Ahasuerus had a huge party that lasted for six months! While he was partying with the men, his lovely queen, Vashti, entertained the women in another part of the palace.

The king got drunk and sent a message to Queen Vashti: "Put on your royal crown and get over here! I want you to show the men at my party what a beautiful queen I have." The queen was modest and dignified, and she refused to show off for those drunken men.

This made the king terribly angry. His advisors said, "If you let the queen get away with this, all the women in the kingdom will start disobeying their husbands. Throw Vashti out and get a queen who will show respect for Your Majesty."

The king agreed, but later he began to miss Vashti and was sorry she was gone. Then his advisors put on a beauty contest among the young women of the kingdom. The winner would be Ahasuerus' new queen.

Many attractive girls competed, but the one Ahasuerus chose was a beautiful Jewish girl named Esther. She and her uncle, Mordecai, were captives from Jerusalem, and Mordecai had a job in the palace. Mordecai said to Esther, "You'd better not tell the king you are a Jew."

Now the king was happy. He had the most beautiful woman in the country for his queen!

ONE day Mordecai discovered a plot to kill Ahasuerus. He told Esther to warn the king, and the traitors were caught and punished. This was written down in the court records and then forgotten.

The king's most powerful official was Haman. He was very proud and liked to have everyone bow down to him. The only person who wouldn't bow was Mordecai. As a Jew, he believed he should bow only to God. Naturally, this made Haman angry—not just with Mordecai but with all Jews.

This is how he planned to get even. He said to the king, "You know, these Israeli captives are getting to be a big problem. They have their own rules and laws, and they refuse to obey yours. We'd better find a way to get rid of them. If you will declare that they must all be killed, I'll pay a lot of money into your treasury."

The king agreed and gave Haman permission to write a law that would get rid of the Jews. Haman made a terrible law—that on a certain day in February, all citizens should kill all the Jews they could find—men, women, and children. When they did this, they could have those Jews' possessions for their own. Haman sent messengers out all over the country to announce the law.

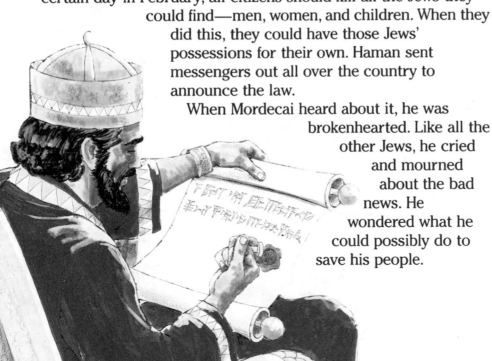

When Mordecai heard about it, he was brokenhearted. Like all the other Jews, he cried and mourned about the bad news. He wondered what he could possibly do to save his people.

9

Mordecai Asks Esther to Help

ESTHER 4

QUEEN Esther didn't know about Haman's law, but she did hear that her uncle was outside the palace, crying. He had taken off his good clothes and was wearing rough clothing made of burlap—like gunny sacks. Esther sent someone to find out what was wrong with him and to offer him some fresh clothing. He sent a message back, telling her about the trouble the Jews were in and asking her to get the king to help.

She replied, "The king is likely to kill anyone who goes to see him without an invitation, unless he is feeling especially kind and holds out his scepter. He hasn't invited me to see him for several weeks, and it would be dangerous for me to go."

Mordecai sent another message: "Even though you are the queen, that won't keep you from being killed in February along with the rest of our people. Perhaps this is the very reason you got to be queen—so you could help your fellow Jews in this emergency!"

Esther asked Mordecai to pray for her and to start prayer meetings all over the city. "Then I will go to see the king. And if he kills me—well, at least I tried to help my people."

While all the Jews were praying for Esther, she worked out a plan to try to get her husband, the king, to help the Jews get out of danger.

ESTHER went to the king, not knowing whether she would live or die. But he held out his scepter! He said, "What can I do for you?"

She replied, "I just want to invite you and Haman to a banquet tonight." The king accepted her invitation and sent for Haman.

They had a fine dinner, then the king asked again, "What do you want me to do for you?"

Again she answered, "I just want you and Haman to come back tomorrow for another banquet."

Haman was very proud to be invited to eat with the king and queen. He bragged about it to his family and said, "I would be completely happy if it weren't for that rude fellow Mordecai."

His wife said, "Build a high gallows and get the king's permission to hang Mordecai tomorrow. Then you can enjoy the banquet." Haman liked that idea, and he had the gallows built.

That night, before the king went to sleep, he found the record of the time Mordecai had saved his life. He realized he had never rewarded Mordecai for this good deed. When Haman came to see him, planning to ask about killing Mordecai, the king spoke first. "Haman, what could I do to honor someone special?"

Haman assumed the king meant him, so he said, "Oh, give him a fine robe and a crown. Let him ride your own horse in a parade through the city. And have a prince shout, 'This is how the king honors someone who is worthy.'"

"That's excellent! Do all these things for Mordecai!"

11

The Brave Queen Saves Her People

ESTHER 7–10

WHAT a shock for Haman! Can you imagine how he felt as Mordecai received all the reward and honor Haman wanted for himself?

The king and Haman went to Esther's second banquet that night. Again the king asked Esther what she wanted. This time Esther said, "O king, if you care about me, please save my life and the lives of all the other Jews who still live here in your kingdom, for we are to be killed."

"What do you mean?" the king cried out. "Who would dare to threaten your life?"

"This wicked man Haman has ordered all Jews to be killed—and I am one of them!" she answered.

The king was terribly angry and stomped out of the room to think about the problem. Haman shook with fear, and he threw himself across Esther's couch to beg for mercy. Just then the king came back and thought Haman was trying to hurt Esther, so he ordered his death.

Haman was hanged on the very gallows he had built for hanging Mordecai!

The king gave Haman's house to Esther and Haman's job as prime minister to Mordecai. Esther asked the king to change the law about killing Jews, but he could not.

Then Esther had another idea. She said, "O king, since you cannot change that law, will you make another one permitting the Jews to fight back against their attackers?"

Ahasuerus was happy to do that, and when the Jews were attacked in February, they fought back and their lives were saved.

MEANWHILE, the Jews who had returned to Jerusalem kept working on the Temple. But some enemies were spying on them. They were the Samaritans, who had been living in Judah while the Jews were in Babylon. They were not true worshipers of God. When they saw that the Temple in Jerusalem was being rebuilt, they pretended they wanted to help.

Joshua and Zerubbabel were wise enough not to trust the Samaritans. Besides, they felt the work was their own responsibility. They said, "No, thanks! We can do the job by ourselves."

The Samaritans didn't like this, so they tried to discourage the workers and cause trouble for them. They even wrote to Artaxerxes, who had become king of Persia when Ahasuerus died.

They told him a lot of lies about the Israelis. "O king, we think it's our duty to tell you that when these people get the Temple and the city rebuilt, they will not be loyal to you. They won't pay taxes as they should. In fact, if you check their history, you will find they have always been troublemakers wherever they live."

After awhile they got the king's answer. "It looks as if you are right. The people of Jerusalem have often caused trouble. I hereby give you authority to tell them to stop building immediately. If I change my mind later, I'll let them know."

This was just what the Samaritans wanted. They waved the king's letter in front of the builders. "See this? You are ordered to stop your work right now!" So as long as Artaxerxes lived, the men of Judah did nothing more to restore their Temple.

EZRA was a religious leader among the prisoners in Babylon. He knew a great deal about the laws of Moses. As he thought about the men and women who had returned to Judah, he wondered who would be responsible for teaching them about the law. How would they know how to worship when they got the Temple finished?

He felt he should go back and be their teacher, so he asked Artaxerxes for permission to leave. The king not only let him go, but he allowed many others to go with Ezra. The group included priests, Levites, singers and other Temple musicians, and many others.

The king gave them a lot of money and other treasures to take with them, and they guarded them very carefully as they made the long trip back to Judah.

They left Babylon in March and arrived safely five months later. Artaxerxes admitted that he was letting all these people go because he was afraid of their God and didn't want him to punish him for keeping the Israelis as captives.

When Ezra arrived in Judah, he worked hard to teach God's law to the people. He was upset to find that Israeli men were marrying heathen women from the tribes around them.

Ezra prayed, confessing the sin of his people and pleading for forgiveness. Then the people were sorry about what they had done, and they stopped marrying heathen women. They had learned the lesson God wants us all to remember: Men and women should marry only those who love and worship the true God.

EZRA was not the only man King Artaxerxes sent back to Judah. The king had in his palace a Jewish servant named Nehemiah, whom he liked and trusted. One day Nehemiah talked to some friends who had recently been to Jerusalem.

Nehemiah asked, "How are things going? Are the city walls being rebuilt as we had hoped?"

The men told him the work was going ahead very slowly and that the walls of Jerusalem were still in ruins. This worried Nehemiah, and he went around looking sad for several weeks.

Finally the king noticed Nehemiah's sadness. "What is the matter, Nehemiah?" he asked.

"Your Majesty, I am unhappy because my countrymen who returned to Judah still have not made much progress with the rebuilding. It makes me sad to think of my beautiful city still in ruins after all these years."

The king asked, "How can I help?"

Nehemiah gathered his courage and asked, "Sir, would you let me go back to Judah and see that the work gets done?"

The king said, "All right, you may go. Just let me know when you will be back." And he gave Nehemiah letters to the rulers of the countries Nehemiah would travel through, asking them to be kind to Nehemiah and let him pass safely.

The rulers all let him travel through their territory, but two of them—Sanballat and Tobiah—weren't pleased about it. They didn't like to have anyone help the Israelis who were resettling Judah.

SEPTEMBER

15

*The Jews
Work on
the City
Walls*
NEHEMIAH

WHEN Nehemiah got to Jerusalem, he knew that enemies—like Sanballat and Tobiah—would not want him to succeed in his project. He sneaked out at night and made a secret inspection of the ruins.

The next day he called his workers together and told them his plans. "We must build the walls first, so that we can keep our enemies out of the city while we do other building. Come on, let's get it done!"

The people got busy right away. Everyone helped, even the priests and Levites and a number of women. Soon Sanballat and Tobiah saw what was happening, and they made cruel remarks to try to discourage the workers:

"Why, those walls are so weak, even the weight of an ant would crumble them!"

"Look at those crazy Jews! How do they think they can build a wall clear around the city without any good stones?"

But the people kept on working. Then their enemies saw that words were not enough; they would have to attack. Nehemiah heard about their plan and told his workers to carry weapons all the time.

Sanballat and Tobiah changed their minds about attacking, but from then on, the Israelis had this system: Half of them stood guard while the other half worked on the wall. And every one of them carried a sword, just in case an attack should come.

No matter what their enemies said or did, the people kept on working. And just fifty-two days after they started, the wall was finished!

16

The Temple Is Finished at Last!

EZRA; HAGGAI

Meanwhile, since Artaxerxes had stopped the work on the Temple, the people had begun building houses for themselves. Gradually they lost interest in the Temple. Even after Artaxerxes died, they didn't bother to ask the new ruler, Darius II, for permission to start the Temple work again.

Their selfishness disappointed God and made him angry. He warned them as he usually did: He spoke through prophets. This time he chose Haggai and Zechariah to be messengers.

Haggai said, "You are neglecting the Temple and thinking only of your own comfort. This is no time to spend your time and money on fancy houses for yourselves, when God's house is still in ruins. Now get out there and get busy!"

The people were ashamed. They started to work on the Temple immediately. The Samaritans said, "Who said you could work on the Temple again?"

The leaders replied, "We are here because King Cyrus sent us to take care of God's house."

The Samaritans wrote to Darius and said, "Are these people telling the truth? Did King Cyrus really tell them to rebuild the Temple?"

Darius checked in the law books and found Cyrus' decree. He wrote, "Now you Samaritans stop bothering the Israelis. Let them get on with their work, or I will punish you. And you must help them by giving them part of the tax money you owe me."

So the people of Judah were able to finish the Temple. They were so happy that they celebrated the feast of Passover in their new house of worship.

17

Joyful Celebrations

NEHEMIAH

THIS was really a wonderful time for the people of Judah. Just think: God had made their Babylonian and Persian rulers be kind to them. Their captivity was over. Many of them had come back to live in their own land. The walls of Jerusalem were built, so the city could be protected from enemies.

Workers had rebuilt the Temple, so the people could worship and serve God in his own house. They had even brought back the gold and silver bowls and cups and many other treasures that had been stolen from the old Temple.

No wonder the Israelis were so happy! They had several celebrations to show their joy.

When the walls were finished, they had a parade around the top of the wall, some marching one direction and some marching the other. They played trumpets and harps and drums and sang songs of praise. Then they marched to the Temple and made sacrifices to God.

They also had a thanksgiving celebration called the Festival of Trumpets. During that time Ezra held the book of the law and read it aloud to all the people. He read for hours, as the people stood and listened. They all told God they were sorry for the times they had disobeyed him, and now they would try to do better.

Next, they signed a paper, promising certain things: "We will obey God, not mingle with the heathen tribes, not marry ungodly women, give the Lord a tenth of our money and grain, and keep the Sabbath day a holy day of rest."

EVEN though the people of Israel were back home, they were not really free. They paid taxes to the Persian kings, who still ruled them. We don't see anything in the Bible about the next 400 years. However, we know a lot about what happened to God's people, because history books tell the events of those times.

One government followed another, but always the Jews were servants. The Greeks, the Egyptians, the Syrians—each ruled the Jews for awhile.

Then for about a hundred years they became free again, while a family of Jewish leaders, called the Maccabees, kept invaders out of Judah. Once more the people could worship God in their Temple.

Think back over the stories about God's people. Do you remember what usually happened to them when things were going well? Were they grateful, and did they show it by being faithful to God? If you answered, "No!" you are absolutely right.

Well, it happened again. The Jews neglected to worship God, and they fought among themselves. So God let another foreign army conquer them. This time it was the Romans, one of the strongest governments in all of history.

The Roman emperor sent a soldier named Herod to be king of Judah. Herod was cruel, and the people hated him. He tried to make friends by rebuilding the Temple, which by now was 500 years old and in bad condition. He spent nine years on it, and it really was beautiful.

But the Jews still were unhappy under Roman rule. How they longed for a great leader to come and free them!

ONE of the priests in the newly rebuilt Temple was Zacharias. He and his wife, Elizabeth, were happy serving God. However, they were both disappointed that they had no children. Now it was too late, because they were so old.

The priests had different duties in the Temple, but they took turns doing each task. One day it was Zacharias' turn to burn incense in the holy place. As he did this, he was frightened to see an angel beside the altar.

The angel said, "Don't be afraid of me, Zacharias. I have good news for you. You and Elizabeth are going to have a baby boy! You must name him John and bring him up in a certain way: He must never drink any wine.

"The Holy Spirit will live in him, and he will be a strong messenger of God, as powerful as Elijah. He will be the one to bring people back to God and get ready for the promised Messiah."

Zacharias was amazed. He said, "How can this possibly happen? My wife and I are too old to have a baby."

"How can you doubt what I say?" the angel replied. "I am Gabriel, and God has sent me directly from his throne in heaven. Because you don't believe, you will become unable to speak until after the baby is born!"

When Zacharias finally came out of the holy place, he couldn't say a word. But he showed everyone by his hand motions what he had seen and heard in the Temple.

20

*A Promise
from an
Angel*
LUKE 1

GOD had another important announcement for the angel
Gabriel to make. He sent Gabriel to Nazareth, a village in
Galilee, to give a message to a young woman named Mary. Mary
was a virgin; that is, she had never slept with a man. She was
engaged to be married to Joseph, a local carpenter.

Of course Mary was startled when the angel suddenly appeared
in her room. Gabriel said, "I've come to congratulate you, Mary.
You have been chosen for a great honor." Mary was puzzled and
troubled by his words.

He continued, "Don't be afraid. This is a great blessing. You will
soon become pregnant, and when your baby boy is born, you will
name him Jesus. He will be very great and will have the throne of
his ancestor David. His kingdom will never end."

Mary was greatly puzzled by the angel's words. She said to
Gabriel, "How is it possible for me to have a baby? I'm a virgin!"

The angel replied, "You will become pregnant by the power of
the Holy Spirit. Your baby will be a holy child—the Son of God.
Your cousin Elizabeth is pregnant too, even though she is beyond
the age for having babies. You see, nothing that God promises is
impossible!"

Mary answered joyfully, "I'm God's servant, and I'm glad to do
whatever he wants me to do. I'm ready for this wonderful thing to
happen."

Then the angel left Mary's room, and she was alone.

21

*Elizabeth
Has a
Baby Boy*

LUKE 1

MARY went to visit Elizabeth and Zacharias when Elizabeth was about six months pregnant. When Mary came into the house, the baby inside Elizabeth gave a sudden leap, and Elizabeth was filled with the Holy Spirit.

She said to Mary, "You are a fortunate woman, and God will honor your baby. As you came in, my baby leaped for joy. God has chosen you for this privilege because you believe and are willing to obey."

Then Mary said some beautiful words, like a song or a poem: "I'm praising God because he has chosen me, a simple village girl. He's going to do a wonderful thing. He's so powerful; he puts down rulers and lifts up lowly people. He has promised to be faithful to Abraham's children forever."

Mary stayed with Elizabeth for three months, then she went home. Elizabeth soon had her baby, and she and Zacharias did as the angel had told them.

The neighbors thought they should name the baby for Zacharias, but Elizabeth said, "No, he is to be named John."

They asked Zacharias, and he wrote on a piece of paper, "His name is John!" Immediately he got his speech back again!

The first thing Zacharias said aloud was, "The Lord is going to send a Savior from the family of David. My child shall be a prophet of God, preparing the way before the Savior."

John grew up to be a strong, godly man. He spent a lot of time in the desert until it was time for him to speak God's messages.

JOSEPH and Mary got married, but they didn't live as husband and wife until after the baby was born. Shortly before the baby came, the Roman emperor said everyone must go to his or her family's hometown for a census. That is how they counted the people. Joseph and Mary both came from David's family, so they had to register in Bethlehem, even though it was a bad time for Mary to travel.

SEPTEMBER

22

God Sends His Son

LUKE 2

They found Bethlehem crowded with people, and all the inns were full. The only space they could find was in a shed with some animals.

That night Mary's baby was born. She wrapped her little boy in warm clothes and put him to bed in a manger, which usually held the animals' food.

At first, the only people who knew what had happened were some shepherds who were tending sheep in a field. They saw many angels in the sky and heard them say, "Glory to God! Peace on earth! A Savior has been born today in Bethlehem, the city of David. You will know this is true when you find him, warmly wrapped and lying in a manger!"

After the angels had disappeared, the shepherds said, "Let's go see!"

They hurried into town and hunted until they found the little baby, with Mary and Joseph. Everything was just as the angels had said. After they had visited the baby, the shepherds went out and told everyone the news.

Mary thought a lot about what had happened and wondered what it all meant.

THE LAW told new parents to do several special things. First, they were to dedicate their first baby boy to God. When the baby was eight days old, the parents were to name him. Of course, Mary and Joseph named their baby Jesus because that is what the angel had told Mary to do.

Later, they traveled to Jerusalem and took baby Jesus to the Temple. They offered a sacrifice of two young pigeons, as the law required.

At the Temple they saw an old man named Simeon. He spent a lot of time in the Temple, because once God had told him he would not die until he had seen the baby who would become the Messiah—the Savior. Simeon had seen many baby boys brought to the Temple, but so far he had not seen the one who was God's Son.

As soon as Simeon saw the baby Jesus, he knew this was the right baby at last! He took Jesus from Mary and held him lovingly.

Simeon prayed, "O Lord, now I can die in peace. I have seen the baby who will bring your salvation to the world."

Another very old person who lived in the Temple was Anna. She had been a prophet for many years. Anna, too, recognized Jesus as the Messiah. She prayed a prayer of thanks for the Savior, then she hurried to tell everyone she met that the Messiah had been born.

MEANWHILE, far away in another country, some wise men watched the stars every night. When a bright new star suddenly appeared, they realized it had special meaning. They knew it was a sign that a great king had been born. They wanted to take gifts to him, so they decided to follow the star until they found him.

They traveled for many days and arrived at last at Jerusalem. They asked everyone, "Where is the new king of the Jews? We have been following his star, because we want to worship him."

King Herod heard about their questions, and he was worried. Was some new king going to take away his throne? Could these foreigners be talking about the Jewish Messiah?

SEPTEMBER

24

The Wise Men

MATTHEW 2

Herod called for the men who knew the most about the prophets. "Do your books tell where the Messiah will be born?" he asked.

"Oh, yes. The prophet Micah said he would come from Bethlehem," they answered.

Herod asked the wise men to come to his court. He asked when they had first seen the star. He told them to go ahead and find the baby king. "Then come back and tell me where he is, so I can worship him too," he said.

The star led the wise men right to the house where Mary, Joseph, and Jesus were staying. The men bowed to little Jesus and gave him valuable gifts—gold, frankincense, and myrrh.

Then they had a dream in which God said, "Don't go back to Herod. Take a different road as you travel home."

SEPTEMBER

25

Hiding from Herod

MATTHEW 2; LUKE 2

WHEN King Herod found that the wise men had left without reporting to him, he was angry. He said, "According to what they told me about the star, this new king must be less than two years old." So he sent soldiers to Bethlehem to kill all little boys younger than two. What a sad day!

Before the soldiers got there, God sent an angel to warn Joseph. "Quick! Take Mary and Jesus to Egypt and stay there until I say it is safe to come back." That is how God protected his Son from Herod's soldiers.

Joseph kept his family in Egypt until King Herod died. Then Joseph had a dream in which God said, "You can safely go back now." God said they should go to Galilee and live in Nazareth. That's where they had lived before going to Bethlehem for the census.

Jesus grew to be a fine, strong boy. Once, when he was twelve, he was in Jerusalem with his parents for the Passover. When the group from Nazareth started home, Jesus stayed behind.

After awhile Mary and Joseph missed him and went back to look for him. They found him in the Temple, talking with the teachers of the law, who were surprised by his wisdom.

Mary said, "Son, how could you cause us such worry?"

Jesus answered, "I thought you would know I'd be in my Father's house!" Then he went home with them and was always an obedient son. He kept getting taller and wiser, and everyone liked him.

DO you remember the baby boy Zacharias and Elizabeth had? Yes, his name was John. He and Jesus were cousins, because their mothers were cousins. John had been chosen to prepare people to receive the Messiah and to announce his coming. ·

He preached many sermons, saying, "You must be sorry for your sins and take care of the poor and the hungry. I baptize people in water, but soon the Messiah will come and he will baptize you with the Holy Spirit." (Because John baptized people, he was called John the Baptist.)

People asked John, "Aren't you the Messiah?"

"No," he answered. "He will come later. He's so great that I'm not worthy even to tie his shoes!"

One day Jesus came to the Jordan River, where John was baptizing. John called out loudly, "Look! There is the one I have been telling you about. He is the Lamb of God—the Messiah!"

Jesus asked John to baptize him.

John answered, "Oh, no! I'm the one who should be baptized by you!"

But Jesus insisted. He said, "I want to do everything the right way." So John baptized Jesus in the river.

Just as Jesus came up out of the water, he saw the heavens open up. God's Holy Spirit, looking like a dove, came down and lighted on Jesus. Then the voice spoke from heaven: "This is my dear Son, whom I love. I am greatly pleased with him."

SEPTEMBER

27

Satan Tempts Jesus

MATTHEW 4;
MARK 1; LUKE 4

AFTER Jesus was baptized, he went into the wilderness. There he went without food for forty days and nights. While Jesus was weak from hunger, Satan came and talked to him. Satan said, "If you're really the Son of God, turn these stones into bread."

Jesus answered, "The Scriptures say we don't live just by eating bread. We live by obeying every word God says to us."

Satan took Jesus into Jerusalem, and they stood on the roof of the Temple. He said, "Go on— jump off! That will prove to everyone that you are the Son of God. The Scriptures say God will send angels to keep you from being hurt."

"What it really says," Jesus answered, "is that we should not test God in such a foolish way!"

Then Satan tried once more. He was determined to make Jesus obey him instead of obeying God. He took Jesus to the top of a high mountain. They could look out over the kingdoms of the world.

Satan said, "This could all be yours! I'll give you these kingdoms to rule if you will just kneel down right here and worship me."

Can you imagine God's Son kneeling and worshiping the devil? Of course not! This time Jesus said, "Listen, Satan. You get out of here. The Scriptures say, 'You must worship and obey the Lord God, and not anyone else!'"

Seeing that Jesus had won, Satan gave up and went away.

JESUS began to ask some men to stop the work they usually did and travel around with him. He taught them important things, so they were called his disciples.

One day he and his disciples were invited to a wedding in the small town of Cana. Jesus' mother, Mary, was there too.

Evidently the host had not planned very well—or perhaps more people came than he expected—because the wine was all gone long before the celebration was over.

Mary spoke to Jesus about it, but he said, "You shouldn't expect me to do anything about it. It isn't time yet for me to do miracles."

Mary didn't argue with him, but she went to the serving men and said to them privately, "If Jesus tells you to do something, you do it."

Six large, empty waterpots were standing there in the kitchen. Jesus said to the servants, "Fill each of these pots with water."

Remembering what Mary had said, the servants obeyed. "Now," Jesus said, "dip out some of it and take it to the host."

The host tasted what they gave him. "Why, this is excellent wine!" he exclaimed. He said to the bridegroom, "Most people give their guests the best wine first. Then, after they have had enough and don't care so much what it tastes like, they receive cheaper wine. But you have saved the very best wine until last!"

That was the first miracle Jesus did.

*Jesus' First
Miracle*

JOHN 2

SEPTEMBER

*How
to Be
Born
Again*

JOHN 3

MORE and more people began to notice Jesus and listen to what he said. Some of them thought he might be the Messiah, but the Pharisees, who were the main church leaders, didn't like him at all.

One Pharisee, named Nicodemus, didn't agree with the rest of them. He made a secret visit to Jesus late one night. He said, "Teacher, I believe you have come from God, or else you wouldn't be able to say and do such wonderful things."

Jesus saw that Nicodemus really meant it. He said, "Nicodemus, I tell you the truth: If you want to be in the Kingdom of God, you must be born again—in a heavenly way."

Nicodemus said, "I don't understand how an adult could be born again like a little baby!"

"No," Jesus replied, "this is a different kind of birth. God's Holy Spirit makes your spirit alive, and that is like being born into a new life. You can't see the Spirit doing this. He is like the wind— invisible but powerful."

"Please explain," said Nicodemus.

"You are a leader and should understand," Jesus said. "The Son of Man has come from heaven and will return there. I am like the brass serpent Moses lifted up in the wilderness. I'll be lifted up so people can be saved."

Then Jesus said the words we all love, the words in John 3:16:

"For God loved the world so much that he gave his only Son so that anyone who believes in him shall not perish but have eternal life."

King Herod— John's Powerful Enemy

LUKE 3; JOHN 3

JOHN the Baptist was still preaching and baptizing. One day his followers said, "Master, that man Jesus is becoming famous. Many people are leaving you to follow him."

John said, "Well, that's the way it should be. I'm like the friend of the bridegroom—not nearly so important as the bridegroom himself. Jesus should become greater, and I should become less important."

Then John did something dangerous. He criticized the king! King Herod, the son of the Herod who was king when Jesus was born, had married Herodias. This was wrong, because she was the wife of Herod's brother.

John the Baptist scolded Herod for his sin. This made Herod so angry that he put John in jail. After awhile, Herod began to realize what a good man John was, so although he kept him in jail, he protected him.

Much later, the king was giving a feast. Herodias' young daughter, Salome, danced for Herod and his guests. She pleased Herod so much that he offered to give her anything she wanted! She asked her mother what she should ask for.

Herodias had never forgiven John for speaking against her marriage. She said, "Ask for John's head on a platter!"

When Herod heard Salome's request, he was sorry he had made such a foolish offer. But he couldn't break his promise in front of all his guests, so he ordered his soldiers to cut off John's head.

When John's disciples heard about his terrible death, they came and buried his body.

OCTOBER

1

*The
Woman
at the
Well*

JOHN 4

ONE hot day, Jesus and his disciples had to travel through Samaria. The men said to Jesus, "You rest here by this well, and we will go find some food."

As Jesus sat there, a woman of the village came to the well with her pitcher. Jesus asked her for a drink. She said, "I'm surprised you would ask me. You Jews don't usually speak to Samaritans." (For many years Jews and Samaritans had been enemies.)

Jesus said, "If you knew who I am, you would ask me for living water!"

"Living water?" she echoed. "You don't even have a rope or pail. How could you get water?"

Jesus replied, "The well water leaves you still thirsty. But the water I give satisfies you forever."

"Oh, I want some of that kind," she said.

"All right. Go and get your husband," said Jesus.

She hesitated. "Well, . . . I don't have a husband."

Jesus said, "The problem is that you have had too many husbands. And you are not married to the man you live with now."

The woman was embarrassed and changed the subject. "Why do you Jews worship in one place and we Samaritans in another?"

Jesus answered, "The important thing is not *where* we worship, but *how*. Remember, salvation will come through the Jews."

"Yes," she answered. "When the Messiah comes, he will tell us everything."

"I am the Messiah!" he said.

The woman hurried into town and called everyone to come and meet Jesus. He preached to them for two days.

WHEN Jesus talked to the people in the Samaritan village, many of them believed he really was the Savior. Then Jesus and his friends continued their trip to Galilee.

They stopped in the town of Cana, where Jesus had once turned water into wine at a wedding. A rich government officer from Capernaum came looking for Jesus. He begged Jesus to help him. He said, "My little boy is very sick and about to die. Please, please come to Capernaum and heal him."

Jesus sighed. "You people are always wanting to see miracles before you will believe in me."

The child's father said again, "Oh, sir! Please come and heal him before it is too late!"

Then Jesus said, "You can go back home now. Your little son has been healed!"

The officer believed what Jesus said, and he started to Capernaum. Even before he arrived, his servants hurried out to meet him. "Oh, master, we have good news! Your son is not going to die. He has recovered!"

The happy father asked his servants, "When did he start to get better?"

They answered, "About one o'clock yesterday afternoon."

The boy's father realized that one o'clock was the exact time at which Jesus had told him his son was healed. How thankful he was! He and his family believed Jesus was the promised Messiah.

OCTOBER

2

Jesus Heals a Sick Boy

JOHN 4

OCTOBER

3

*From
Fishermen
to Followers*

MATTHEW 4;
MARK 1; LUKE 5

ONE day Jesus was walking by the Sea of Galilee—which was a large lake—and he watched the fishermen. They were not fishing just for fun; this was their work. They caught great numbers of fish in big nets, then sold them to make a living.

Jesus noticed two brothers named Simon and Andrew and called to them, "If you were working with me, you would be fishing for men instead of fish!"

He said the same thing to two other brothers, James and John, who were fishing with their father, Zebedee. All four of these brothers were interested and listened to what Jesus was teaching.

Such crowds came to hear Jesus that he hardly had room to move. He got into Simon's boat and said, "Push the boat out into the water a little way, and I'll speak to the people from there."

After he had finished preaching, he said, "Now let's go out where it's deeper, and you can get some fish."

Simon answered, "Oh, we tried all night, but couldn't find any. But if you say so, we'll try again."

They threw the nets out and were amazed at how many fish they caught. In fact, the nets broke from the weight. They had to call other fishermen to come and help them.

They could tell that Jesus had done a real miracle for them, and they were awed and a little bit afraid.

Then Jesus asked both pairs of brothers to leave their fishing business and become his disciples. All four men came immediately.

ALTHOUGH God's people went to the Temple in Jerusalem to make their sacrifices at certain times of the year, they did have small places of worship in each town. These were called synagogues. Whenever a famous speaker came to town, he was invited to teach there. The people of Capernaum asked Jesus to speak in their synagogue.

While he was there, a demon-possessed man began to disturb the meeting. He called out, "Go away! We don't want anything to do with you, Jesus of Nazareth! You've just come to make trouble for us because you are the Son of God!"

Jesus spoke sternly to the demon in the man. "Be still! Come out of him!" The demon threw the man to the ground, but he left him alone after that, and the man was normal.

The crowd was excited at what they saw. "Imagine that! He has the power to make demons come out of people!"

Then Simon took Jesus and the other followers to his home. They found that Simon's wife's mother was very sick with a high fever. Jesus went to her bedside and told the fever to leave her. She felt better right away. She even felt well enough to get up and help cook a meal for Jesus and his friends.

That evening many other sick and demon-possessed people heard Jesus was there. They came and asked to be healed, and Jesus touched each one. They were all healed, no matter what diseases they had.

OCTOBER

5

Down through the Roof!

MATTHEW 9;
MARK 1; LUKE 5

ONE man in Capernaum was too badly paralyzed to go to see Jesus and ask for healing. But he did have good friends. Four of his closest friends made a kind of stretcher-bed for him. Each man took a corner of the stretcher, and they carried their paralyzed friend to the house where Jesus was staying.

When they saw the huge crowds and the long lines, they were discouraged. What could they do? Then one of them got an idea.

"Let's lift the stretcher up onto the flat roof," he said. "We can take out some of the tiles and lower our friend into the room where Jesus is healing people."

They could hardly pull their friend's weight up that high, but they finally succeeded. They made a hole by removing some roofing tiles, then slowly and carefully they eased the stretcher down until their friend was lying right in front of Jesus!

Jesus was pleased when he saw the faith of the man's friends. He said to him, "I forgive your sins."

The religious leaders who didn't like Jesus said, "Huh! Who does he think he is? Only God can forgive sin."

Jesus knew exactly what they were thinking. He said, "Which do you think is harder—to forgive sin or to heal the body? Well, I'll do both!" He said to the paralyzed man, "Stand up; you are well. Now go on home."

The man jumped to his feet, completely healed. He picked up the stretcher and hurried home. Everyone was absolutely amazed!

ONE Sabbath day Jesus went to Jerusalem. There he passed Bethesda Pool, where people were healed. Once in awhile the water moved, as if it were bubbling. When that happened, the first person into the water was healed. Of course, many sick people gathered, hoping to be the fortunate ones.

Jesus felt especially sorry for a man who had been sick for thirty-eight years. He said, "Do you want to be healed?"

The man answered, "Of course! But I'm too weak to move quickly into the pool."

Jesus said, "Well, now you are healed! Get up, roll up your mat, and go home."

When the religious leaders saw the man, they said, "Carrying that mat is work. By working on the Sabbath, you are breaking the law."

The man replied, "The man who healed me told me to carry it."

"Who would tell you that?" they asked.

"I don't know his name," he answered.

Later Jesus saw him in the Temple and warned him not to go on being a sinner. Then the man told the leaders who had healed him.

They scolded Jesus for not respecting the Sabbath laws. But he said, "My Father does good things for people, no matter what day it is. I just do as he does."

The leaders were shocked that Jesus called God his own father. He continued, "If you don't honor the Son, you dishonor the Father. Whoever listens to what I say and believes God sent me shall have life forever and not be punished."

OCTOBER

6

Jesus and the Sabbath

JOHN 5

I N SPITE of the disapproval of the official religious leaders, Jesus kept on doing kind things for people, even on the Sabbath day.

Once when he and his followers were walking through a field on the Sabbath, some of them were hungry, so they picked some grain. They rubbed the husks off and ate the good kernels. Again the Pharisees were displeased. They said that rubbing the husks from the grain was like doing farm work, which was forbidden on the Sabbath.

Jesus said, "I have been made the master of the Sabbath. I should know what is permitted and what is not!"

This made the leaders angrier than ever. They actually began to make plans to kill Jesus. When Jesus heard this, he took his followers away. They went back to the Sea of Galilee, and again he made many sick people well.

Jesus went off alone into the desert and spent a whole night praying. When he came back to his followers, he chose twelve of them to be an inner circle of companions and helpers. They would travel with him, preach, help heal the sick, and send evil spirits out of demon-possessed people.

Here are the names of the twelve special disciples: Peter (the new name Jesus gave Simon the fisherman), Andrew (Peter's brother), James, his brother John, Philip, Bartholomew, Thomas, Matthew (who had been a tax collector), another man named James, Thaddeus, Simon, and Judas Iscariot.

8

Jesus Preaches on a Mountain

MATTHEW 5; LUKE 6

EVERYWHERE Jesus went, people crowded around him. He decided the best way to speak to so many people was to climb up high on a hill. That way, everyone would be able to see and hear what went on.

One time when he taught on a mountain, he was especially teaching his disciples, but everyone wanted to hear.

We usually call this The Sermon on the Mount, but it wasn't like a sermon you would hear at church, lasting just a few minutes. This message was probably given on several days. People came and went, they ate picnic lunches, and children played on the hillside while their parents listened to Jesus.

Jesus started this long talk by telling the people how they could be happy and enjoy God's blessing.

Be humble, not proud and stubborn.

Be sorry for their sins.

Be meek and listen to other people's opinions.

Be eager to do right.

Be kind to everyone else.

Be pure in their hearts, thinking only about good things.

Be peaceable and help others not to quarrel.

Then he told them something that sounds very strange. We usually feel bad when people treat us unkindly, don't we? What Jesus said sounds just the opposite:

"Be *glad* when others are mean to you because you believe in me and obey me! God will give you a great reward if you suffer for being my followers."

9

Jesus Tells How We Should Live

MATTHEW 6; LUKE 6

IN HIS rules for being happy, Jesus said a lot about being good. But what does it mean to "be good" and "do right"? We want to know too, don't we? So we can be glad Jesus gave details about what we should and should not do. His talk on the mountain is just as helpful to us today as it was to those people a couple of thousand years ago!

Here is a list of some of his instructions:

Be like a bright light, helping people see how good God is.

Do all the good things God told Moses in the law.

Not only must you not kill anyone, but you must not even hate anyone, for hatred is like murder in the heart.

Settle your arguments and disagreements quickly.

Men and women must have only pure thoughts about one another.

Married couples must not get divorces.

If you make a serious promise, you must keep it.

Be generous with others, even if they treat you unfairly.

Be just as nice to your enemies as you are to your friends.

Don't show off when you do generous things for others.

Don't show off when you pray, but do it quietly and privately.

Don't try to store up a lot of money on earth. Give your money generously to people in need, and God will take care of your needs.

Don't worry about what is going to happen. God is in control of your life. Live one day at a time.

JESUS told his disciples and the other people on the mountain many important things about life. He told them not to be too quick to criticize other people but to check up on their own lives too. And he promised that when they asked for God's help, he would always answer their call.

One of the most important things Jesus said has been quoted over and over. Probably your parents and your grandparents learned it when they were boys and girls. In fact, it is such good advice that it is called The Golden Rule. He said, "Do for other people the things you would like them to do for you!"

Then Jesus told an interesting story. He said, "If you listen to what I say and obey my rules, you will be like a man who built his house on a solid rock. Heavy rainstorms came, the wind blew, and flood water washed against his house; but it stood firm, because it was built on a solid foundation.

"But if you hear what I tell you and do not pay any attention to my instructions, you will be like a man who built his house on sand. When the rain and wind and flood came, his house fell down with a mighty crash. It was a complete wreck, because it had a poor foundation."

All the people who heard Jesus talk were surprised at how well he taught. They said, "That's the best thing we've ever heard! We think God has given him authority to speak."

THE POWERFUL country of Rome now ruled the Jews. Often the Romans were cruel; however, a few Roman officials were kind to the Jews.

One of those friendly Romans even paid to have a synagogue built in Capernaum, so the Jews liked him. He had a servant who became very sick. The Roman sent word to Jesus, asking him to come and heal his servant. Jesus agreed to come.

But even before Jesus got there, the Roman hurried out to meet him. "Oh, master," he said, "I'm not good enough to have you enter my home. You can heal my servant without seeing him. Just speak the word, and he will be well."

Jesus said to the people around him, "This man has more faith than any Jew I know!" And he said to the Roman, "Your servant is now healed. You may go home."

When the man got home, he found the servant entirely well.

Later, in the village of Nain, Jesus saw a funeral procession. The only son of a widow had died, and she was heartbroken. Now she would have no one to love her and take care of her.

Her sorrow touched Jesus' heart, so he said to her, "Don't cry." He stopped the procession and touched the casket.

"Young man! Come back to life!" The boy sat up and was able to talk and walk. Jesus led him to his mother, and they were together again!

Everyone was amazed. People said, "This man is a great prophet. He can do the works of God!"

OCTOBER

11

Jesus Shows Great Power

MATTHEW 8; LUKE 7

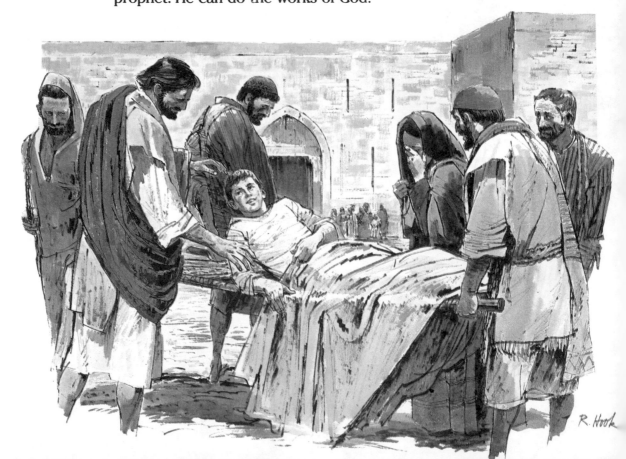

R. Hook

12

Showing Love to Jesus

LUKE 7

ONE day a Pharisee invited Jesus to his home for dinner. A sinful woman heard Jesus was there, and she came to see him. She brought an expensive jar of perfume.

She was crying because she was sorry about her sins. Her tears fell on Jesus' feet, and she wiped them with her long hair. Then she poured the perfume on his feet to show her love and respect for him.

Simon the Pharisee, Jesus' host, said to himself, "Well! Jesus must not be a prophet, or he would know how bad she is, and he wouldn't let her touch him."

Jesus always knew what people were thinking. He said, "Simon, let me ask you a question. If a man lends $500 to one person and $5,000 to another and then tells them they don't have to pay the money back, which debtor would love him more?"

Simon answered, "The one who owed him the larger amount."

Jesus said, "Right! Now look at this woman. When I came to your house today, you didn't wash the dust from my feet—but this woman washed them with her tears. You didn't give me the usual kiss of greeting—but she kissed my feet. You didn't give me oil for my head—but she poured expensive perfume on my feet.

"Yes, she is a sinful woman, but I am forgiving her sins because she loves me so much. You, however, have shown me very little love and are forgiven very little."

Some people grumbled because Jesus said he could forgive sin, but the woman went away happy!

OCTOBER

13

*A Story
about
Money*

LUKE 12

ONE day a man called to Jesus from the crowd, "Master, I wish you would tell my brother to divide our father's money fairly."

Jesus replied, "I wish you would not ask me to settle your arguments! Besides, you shouldn't be worrying about money. Money won't make you happy.

"I'll tell you a story: One year a farmer got such good crops that he became rich. His barns were full, and he didn't have room to store all the grain!

"He thought, 'I'll tear down these old barns and build bigger ones. I'll be able to relax and have fun, because I'll be so rich that I won't ever have to worry about money again!'

"But that night the rich farmer heard the voice of God warning him: 'You think you are safe because you are rich. What a fool you are! Tonight you will die, and then what will become of your riches?'"

Jesus said, "Don't waste time worrying about money, clothes, and food. Birds don't plant crops and build barns, yet God provides food for them. Aren't you more valuable to God than birds are?

"And the flowers don't make cloth and sew clothes for themselves—but just see how beautifully God dresses them! If God takes care of flowers, won't he take care of you? Spend most of your time thinking about God, and he will give you everything else you need!"

JESUS was good at telling stories that taught lessons. One of his best stories was about seeds.

"A farmer went out to plant his seed. As he threw out handfuls of seed, some of it fell on the path. People walked on it, and birds flew down and ate some of it.

"Some of the seed fell on rocky soil that wasn't deep. It started to grow, but there wasn't enough dirt to nourish the roots, so the little plants died.

"Some seed fell into patches of weeds. The weeds were stronger than the grain seedlings, and the seedlings died.

"And some seed fell on good rich soil. It started to grow, and it got tall and strong. At harvest time the farmer got a hundred times more than he had planted!"

The disciples asked him what the story meant. Jesus said, "You can understand it, but most people can't. The seed is what God says to men and women. Some of his words come to hard hearts, and the devil steals it away.

OCTOBER

14

A Story about Seeds

MATTHEW 13; MARK 4; LUKE 8

"Some of God's messages come to shallow hearts. They believe for awhile, but then they lose interest. Some people's hearts are like a weed patch. The other things they are interested in crowd out God's truth.

"But some people are like the rich soil. They listen and believe God's word. Therefore the message grows and produces fruit— many times more than was 'planted' in them!"

Which kind of soil is your heart most like?

15

A Story about Faith

MATTHEW 13; MARK 4

JESUS told other stories about seeds. He said, "You know how tiny a mustard seed is. But when it is planted, it becomes a plant that grows very large—as tall as a tree. That's the way it is with faith. If you believe even a little bit, your faith can grow and become strong."

Then he said, "Once upon a time a farmer planted good seed in a field. But while he wasn't watching, some enemies came into his field and planted a lot of weeds, called thistles, among his good seeds. Of course both kinds of plants grew. The weeds grew big and strong right along with the good grain.

"When the seeds sprouted and the plants grew, the farmer's servants said, 'Master, did you know your field has a lot of thistles among the grain?'

"'Yes,' he said, 'an enemy did that.'

"'Well, don't you think we should pull up the weeds?' they asked.

"'If you do that,' he replied, 'you will pull up grain along with the weeds. Just leave the field alone until the harvest time. Then the reapers can separate the weeds from the grain.'

"That's the way it is with my kingdom. The good seed is like the people who have faith in me. The weeds are those whom Satan has planted among my people. But someday the angels will take out all my true people. Then the ones who are wicked unbelievers will be thrown out and burned up."

ONE day Jesus and his disciples were crossing the Sea of Galilee. Suddenly a terrible storm swept over the water. The boat was tossed around, and the men thought it would sink.

Jesus was tired from teaching and was taking a nap. He slept soundly through the storm. The disciples woke him up and yelled, "Oh, Master! Do something to save us or we'll all drown!"

Jesus got up and spoke to the wind and the waves. "Stop! Be still!" Instantly the wind stopped, and the sea was completely calm.

Jesus said to his companions, "Why were you afraid? You don't have very much faith!"

On the other side of the lake they saw a strange man. He had evil spirits living in him, so he did wild and frightening things. He wouldn't wear clothes, and he went around screaming and hurting himself with stones. Everyone in town was afraid of him.

The wild man knelt at Jesus' feet. The demon in him cried out, "Don't hurt me! I'm just one of many demons here. Please let us go into the pigs in this field."

Jesus said, "All right. Leave the man and go into the pigs."

When they did, the large herd of pigs became wild too. They ran down the hill, jumped into the lake, and were drowned.

Then the man sat quietly with Jesus, acting perfectly normal. He wanted to join Jesus' group, but Jesus said, "No, go home and let your family and friends know what has happened to you."

OCTOBER

16

Two Wonderful Miracles

MATTHEW 8;
MARK 4–5; LUKE 8

OCTOBER

17

*Jesus Gives
Health and
Strength*

MATTHEW 9;
MARK 5; LUKE 8

WHEN Jesus returned from his trip across the Sea of Galilee, a religious leader named Jairus was waiting for him. Jairus knelt at Jesus' feet and said, "Please come to my home and heal my twelve-year-old daughter. I'm afraid she is dying!"

Jesus agreed, but as they walked along, another person came to Jesus for help. This was a woman who had been sick for twelve years. She was shy about stopping Jesus, so she just reached out and touched his robe. Immediately she was healed.

But Jesus knew something had happened. He asked his disciples, "Who touched me?"

They said, "Master, many people are bumping against you!"

Jesus said, "This was different. I felt healing strength go out from me."

The woman admitted that she was the one and that she was healed. Jesus said, "You are well because you believed in me!"

The group went on, but as they came near Jairus' house, a messenger came and said, "You won't need Jesus now, sir. Your little girl is dead."

Jesus said to Jairus, "Don't worry. She'll be all right." He went into the house and spoke to the people. "Don't cry. She's only sleeping."

The mourners were sure she was dead, and they laughed at Jesus. He took Peter, James, John, and the child's parents into the bedroom. Jesus held the girl's hand and said, "Little girl, get up!"

She jumped up, completely well!

A S HE left Jairus' house, Jesus noticed two blind men following him. One of them called, "Please take pity on me, O Son of David!"

The men followed him into the house where he was staying. Jesus turned and said to them, "Do you really believe I can heal your blindness?"

"Oh, yes, Lord," they answered eagerly.

"All right, then," Jesus said, "I will."

He touched their eyes, and they could see clearly. Jesus told them not to go around talking about what had happened to them, but they just couldn't keep still. They told their story everywhere.

That same day Jesus saw a pitiful man who could not say a word because a demon controlled his tongue. Jesus drove the demon out of the man, and he could speak again. Everyone was amazed at what Jesus could do. "We've never seen anything like this in all of Israel," they marveled.

But as usual, the Pharisees were jealous of Jesus' success and fame. They said, "The only reason he can drive out demons is that he himself is demon-possessed!" But of course you and I know the real reason Jesus could do such miracles: he was the Son of God!

Jesus kept on preaching, teaching, and healing throughout the countryside and in the villages. He did this because his heart was loving, and he didn't want anyone to suffer.

He told his disciples, "All around us the harvest is ready, but we don't have enough people to help with the harvest. Let's pray for more workers."

OCTOBER

19

*The Disciples
Tell the
Good News*

MATTHEW 10;
MARK 6; LUKE 9

JESUS wanted everyone to hear the Good News (another word for it is "gospel") about being born again and being forgiven. He sent his twelve special disciples out to tell that Good News.

After learning from Jesus, they were able to teach and preach his message. Jesus gave them the ability to heal the sick and set people free from demons. They could even raise the dead!

Jesus said, "God has chosen the Jews to be his special people, so tell the Good News only to them. They won't all receive you warmly. In fact, some of them will be cruel to you—beating you and throwing you into jail. But even if they hurt your bodies, they can't harm your spirits.

"Don't take money and food with you. And don't pack a suitcase with extra clothing and shoes. God will give you what you need as you travel along.

"You will be like the sparrows. God feeds them, even though they are rather unimportant. You are much more important than sparrows, so you can be sure God will provide everything you need.

"When people receive you kindly, give God's blessing to their homes. But if some people treat you badly, just leave their town and don't have anything to do with them.

"Go on now; represent me wherever you go. If you try to hold onto your lives, you will lose them. But if you are willing to spend your lives serving me—even if you should die—you will be saving your lives for eternity."

JESUS' disciples went out and preached the gospel and healed the sick. When they came back, Jesus took them to a quiet place to rest.

Soon crowds of people found out where they were and followed them. Jesus didn't turn any of them away but healed their sicknesses and cast out demons.

Some people even followed him to the other side of the lake, a long way from their homes. When lunchtime came, the disciples said, "We'd better send these people away so they can get lunch somewhere."

Jesus said, "That's not necessary. You can give them something to eat."

They answered, "It would take a lot of money to buy food enough for this crowd!"

Jesus asked, "How much food do we have here?"

Andrew said, "A young boy has five small loaves of bread and a couple of fish."

"Give it to me," he said. The boy was willing to share, so Jesus took the food and thanked God for it. "Have all the people sit down, then pass out this food. It will be enough for everyone."

And it was! Everyone received plenty of bread and fish. A lot of food was left over, and the disciples gathered it up in baskets so it wouldn't be wasted.

How many people do you think had lunch with Jesus that day? Dozens? Hundreds? No, many more than that. Five thousand men, plus some of their wives and children, ate all they could hold! Don't you suppose that boy was glad he had shared his lunch?

OCTOBER

21

Jesus Walks across the Lake

MATTHEW 14;
MARK 6; JOHN 6

THE PEOPLE were excited about Jesus' power to feed so many people from such a small amount of food. They said, "This man is a great prophet!" Jesus was afraid they would try to make him their king. He went up into the mountains alone.

The disciples waited for him for awhile, but when he didn't come, they decided he must have gone home some other way. They got into the boat and started back toward Capernaum.

A storm came up quickly, as so often happened on the Sea of Galilee, and the men were having trouble controlling their boat. From the shore, Jesus saw their problem, so he started walking across the lake, right on top of the water!

When they saw him coming, they were terrified. Of course they had never seen anything like that before. They even thought he might be a ghost! He called to them and told them who he was.

Peter said, "If it's really you, let me walk on the water too."

"Come on!" Jesus said.

Peter started out bravely, but after a few steps he looked around at the storm. He became afraid, and immediately he started to sink. Jesus reached out and helped him.

"Why didn't you have more faith in me?" Jesus asked. They both got into the boat, and the storm stopped. They quickly finished their trip to Capernaum.

Jesus' disciples were just amazed at what he had done. They said, "You really must be God's Son!"

OF COURSE Jesus was healing sick people everywhere he went—the deaf, blind, lame, and people with fevers. Often the sick people were too weak or too afraid to come to Jesus by themselves, so friends would bring them.

One day some friends came bringing a man who had two problems. He was deaf and could hardly speak at all. The friends begged Jesus to put his hands on the man and heal him.

Jesus led the man away to a quiet place where they could be alone. He put his fingers in the man's ears. Then he used some of his own spit and touched the man's tongue with it.

Jesus looked up to heaven and prayed. Then he said, "Be opened!" Instantly the fellow could hear and speak perfectly.

Of course, when the people realized he was healed, they were terribly excited. Although Jesus asked them not to tell what had happened, they talked about it everywhere.

After that experience, a huge crowd gathered. As before, the disciples were concerned about what the people would eat. Again Jesus took a small amount of food they could find—just seven little loaves of bread and a few fish—and did a miracle with it. He made it into enough to feed everyone.

This time the crowd was more than 4,000 people! After everyone was full, the disciples gathered up seven baskets full of leftovers.

OCTOBER

22

Another Picnic and a Miracle

MATTHEW 15;
MARK 7–8

ONE day some people brought a blind man and asked Jesus to heal him. Jesus led the man outside the village, then he put some spit on the man's eyes and covered them with his hands. When he took his hands away, he asked, "Now can you see?"

The man looked around eagerly, then he said, "Well, yes. I can see people's shapes, but they look like trees walking around!"

Then Jesus put his hands on the man's eyes again. That time the eyes were perfectly clear, and the man was thrilled to be able to see everything very plainly.

As Jesus and his disciples were walking away from that town, he said to them, "When people talk about me, who do they say I am?"

"Some of them think you are John the Baptist," said one.

Another said, "They think you are Elijah, come back to life again. Or maybe one of the other prophets."

Jesus asked them, "But who do you say I am?"

Peter, who often was the first to answer, said, "You are Christ, the Messiah."

Jesus was pleased that they understood who he was, but he asked them not to tell everyone just yet. He explained to them that the powerful religious leaders would not be satisfied until they had killed him. But he promised he would rise again just three days later.

Peter said, "Oh, Lord, don't let that happen to you!"

But Jesus answered, "Don't be like Satan, the tempter. You just don't understand God's plan."

R. Hork

OCTOBER

24

*A Miracle
on a
Mountain*

MATTHEW 17;
MARK 9; LUKE 9

AMONG the twelve disciples, Peter, James, and John were the
ones who were Jesus' closest friends. One day he took those
three friends with him to the top of a mountain. There a
remarkable thing happened to Jesus. He began to shine all over—
his face and his clothing just glowed with a bright light.

The three disciples saw two men standing with Jesus, talking to
him about things that would happen to him at the end of his life.
Somehow the Lord let the disciples know that the two men were
Elijah and Moses, who had, of course, been dead for many years.

Peter—always so quick to speak before thinking—said, "Oh,
Lord, shall we put up three little tents for you and Moses and
Elijah to stay in?"

As he said this, God spoke from heaven and said, "This is my
Son, whom I love. Pay attention to him and to what he says!"

The disciples were terrified at hearing the voice of God, and
they fell down on the ground. Jesus touched them and said, "You
can get up. You don't need to be afraid."

When they got up, they realized that the two prophets from long
ago had disappeared.

Jesus said, "You must not talk about what has happened up here
on the mountain. Wait until after my death and after I come to life
again." The disciples were really puzzled. What could he mean by
"come to life again"?

Do *you* know what he meant?

OCTOBER

25

*Jesus
Teaches
about
Pride*

MATTHEW 18;
MARK 9; LUKE 9

HERE'S a question that might embarrass you. Have you and your friends ever said things like this: "I'm smarter than you are!" or "My dad has a nicer car than your dad has!" or "I get more allowance than you do!"

Well, sometimes even grown-ups talk like that, and that's what the disciples were doing one day as they walked along the road on one of their trips. What do you think they were bragging about? It was about which one of them was going to be the greatest person in the kingdom Jesus was going to have!

When they finished their trip, Jesus asked them, "What were you quarreling about back there?"

They didn't want to talk about it, but of course Jesus already knew the answer, because he could always tell what people were thinking and saying.

He sat down with them and said, "Listen! If you want to be 'great,' you must do it by becoming a servant to other people. If you want to be first, you must be willing to be last."

Then he picked up a child and held him in his arms. "Look at this little fellow. If you welcome a little child because of your love for me, then you are welcoming me and my Father. Don't act so proud and selfish. Believe in me the way little children do.

"And don't ever do anything to hurt a child. People who do cruel things to children would be better off if they had never even been born."

ONE day a man who knew a lot about the Jewish law asked Jesus, "Master, how can I be saved?"

Jesus answered, "You know the law. What does it say?"

The man said, "It says to love God and my neighbor."

"That's true," said Jesus. "Now you know what to do."

"But what does the law mean by 'neighbor'?" the lawyer asked.

Jesus said, "Let me tell you a story. One day a man was taking a trip from Jerusalem to Jericho. Robbers attacked him and beat him. They stole his clothing and left him there, badly hurt.

"A priest came along the road, but he ignored the injured man and hurried by. Then came a Levite, or Temple worker. He didn't stop either.

"Then came a Samaritan man. Samaritans don't usually do anything kind for Jews. But this man felt sorry for the fellow who had been attacked. He took care of his injuries and bandaged the wounds.

"He put him on his own donkey and took him to a hotel and paid for a room where he could rest while recovering. He even told the hotel clerk he would pay more later, if that much money wasn't enough."

Jesus asked the lawyer, "Which of the three men who saw the victim on the road acted like his neighbor?"

The lawyer said, "Well, of course, it was the one who took care of him."

"That's right," Jesus answered. "Now, you do the same kind of things for needy people. That's the way to 'love your neighbor.'"

26

A Really Good Neighbor

LUKE 10

JESUS had good friends in a village called Bethany. They were two unmarried sisters named Mary and Martha and their brother, Lazarus. When Jesus would visit them, Martha—who was a very good housekeeper and cook—wanted to prepare fancy meals for him. She wanted her sister, Mary, to come to the kitchen and help her, but Mary would rather sit beside Jesus in the living room and listen to him talk.

Martha finally became angry with Mary. She said to Jesus, "I wish you would tell that sister of mine to come out and help me with the cooking."

Jesus said, "Don't worry so much about the housework, Martha. Learning about God is more important than food. Mary has made a good choice."

Later Jesus talked to his disciples about how they should pray. He taught them a prayer that we usually call The Lord's Prayer:

"Our Father in heaven, your name is holy and should be respected by everyone. We want your kingdom to come. We want people on earth to do what you want, just as the angels in heaven do.

"Please give us the food we need today. Forgive our sins, just the way we forgive the sins of people who wrong us. Don't let us be tempted to do evil things, but keep us away from sin. You are the glorious and powerful ruler. Amen."

ONE day Jesus and his disciples saw a beggar beside the road. He had been blind all of his life, and he couldn't work. The disciples asked Jesus, "Is this man blind because of some sin he has done? Or is it because of the sin of his parents?"

Jesus answered, "Neither one. His blindness is an opportunity for God to show his glory and power."

Then he mixed up a sort of clay by spitting on some dirt. He put the clay on the blind man's eyes and said, "Now go and wash off the clay in Siloam Pool."

The blind man obeyed, and immediately he could see.

People looked at him and said, "Why, isn't this the blind beggar?" Some thought he was, and others thought he just looked like the beggar.

The man himself said, "Yes, I am the one who was blind, but now I can see perfectly."

"How did that happen?" people asked.

"That preacher named Jesus put clay on my eyes and told me to wash it off at the pool," he explained.

The people looked around, but couldn't see Jesus. "Where did he go?" they asked.

"I really don't know," the man replied.

His friends and neighbors said, "We had better take you to the Pharisee leaders to be examined."

OCTOBER

29

*Open Eyes,
Open Heart*

JOHN 9

PEOPLE took the formerly blind man to see the Pharisees. These leaders asked him how he had been healed. He told them everything Jesus had done.

They were always finding fault with Jesus, so they said, "He did it on the Sabbath, so he can't be a very good man! Who do you think he is?"

The man said, "I think he is a prophet!"

The leaders still doubted the man's story so they called his parents and asked them, "Is this really your son, who was blind?"

"Oh, yes," they said. "But we don't know how he received his sight. He's an adult; he can tell you." The parents were afraid to let the Pharisees know they believed that Jesus had done a miracle.

Jesus' enemies talked to the man again. "You ought to give God the credit for healing you, not this Jesus. He is a sinner."

The man answered, "I don't know about that. I only know that I was blind before, but I can see now."

The Pharisees kept asking him to tell the story over and over. Finally he became angry. "Why do you keep asking me about it? Is it because you want to believe in him too?"

Then they scolded him and said he couldn't come back to the synagogue anymore.

Jesus talked to him again and asked, "Do you believe in God's Son?"

"I would if I knew who he was," the man answered.

"I am the one," Jesus said.

Then the man said, "I do believe in you!"

WHEN Jesus finished talking to the man who had been blind, he said something to everyone in the group: "One of the reasons I have come into the world is to make blind people see—and to make some people who think they can see realize how blind they are!"

The Pharisees asked him if he was speaking about them, and he answered, "If you knew you were blind, you would not be sinful; but because you think you have such good eyes, you are guilty of sin!"

Then he said, "If a person doesn't walk into a sheep pen through the door but climbs over the fence, we know he is a thief. The one who enters the right way is the real shepherd. His sheep recognize him and know his voice.

"I am like a good shepherd to those who love me. I am willing to sacrifice my life for my sheep. I know my sheep and they know me."

Then Jesus talked about God, his Father. "My Father loves me because I give up my life and will get it back again. My Father has given me this power."

When the Pharisees heard him say God was his Father, some of them were shocked and angry. They even thought an evil spirit was controlling him.

But some of the people who had seen his miracles said, "We don't think he has an evil spirit. Look at the good things he does for people! How could he heal a blind man if he had a demon?"

YOU remember Jesus' good friends in Bethany—Martha, Mary, and Lazarus? One day Lazarus became very sick. His sisters were afraid he might die, so they sent word to Jesus, asking him to come and heal him.

His disciples expected him to rush to Bethany at once, but Jesus didn't do that. When he heard about it, he said, "The purpose for this illness is not Lazarus' death, but it is intended to bring glory to me, the Son of God." And he stayed away from Bethany for two more days.

Then at last he said, "Let's go to Bethany now. My dear friend Lazarus has gone to sleep, and I must wake him up."

At first his disciples didn't understand what he meant, but then he said, "Lazarus is dead, and when you see what I will do, you will believe in me."

When Lazarus' sisters heard Jesus was coming, Martha ran out to meet him, but Mary stayed in the house, grieving for her brother.

Martha said to Jesus, "Master, if you had been here, Lazarus wouldn't have died. But even now he would come back to life if you would tell him to."

JESUS said, "Yes, your brother will rise again."
   Martha thought he meant at the great resurrection day at the end of the world, but he said, "I am the Resurrection and the Life. Anyone who believes in me shall rise from the dead and live forever. Do you believe this?"
   Then Martha said, "Yes, Master. I believe you are the Messiah."
   Martha went home and told Mary that Jesus wanted to talk to her. Mary hurried out to see him. Everyone thought she was going to her brother's grave, so they followed her.
   Mary said the same thing to Jesus that Martha had said. "If you had come sooner, our brother would not have died."

   When Jesus saw her crying, he felt very sad and he cried too. He asked them to take him to the grave. It was a cave in the side of a hill, with a big stone in front to seal it shut.
   Jesus said, "Roll the stone away."
   Martha said, "Oh, we'd better not. He's been dead for four days, and his body has decayed. It would smell terrible."
   Jesus answered, "Don't you remember I told you I would do a miracle?" So the men in the group rolled away the heavy stone.
   Jesus prayed, "Father, thank you for hearing me. I know you always do, but I want these people to know it too."
   Then Jesus called loudly, "Lazarus, come out of the grave!"
   How surprised and frightened all the people were when Lazarus walked out of that cave! He was still wrapped tightly with the strips of cloth people used when they prepared a body for burial.
   Jesus said, "Unwrap those cloths and let him go!" And Lazarus was alive and well and could go home with his sisters.

NOVEMBER

1

New Life for Lazarus
JOHN 11

ONE day Jesus talked to the disciples about the importance of forgiveness. He said, "If a friend commits a sin, tell him it is wrong. If he is sorry and makes things right, be sure to forgive him. Even if he does it again and again, you must be willing to keep on forgiving him."

Another time, ten men who had the skin disease called leprosy came to meet Jesus. They couldn't come close, because the law said a leper must stay away from other people. Everyone thought leprosy was very contagious.

The lepers called to Jesus, "Oh, Master, please take pity on us."

Jesus always felt sorry for sick and hurting people. He said, "Go and show yourselves to the priest." That is what the law said lepers must do when they thought their disease was cured. The priest had to agree that they were well before they could go home and live normally.

As the ten men obeyed Jesus and walked toward the Temple to see the priest, their skin became clear and healthy!

One of the ten, a Samaritan, turned around and hurried back to where Jesus was standing. He was so sure he was well that he came right up to Jesus and fell down at his feet. He cried out with joy, "Oh, praise God! I'm completely healed!"

Jesus said, "Didn't I heal ten men? Where are the other nine? Isn't it strange that the only one to come back and give thanks is this Samaritan!"

Then he said to the man, "Because you have faith, you have been healed."

NOVEMBER

2

Ten Are Healed; One Is Grateful

LUKE 17

YOU and I don't like to be sick for even a few days, do we? This story is about a woman whose back had been crippled for eighteen years so she could not stand up straight. One Sabbath day she went to the synagogue in her town, and Jesus was there to teach. Jesus saw her stiff, bent back, and he felt sad about her pain.

He said to her, "Woman, I am making you well. Your back is completely healed."

As soon as he had said these words, she was able to straighten up and stand like everyone else! She was so happy that she praised God and thanked him.

You can probably guess what the synagogue leader said about this healing. He was angry because Jesus had healed on the Sabbath day, when no one was supposed to do any work. He yelled, "You have plenty of other days when you could heal people. You don't need to break the Sabbath!"

Jesus answered, "Well, that doesn't make any sense! You yourself do some kinds of work on the Sabbath. For instance, you take your animals from their stalls and lead them out to get water, don't you? If you do that for a mere animal, shouldn't I do a kindness to this human being—a daughter of Abraham—after Satan has kept her in this terrible condition for eighteen years?"

These words made his enemies feel ashamed of themselves. And the crowds of people were happy because of this miracle Jesus had done.

MANY people didn't understand why Jesus did some of the things he did. For instance, he seemed glad to have people around him who were not good people at all. One day some Pharisees were grumbling about the bad people Jesus spent time with.

Jesus heard them, and he said, "Suppose you were a shepherd with a hundred sheep to care for. If one of them wandered away from the flock and got lost, what would you do? Wouldn't you leave the other ninety-nine sheep safe in the sheep pen and go out to look for the lost one?

"You would hunt until you found it. Then you would carry it home and call in your friends and neighbors to celebrate with you!

"Well, that's the way I feel about wandering sinners. I'm more concerned about the one who wanders than I am about the ninety-nine who do not stray away."

Then he said, "If a woman has ten coins, worth a lot of money, and she loses one in her home, don't you think she will look for it very hard? Yes, she will turn on all the lights and look in every corner and crack.

"She will look under beds and will sweep the floor carefully until, aha! There it is! She is so happy because she has found her valuable coin. She too will call in her friends to have a party and rejoice with her.

"Just so, the angels in heaven are happy when a sinner is sorry for his sins and the Lord finds him."

JESUS told another story, this time about a young man. He was the younger son of a farmer. He got tired of helping on his father's farm, so he said, "Father, give me my share of your money so I can leave home and live on my own."

The father divided his property between his two sons, and the younger one took his share, packed up his clothes, and went far away from home.

He had a great time for awhile. He had lots of friends because he had plenty of money. But after he had carelessly wasted everything, his "friends" disappeared. He had no money, no fun, no friends, no food.

The only job he could find was tending pigs. No Jewish boy liked pigs, because they were unclean. But it was the best he could do. He was so hungry he could have eaten even the dry husks of the pigs' food. He was miserable.

He got to thinking about how comfortable his home had been. He thought, "Even the servants on the farm have a better life than I have here. I think I'll go home and confess to my father that I did the wrong thing. I don't deserve to be a son in his home anymore, but maybe he would let me be one of his servants."

His father had always hoped his boy would come back. He often looked down the road, hoping to see him. Finally, one day, there he came! The father rushed out and hugged and kissed his boy.

THE RUNAWAY son started his speech: "Father, I have sinned against you. . . ."

But before he got to the part about becoming a servant, his father called to one of his slaves, "Bring him some good clothes. And get him some decent shoes for his feet and a ring for his finger." When he said that, his son knew he was received back into the family, because servants didn't wear shoes and jewelry.

His father went on with his plans: "And kill that fat calf in the pen, and we'll have a feast to celebrate."

The older son came in later from working in the fields. He heard the sound of music and fun. When someone told him the party was in honor of his younger brother, he was not so happy as his father had been. He was jealous of all the attention the boy got after he had behaved so badly.

He said to his father, "I've always been a good son and a hard worker, but nobody ever gave *me* a big party! This kid has been out wasting your hard-earned money in wild living, and when he comes home broke, you invite friends in and have a celebration. You even killed that fat calf, the best one we have!"

His father said, "Don't be angry. You are my dear son, and everything I have is yours. But we should be happy because this boy who was lost is found. It is as if he has come back from the dead!"

THE PHARISEES, who always criticized Jesus, were very proud, and they loved being rich. One day Jesus told them this story: "A very rich man lived in a large, expensive home. He had beautiful clothes and everything else he wanted. Out at the gate to his property a poor dirty beggar lay, begging money from people who passed by. The beggar's name was Lazarus. He was covered with sores because he never got to take a bath, and he didn't have proper food.

"Finally the beggar became so ill that he died. Angels took him to heaven, and there he was with Abraham. Soon after that, the rich man died too, but he went to the place of fiery torment called hell. As he lay there in agony, he could see up into heaven, where the beggar was now happy and comfortable.

"The rich man called to Abraham, 'Oh, please send Lazarus down here to touch my tongue with water and relieve my suffering.'

"Abraham answered, 'You had every comfort when you were on earth. This poor beggar had nothing. Now it is the other way around. The great space between heaven and hell cannot be crossed by anyone.'

"Then the rich man cried out, 'Well, at least send Lazarus back to earth to warn my brothers, so they can escape this place.'

"But Abraham said, 'No, they have the Scriptures to warn them. If they won't believe them, they won't believe a person who comes back from the dead.'"

NOVEMBER

8

Jesus Loves Little Children

MATTHEW 19;
MARK 10; LUKE 18

WE read many stories about the kind things Jesus did for men and women when he was on earth. But Jesus loved children, too. Remember how he raised the little girl from the dead and how he healed the young boy who was demon-possessed?

One day while he was teaching the people who gathered to learn, some mothers were there with their children. They brought the children up close to Jesus, because they wanted him to give them a special blessing.

The disciples thought they should not interrupt Jesus while he was talking, so they scolded the women and tried to get them to leave.

Jesus saw what they were doing, and he stopped them at once. "Don't send them away. Don't ever prevent children from coming to me. They are the very ones for whom my kingdom is intended. Everyone who wants to be in my kingdom should be like these little children—pure and trusting and loving."

Then he picked the children up and held them in his arms and on his lap. He often warned people not ever to do any harm to a child. In fact, he was very stern about it, saying that if anyone does anything cruel to a child, it would be better for him if he were killed! That's a very strong warning, but it shows how important children are to Jesus and how much he loves them.

No matter how bad you feel sometimes, and no matter what sad things happen to you, always remember: Jesus loves you!

A BLIND man named Bartimaeus lived near the city of Jericho. One day Jesus and his disciples were in that area, preaching to the crowds.

Bartimaeus heard he was coming, and he knew Jesus had often healed people with serious problems like his. He couldn't see Jesus, of course, but he sat by the side of the road and called out, "Jesus, Son of David, please have mercy on me. Oh, Son of David, have pity on me!"

Some of the people around him were cross with him. "Oh, be quiet!" they growled.

But he was determined to get Jesus' attention, so he called out all the louder, "Please, Jesus, help me!"

When Jesus finally heard him, he said, "Tell that man I want to talk to him."

The people said to the blind man, "Well, this is your lucky day! Come on, he is willing to see you." And they led him to Jesus.

Jesus said to Bartimaeus, "What do you want me to do for you?"

Bartimaeus replied eagerly, "Oh, Teacher, I want you to give me my sight!"

"All right," said Jesus, "it's done. Your faith has healed you." This time Jesus didn't touch the man's eyes or spit on the ground and make clay or anything like that. He just said those words, and Bartimaeus was able to see perfectly!

As Jesus walked away, Bartimaeus followed him, because he wanted to stay with the one who had healed his blind eyes.

NOVEMBER

9

Jesus Heals Bartimaeus's Eyes

MATTHEW 20; MARK 10; LUKE 18

ANOTHER man in Jericho was eager to see Jesus. Zacchaeus collected taxes for the Roman government. The people hated the Romans, so they disliked Jews who worked for the Romans.

People especially hated tax collectors because most of them were dishonest. They would raise the taxes so they could keep some of the money for themselves before giving the required amount to the government.

Zacchaeus was a very short man. He found it hard to see over taller people in front of him. Because he was so determined to see Jesus, he climbed into a sycamore tree and sat on one of the branches. There he could see everyone who passed.

Finally Jesus and his disciples came by. Jesus looked up into the tree and spoke directly to the little man: "Zacchaeus, come down from the tree. I am going to your home today."

Some people in the crowd were shocked. "Look! He's going to the home of a terrible sinner!" they muttered.

Like most tax collectors, Zacchaeus was rich and had a beautiful home. He welcomed Jesus gladly.

He had something important to say. "Master, I want to give half of my money to poor people. And since I got some of my riches by cheating the taxpayers, I will give back four times as much as I stole."

Jesus could see that Zacchaeus's faith had changed his heart. He said, "I came to look for lost people and save them. Today salvation has come to this house."

JESUS decided to go to Jerusalem. First he stopped in Bethany to visit Martha, Mary, and Lazarus. Everyone remembered how Jesus had raised Lazarus from the dead, so crowds came out to see him. This displeased the religious leaders, and they continued their plans to kill Jesus.

Jesus sent two of his disciples to a nearby town to find a donkey's colt on which he could ride into the city. They brought the animal and put their coats on it to make it more comfortable for Jesus.

As he rode into Jerusalem, great crowds of people gathered to welcome him. They put their coats and branches of palm trees down in the road. They shouted their welcome to him: "God bless the Son of David! Praise God for sending him! He comes in the name of the Lord!"

Some people asked, "Who *is* that?"

Others answered, "It's Jesus, the great prophet from Galilee!"

Jesus went into the Temple as usual. He was upset when he saw merchants and moneychangers cheating the people. He shouted, "My Temple should be a place of prayer, but you have turned it into a robbers' den!" And he drove them out of the Temple.

Then sick people came to him, and he healed them there in the Temple. Children called out, "God bless David's Son!" The leaders were angry and asked Jesus if he heard what they were saying.

"Yes! The eighth Psalm says that babies and children shall praise the Lord!"

We still celebrate that day in our churches, and we call it Palm Sunday.

NOVEMBER

11

Crowds Welcome Jesus to Jerusalem

MATTHEW 21; MARK 11;
LUKE 19; JOHN 12

12

The Farmer's Son

MATTHEW 21;
MARK 12; LUKE 20

JESUS taught in the Temple every day, and many people came to hear. This is one of his story/lessons.

"Once a rich farmer had a large vineyard. He rented it to a fellow who was supposed to take care of it and divide the grapes with him at harvest time. Then the owner went out of town.

"At harvest time he sent a man to get his share of the grapes. But the renter beat him up and wouldn't give him anything.

"Then the owner sent another helper, but the same thing happened. He even sent a third one, but he too was beaten and chased away.

"Then the owner thought, 'If I send my own son, surely they will respect him and I'll get my share of the crop.' But when his son got there, the tenant farmers said, 'Aha! This is the one who will inherit the farm. If we kill him, we can keep the land.' So they attacked the son and killed him."

Then Jesus asked, "What do you think the owner will do then? He will come and kill those wicked renters and find new people to take care of his farm."

The Temple leaders realized they were the tenant farmers of Jesus' story and he was the owner's Son, whom they were planning to kill.

They wanted to arrest Jesus, but he was so popular with the people that they didn't dare.

JESUS knew he would not be with his followers much longer. He wanted them to be ready to get along without him. He told them this story/lesson:

"A certain king had a son who was to be married. He invited many friends to the wedding feast, but when the time came, they didn't show up. He sent servants out to bring them to the feast.

"Some refused because they were too busy. Some even were cruel to the servants and killed them. This made the king so angry that he sent soldiers to kill the cruel men.

"Then he sent more servants out to invite a new group of people to the wedding. 'Bring everyone you can find on the street or anywhere else.'

"As each guest came, the king gave him or her a beautiful outfit of clothing to wear at the wedding feast. Soon the room was full.

"The king came in to greet his guests. He noticed one man who was not wearing the special wedding clothing. The king said, 'How did you get in here without the proper clothing?'

"The man had no answer, so the king ordered the servants to tie up his hands and his feet and to throw him out into the darkness where he couldn't see the wedding or have any of the food.

"The king said, 'I called many, but I chose only a few.'"

The parables of Jesus were something like puzzles. Can you figure out who each person in this story stands for?

*Oil
for the
Lamps*

MATTHEW 25

JESUS told the people another story about a wedding. He said that getting ready for his kingdom would be like a group of ten bridesmaids getting ready to welcome home a bridegroom and his bride after a wedding.

Five of the bridesmaids brought extra oil so they could refill and relight their lamps when they heard the bridegroom coming. The other five girls didn't bother to fill the lamps or to bring extra oil.

The bridegroom didn't come as soon as they expected, so the girls lay down to have a short nap. While they were sleeping, someone shouted, "He's coming! Quick! Get up and light your lamps!" But some of them didn't have any more oil, so they couldn't light their lamps.

They said to the other five girls, "Please give us some of your extra oil. Our lamps have gone out."

But the other girls said, "We have used it all. You will have to go out and buy some at the store."

So the girls hurried away to find more oil. While they were gone, the bridegroom came, and the wedding feast began.

When the five girls came back from the store, they knocked loudly on the locked door and asked permission to come in. But the bridegroom didn't let them come in.

When the Lord Jesus comes back for us, will we be like the five girls who had extra oil in their lamps—ready and waiting for him?

H ERE'S another story about living wisely while we wait for
Jesus to come back. This one is about a rich boss who gave
his employees money to invest while he was away on a business
trip.

He didn't give them all the same amount of money. He gave
$5,000 to one, $2,000 to another, and only $1,000 to the third.

The first man used his money to buy a store. He sold things
there and made twice as much as he spent, so he doubled his
money.

The second man used his money wisely too, and he had extra
money as a result.

The third man wasn't so smart. He just hid his thousand dollars
so it wouldn't get lost or stolen.

When the employer came back, he asked each one how he had
used the money. The first one told his story and showed his boss
the large profit he had made. The employer was really pleased,
and he gave him a big reward.

The second fellow then told his story and showed how much
money his $2,000 had made. Again the boss was pleased, and he
rewarded that employee too.

When the third man came, the boss asked him what he had
done. The man was embarrassed, but he said, "Well, I knew you
would demand a report, so I was careful not to lose your money. I
kept it safe in a hidden place."

The employer was disappointed with that third man, and he
took back his thousand dollars. He
punished the employee for not
using the money more wisely.

R. Htode

JESUS talked a lot to his disciples about his kingdom—what it was like and how to get ready for it. One day he told them how he would choose the people for his kingdom.

He said, "I'll come back to the earth in great glory, and I'll have angels with me. Everyone will stand before my throne, and I will be like a shepherd separating the sheep from the goats.

"I'll have the 'sheep' stand on my right side and the 'goats' on my left.

"Then I'll say to the ones on the right side, 'Come on into my kingdom. I want you because when I was hungry, you fed me. When I was thirsty, you gave me something to drink. When I was a stranger, you invited me to your homes, and when I was sick or in prison, you visited me.'

"They will answer, 'Lord, we don't remember doing those things for you.'

"And I will say, 'When you cared for needy people, it was just as if you were caring for me.'

"Then I will say to the ones on the left side, 'You must be thrown into the everlasting fire prepared for the devil and his angels. When I was hungry and thirsty, or a stranger, or in prison, you didn't take care of me.'

"They will answer, 'When did we ever see you in need and not take care of you?'

"And I will say, 'When poor people needed help, you neglected them—but you were really neglecting me.'"

THOUGH Jesus taught in Jerusalem during the day, he spent the evenings at his friends' home in Bethany, just a few miles from the city.

On one of those evenings Jesus' friends had a dinner for him. Martha served the meal, as usual. The guests leaned back on couches around the table, which was the way they had banquets in those days.

Mary came into the room, carrying a large jar of very expensive perfume. She came and knelt in front of Jesus. She broke the jar and poured the perfume on his feet. Then she dried them—not with a towel, but with her long hair.

Judas Iscariot was the treasurer of the group of disciples. He was greedy and was always thinking about money. He was shocked at what Mary had done, and he said, "Master! A big jar of perfume like that could have been sold, and we could have taken care of a lot of poor people with the money we got for it."

Jesus knew what was in Judas' heart. He knew Judas wasn't so interested in the poor as he was in getting more money into his bag, so he could sometimes sneak some out for himself.

Jesus said, "Don't complain about what Mary has done. She has shown her love for me in a beautiful way, and the world will never forget what she has done.

"You will always have poor people to take care of, but I won't always be here. This woman has anointed me in advance for my burial!"

18

The Disciples Celebrate Passover

MATTHEW 26;
MARK 14; LUKE 22

THE DISCIPLES asked Jesus where they should prepare the Passover feast. They didn't have a home in Jerusalem, so they needed a large room where they could gather for the meal.

Jesus said, "Walk to the edge of the city, and you will see a man carrying a pitcher of water."

The disciples were surprised at this because men didn't usually carry water. (That was women's work!) But Jesus went on, "Follow that man to his house. Then say to him, 'Please show us the room you have prepared for the Master.' He will show you a room that is all ready for Passover. That is where you can roast the lamb for the feast."

They did as Jesus told them, and everything worked out perfectly. They cooked the lamb, and later in the day Jesus and more of his followers came for the dinner.

Jesus said, "I've been looking forward to this Passover with you, because it is the last one I will celebrate before I am sacrificed for the world's sins."

The disciples couldn't understand this. They had always supposed Jesus would become the powerful king who would free them from the Roman government. Why should he talk about being sacrificed? They even started arguing again about who was going to be the most important one in Jesus' kingdom.

Jesus heard what they were saying, and he said to them, "Anyone who wants to be the most important one must become unimportant. To be great, you must become small. The way to be a leader is to be a servant!"

AFTER Jesus told his disciples they should become servants, he showed them exactly what he meant. He asked them, "Who is greater, the master of the feast or the servant who waits on tables?"

Of course they said, "The master of the feast!"

He said, "Well, I am the master of this feast, but I am also your servant."

He got up and took off his outer robe. Then he wrapped a towel around his waist and brought a pan of water. He stooped down and washed each disciple's feet and dried them with the towel.

Peter thought Jesus shouldn't do this. He said, "Lord, I don't want you to wash my feet!"

Jesus answered, "If I don't, you won't really belong to me."

"Oh! Well, then," Peter said, "wash every part of me!"

"That isn't necessary, Peter," Jesus said. "If I have washed your feet, you are clean all over. But that isn't true of everyone in this room." He said that because he knew that one of the disciples was going to tell his enemies how they could capture him.

When he had washed all the feet, he put his robe on again and sat down with the disciples.

"Do you understand what I just did? You often call me 'Master' and 'Lord,' and those are good titles for me. But if I, the Master, have washed your feet, how much more important it is that you wash one another's feet. I've given you a good example; now you follow it."

NOVEMBER

19

*Jesus
Washes the
Disciples'
Feet*

JOHN 13

NOVEMBER

20

*The Last
Supper*

MATTHEW 26;
MARK 14; LUKE 22;
JOHN 13

THE DISCIPLES wondered who Jesus meant when he said one of them was not loyal. John was sitting closest to Jesus, so he asked him.

Jesus said, "It will be the one to whom I give this piece of bread after I dip it into the bowl."

He handed the bread to Judas Iscariot and said, "Go and do what you have to do."

When that happened, Satan made Judas even more determined to betray Jesus, so he left the table and went out into the night.

Jesus went on talking to the rest of the disciples. "I won't be with you much longer," he said. "But first I want to give you a new commandment. You must love one another as I have loved you! This love will show the world that you really belong to me."

Then Jesus took a piece of bread and broke it. "This is my body, which will be broken for you. When you eat this bread, you will show my death to everyone."

Next he took a cup of wine and blessed it. "This wine is my blood, poured out for you so God will forgive your sins. Drink this in memory of me."

Jesus said his followers should do this over and over until he comes back to earth again. This ceremony has different names— the Last Supper, Holy Communion, the Eucharist, the Breaking of Bread—but no matter what we call it, we do it to remind ourselves and one another of Jesus' death, just as he commanded that night.

PETER didn't want Jesus to leave them. He said, "I love you so much that I would even die for you!"

Jesus shook his head sadly, "Oh, Peter. Before the rooster crows tomorrow morning, you'll say three times that you don't even know me!"

Jesus promised to come back for them someday. Meanwhile, he would prepare a home for them in heaven so they could be with him forever. He said that while he was gone, the Holy Spirit would live in them and comfort them.

Then he took them to the Garden of Gethsemane for prayer. In the garden, he took Peter, James, and John with him to a private place. He said, "Wait here and pray."

As Jesus prayed alone, he thought about how terrible his death would be. He would also be cut off from fellowship with his heavenly Father, because he would be dying a sinner's death. He prayed for awhile, then went back and found the disciples sleeping.

He said, "Can't you even stay awake and pray for me?"

He went back to pray some more. His heart was in such pain that he sweat drops of blood. He cried out, "Father, if it is possible, keep me from this death. However, I want to do your will, not my own."

Angels comforted him, then he returned to the disciples. Again he found them asleep, but this time he didn't scold them. He just said, "Go on sleeping. You need your rest."

NOVEMBER
21
Jesus Prays in the Garden

MATTHEW 26;
MARK 14; LUKE 22;
JOHN 13–14

NOVEMBER

22

*Soldiers
Arrest Jesus*

MATTHEW 26;
MARK 14; LUKE 22;
JOHN 18

JESUS prayed a while longer, then he went back to Peter, James, and John. He said, "Get up now. Judas is coming to betray me."

They all jumped up and saw a group of soldiers and Temple officials coming through the garden. Judas knew just where to find Jesus, because it was a place where Jesus often took his disciples. The soldiers had lanterns and torches and were carrying weapons.

Of course Jesus knew what was going to happen, but he asked, "What do you want?"

They answered, "We've come for Jesus of Nazareth."

He said, "I am he." The words "I am" were used to mean the name of God, and when he said that, the soldiers drew back and some of them fell down.

He asked his question again, and again they said, "Jesus."

He said, "I told you I am the one you want. Take me, but let my disciples go."

Peter was so angry with Jesus' enemies that he grabbed his sword and cut off the ear of the High Priest's servant, Malchus.

Jesus said, "Put your sword away, Peter. Shouldn't I do whatever the Father requires?" Then Jesus healed Malchus's ear.

Jesus said, "You fellows come after me as if I were a robber. Why didn't you arrest me when I was teaching in the Temple? Well, of course, this is the time when Satan is in control!"

The soldiers arrested Jesus and took him to the High Priest.

AS THE SOLDIERS took Jesus away, Peter followed along, but he stayed far back so they wouldn't notice him. While Jesus was being questioned inside the house, Peter waited in the courtyard where people were gathered around a fire to keep warm.

A servant girl looked at Peter as he sat by the fire. She said, "Why, I think I've seen that man with Jesus."

Peter was afraid of what might happen to him, so he said, "No! I don't even know him."

Later another person looked at him closely and said, "Yes, this man is a disciple of the man from Nazareth."

But again Peter said, "I certainly am not!"

A third person said, "Well, he must be one of Jesus' people. You can tell by the way he talks that he is a Galilean."

This time Peter was more frightened than ever, and he shouted, "You don't know what you are talking about! I've had nothing to do with that man Jesus."

Just as he said those words, he saw Jesus being led across the courtyard. Jesus turned and looked at Peter, and at that moment a rooster crowed!

Immediately, Peter remembered that Jesus had said Peter would deny that he knew him—not just once, but three times—before the rooster crowed.

He was so ashamed of himself that he cried. How could he have been so unfaithful to the Master he loved?

NOVEMBER

23

Peter Hears the Rooster Crow

MATTHEW 26; MARK 14;
LUKE 22; JOHN 18

WHEN anyone is arrested, different officers of the law ask many questions. They did this with Jesus, too.

First, members of the Jewish high court questioned him and other people about his teachings. Many people lied about Jesus, trying to get him into trouble.

The High Priest asked Jesus himself if he was the Son of God, and Jesus answered, "Yes, I am. And someday you will see me sitting beside God the Father in heaven. Then I will come back to earth in the clouds."

The court was shocked to hear him say, "I am." When he said that, he was claiming one of the names of God!

The High Priest yelled, "There! You see? He does claim to be God's Son! What shall we do with him?"

All the people thought he should be killed. They all made fun of him and did shameful things to him— spitting on him and hitting him.

They led him to the Roman governor, whose name was Pontius Pilate. They told Pilate lies about Jesus, saying he tried to get Jews to rebel against the Roman government. "He even says he is the king of the Jews," they said.

Pilate asked Jesus, "Is that true? Are you a king?"

Jesus answered, "Yes, I am, but not in the way you mean. I have a kingdom, but it is not on earth."

Pilate said to the Jewish court officials, "I don't see any problem here. He doesn't seem to have done anything wrong."

But the officials and the people made such an uproar about it that Pilate decided to send Jesus to be questioned by Herod. He thought maybe Herod could get to the bottom of this problem.

NOVEMBER

24

*Officials
Question
Jesus*

MATTHEW 26;
MARK 14; LUKE 22;
JOHN 18

340

HEROD talked to Jesus, but Jesus wouldn't answer. His enemies twisted things Jesus had said so it sounded as if he were an enemy of the government.

Finally Herod gave up. He and his soldiers also mocked Jesus and mistreated him. They put a purple robe on him, making fun of his saying he was a king. Then Herod sent him back to Pilate.

Pilate said, "This man hasn't done anything bad enough to die for. Herod didn't find him guilty either."

Each year Pilate had the privilege of setting one Jewish prisoner free at the time of the Passover. He asked the crowds and their leaders which prisoner he should set free that year—Jesus or a murderer named Barabbas. Probably Pilate thought Jesus should be the one to be set free, but instead the crowds shouted, "Barabbas! Set Barabbas free!"

Pilate asked, "Well, if I free Barabbas, what shall I do with Jesus?"

And everyone screamed, "Crucify him! Crucify him!"

Pilate's wife came to him and whispered, "Don't condemn Jesus. I had a dream about him last night, and I know he is innocent!"

But Pilate thought he had to give the people what they wanted. He called for a bowl of water and washed his hands in front of them. "All right. Take him and crucify him. I wash my hands of responsibility. Don't blame me for Jesus' death."

The people all shouted back, "His blood shall be on our heads. We will be responsible for his death."

NOVEMBER

26

*A Crown
of Thorns*

MATTHEW 17;
MARK 15; JOHN 19

PILATE'S soldiers kept teasing and mocking Jesus. They took some branches with sharp thorns on them and twisted them into the shape of a crown. Then they pushed it down onto Jesus' head. Of course the thorns stuck into his forehead and made it bleed. They were making fun of his being a "king."

Pilate kept hoping he could get the religious leaders to leave Jesus alone. He said again, "You know, he really doesn't deserve to die."

But the leaders insisted, and they said, "If you don't let us crucify him, we'll tell the emperor, Caesar, that you let one of his enemies escape!"

So Pilate stopped objecting and said, "Oh, all right. You may crucify him. But I don't think he is guilty!"

About that time Judas, the one who had betrayed him to the soldiers, got to thinking about what he had done, and he was sorry. He took back the thirty pieces of silver money the religious leaders had paid him.

He said, "I don't want your money. I did the wrong thing when I betrayed the Lord."

They just laughed at him and said, "That's just too bad! It's too late now!"

Judas was so sad about turning against Jesus that he took his own life by hanging himself. But nothing could undo the harm he had done. The religious leaders were going to get rid of Jesus at last.

THE SOLDIERS stripped the royal robe from Jesus and gave him his own clothes again. They they made him pick up the heavy wooden cross and start to climb up a hill called Calvary.

Jesus stumbled under the heavy weight. Then the soldiers called a large, strong farmer out of the crowd to carry it for him.

They had Jesus lie down on the cross with his arms stretched out at each side. Then they hammered nails through his hands and feet, right into the wood. They stood the cross upright and dropped the bottom of it into a hole so it would stand straight.

There Jesus hung, in great pain, for several hours.

He wasn't angry with his enemies. In fact, he prayed that his heavenly Father would forgive them. "They don't understand what they are doing," he said.

The soldiers watched him as he hung there, and they divided up his clothes. They rolled dice to see which one would get his robe.

Pilate had told them to put a sign on the cross over Jesus' head, saying JESUS OF NAZARETH, THE KING OF THE JEWS. Some people thought it should say, "He *said* he was the king of the Jews."

But Pilate said, "Don't change what I have written."

Two criminals were crucified at the same time Jesus was, and one of them believed in Jesus. He said, "Please remember me when you have your kingdom."

Jesus answered, "This very day you will be with me in heaven!"

NOVEMBER

27

The Crucifixion

MATTHEW 27;
MARK 15; LUKE 23;
JOHN 19

28

Jesus Dies on the Cross

MATTHEW 27;
MARK 15; LUKE 23;
JOHN 19

JESUS' family and friends came and stayed nearby while Jesus was on the cross. What a sad day it was for those who loved him! His mother, Mary, and the other women who were his followers were there, as well as the eleven disciples.

Jesus said to the disciple John, his closest friend, "John, treat Mary as if she were your own mother." And he said to Mary, "John is to be like your son."

Of course Jesus' body was in terrible pain, but he suffered most because he was dying as a sinner even though he had never sinned.

We know now that he did it to accept the punishment that should have been ours. The sin that separated him from his Father was our sin! If we believe this and ask God to forgive us because of what Jesus did, he will forgive all our sin.

Why do you think he did this? Yes, it was because he loved us! How lonely he was as he died. He cried out, "O my God, why have you left me?"

The sky turned dark, even though it was early afternoon. Jesus said he was thirsty, and someone gave him a taste of sour wine.

Then he cried out loudly, "It is finished!" And he died.

At that moment an earthquake shook the ground. The curtain in front of the Most Holy Place in the Temple was torn from top to bottom.

One of the Roman soldiers near the cross said in amazement, "Why, this man really *was* God's Son!"

THE DAY after the crucifixion would be the Sabbath, so the religious leaders wanted Jesus' body removed from the cross before sundown, which was the beginning of the Sabbath.

They said, "Be sure all the men you crucified are really dead, then take them down."

One way to get them to die faster was to break their legs. When the soldiers looked at Jesus, however, they saw he was already dead, so they didn't break his legs. This is interesting because many years before, one of the prophets had said that when the Savior died, none of his bones would be broken!

A man named Joseph of Arimathea had admired and respected Jesus very much. He had kept his interest in Jesus a secret because he was a member of the Jewish religious council, and the rest of the members of the council were Jesus' enemies.

Joseph owned a burial cave in a garden not far from where Jesus was crucified. He asked Pilate for permission to bury Jesus' body in his tomb. Pilate was surprised to hear that Jesus was already dead, but when he was sure it was true, he gave Joseph permission.

Joseph took Jesus' body, wrapped it in a linen cloth, and laid it in his tomb. He had no time to prepare the body properly for burial because it was almost time for the Sabbath to begin.

Jesus' mother and the other women watched as Joseph rolled a huge, heavy stone in front of the tomb, then they went away, feeling very sad and lonely.

NOVEMBER

29

Jesus Is Buried

MATTHEW 27;
MARK 15; LUKE 23;
JOHN 19

JESUS' enemies asked Pilate to put guards by Jesus' tomb. "We think his disciples might come and steal his body and then pretend he has risen from the dead," they said.

The women wanted to prepare Jesus' body in the usual way for burial, but they couldn't do it until the Sabbath was over. Very early in the morning on the day after the Sabbath, they started toward the tomb, carrying the necessary spices.

They said to one another, "What are we going to do about that heavy rock? We're not strong enough to push it aside."

But when they got there, they were surprised to see that the rock was already rolled away from the tomb. They looked in and saw a wonderful sight: An angel was sitting at the place where Jesus' body had been!

Of course the women were afraid, but the angel said, "Don't be afraid of me. You are looking for Jesus, aren't you? Well, he is not here. He has come to life. Look! That's where his body lay. Tell his disciples he is alive and will meet them in Galilee."

As the women hurried away, they saw Jesus in the garden and touched his feet. He said, "Good morning! Now don't hold onto me. Just go and tell my disciples—Peter included—that I'm alive and will see them in Galilee."

When the women told their story, the disciples could hardly believe them. Peter and John hurried to the tomb to see for themselves, and they found that the tomb was indeed empty!

DECEMBER

1

*The Disciples
See Jesus
Alive*

MARK 16;
LUKE 24; JOHN 20

THE DISCIPLES could hardly believe that Jesus had actually come to life. But soon they began to see proof.

For instance, two of them were walking along a country road, going to Emmaus. They were still very sad about Jesus' death. All of a sudden, he was there with them, but they didn't recognize him.

Jesus asked them why they were so sad, and they said, "Don't you know the terrible thing that happened to Jesus last week? His enemies crucified him! We had hoped he would set the Jews free, but now he is gone. Some of our people heard he had risen, but how can we tell?"

Jesus talked to them for a long time, explaining all the Scriptures that told about the Savior and how they applied to him.

The disciples invited him to supper, and when they sat down at the table, Jesus broke bread. Suddenly, as they saw him do that familiar act, they realized they had been walking and talking with Jesus all that time!

He disappeared, but they hurried back to Jerusalem to tell everyone Jesus was alive.

When they talked to the other disciples, they learned that Peter had seen Jesus too. While they were talking about him, Jesus appeared to all of them!

He assured them that it was really he. He showed them the nail wounds in his hands and feet; then he ate some supper with them. That certainly proved he was really, truly alive.

THE DISCIPLES didn't see Jesus every day, and sometimes they became confused about what they should do. One day Peter decided to go out on the lake and fish. Several of the other disciples went with him. All night they fished but didn't catch anything.

Toward morning they looked at the shore, and there stood a man. They didn't recognize him as Jesus. He called to them, "How's the fishing?"

They answered, "We haven't caught a thing!"

He said, "Try throwing the nets on the other side of the boat."

They did, and right away the nets were so full of fish the men couldn't pull them aboard.

John shouted, "It must be our Lord!"

Peter jumped out into shallow water and waded ashore, he was so happy to see Jesus. The men dragged the net in, and when they counted the fish, they had about 150 of them.

Jesus had started a small fire on the shore and had some fish cooking over the coals.

After breakfast Jesus talked to Peter alone. He asked Peter if he really loved him, and when Peter said he did, Jesus said, "Then you must spend your life feeding my sheep and my lambs."

He meant that Peter must tell others about what Jesus had done for them and show them how to live as faithful followers of the Lord.

DECEMBER

2

*The
Disciples
Go Fishing*

JOHN 21

ONE day Jesus went up on a mountain with a group of his followers. There he told them what he wanted all people who love him to do.

He said, "God has given me all power and authority. Go all over the world and preach to people everywhere. Teach them to obey all the rules and advice I have given you. When they believe in me, baptize them in the name of the Father, the Son, and the Holy Spirit. And I will always be with you, right up to the end of the world."

He told his disciples to stay there in Jerusalem because in just a few days the Holy Spirit would come to them and give them special power to do the things Jesus had told them.

Then he led the group out toward Bethany, where Martha, Mary, and Lazarus lived. He gave his blessing to all his friends. Then—right before their eyes—he started to go up into the sky. They watched him until finally he disappeared into the clouds.

Then they saw an angel who said to them, "Why are you staring at the sky? This Jesus, who has just gone away from you to heaven, is someday going to come back to the earth again!"

So the disciples went back into the city and waited for God to send the Holy Spirit as Jesus had promised.

349

4

The Holy Spirit Comes

ACTS 2

IN JERUSALEM the disciples and other followers gathered in a large room to have prayer meetings. They missed Jesus, but they had his promise of sending the Holy Spirit to live in them.

Because Judas was gone, they needed someone to take his place in the inner group of twelve. They made the choice by casting lots. (This is like drawing straws to decide something.) Matthias was the one chosen to be the new disciple.

After about seven weeks, the disciples were still meeting regularly and waiting for the Spirit. One day they suddenly heard a loud noise, like the roaring of a big storm. Then they saw little flames of fire over their heads, and they were all filled with the Holy Spirit.

Immediately they all began to speak in languages they had never known before. People who gathered to see what was happening were amazed to hear these Galilean disciples saying things in languages from different places all over the world!

Most of the listeners thought it was wonderful, but a few laughed and said, "They've been drinking!"

Peter began to preach to the crowd. "No, we aren't drunk!" he said. "People don't get drunk in the morning! The thing that has happened to us is exactly what the prophet Joel predicted."

Then he preached a wonderful sermon about how Jesus had died and risen again to take away the world's sin. About 3,000 people believed this message and were baptized—and that was the start of the Christian church.

A MAN in Jerusalem had been crippled all of his life. He could not work and earn money. Each day his friends carried him to the gate of the Temple. There he begged passersby for money to live on.

Peter and John saw him one day as they went to the Temple to pray. The beggar asked them for money.

Peter said, "I don't have any money either, but I can give you something better. In the name of Jesus, get up and walk!"

Right away the man's legs and feet became straight and strong. He not only walked, but he jumped around, shouting praises to God. Everyone who saw this was amazed at this miracle.

This was a good chance for Peter to tell them about Jesus, and that's just what he did. "Jesus gave us power to do miracles," he told them. "We want all of you to become his followers!"

Many of the religious leaders still hated to hear about Jesus, so they arrested Peter and John and put them into prison for preaching about him. When they questioned the disciples, the leaders had to admit that healing the man was not illegal, so they let them go.

But first they gave them this command: "You must not preach anymore about this Jesus of Nazareth."

Peter and John wouldn't promise that. They said, "Jesus told us to preach, and you say not to. Should we obey God or men?"

The leaders had no answer to that question!

DECEMBER

5

Obeying God, Not Men

ACTS 3–4

DECEMBER

6

Lying to God

ACTS 4–5

PETER and John told the other disciples, "We must not be afraid. Jesus told us to preach the Good News. He will protect us from the authorities."

So the believers went on telling about Jesus. They met together for prayer and worship. They loved one another and shared with poor people. Sometimes they even sold their property and put the money into a fund that all could use.

One day Ananias brought in some money and said, "I sold my house, and I am giving the money to the treasury." But he had really sold the house for much more money and was only pretending to share it all. Somehow God told Peter what was going on.

Peter asked Ananias, "Is this all the money you got for your house?"

Ananias lied, "Yes, that's all."

Peter said, "Why do you lie to us and to God? The money was yours. You could have kept some or all of it. But because you tried to deceive us, you have sinned."

And immediately Ananias fell down dead. The men took him out for burial.

Soon his wife, Sapphira, came in. Peter said, "Sapphira, did Ananias bring all the money from the sale of your house?"

"Yes," she replied—for she and her husband had agreed to lie.

"Why do you try to fool God? The men who buried your husband have come back for you." She fell dead too, and they buried her next to Ananias.

All the disciples saw how terrible it is to lie to God.

THE JEWISH religious leaders had warned Peter and John not to preach about Jesus, but they went right on doing it. The Holy Spirit came again and gave them courage. They healed the sick and cast out evil spirits.

Before long, the High Priest and other leaders saw that the disciples were becoming more and more popular among the people. So they arrested them again and put them back into prison.

But that night, before they could even have a trial, an angel came and opened the prison door and let them out. They went back and taught in the Temple again.

When the officials sent for them to accuse them, they were gone! Someone reported that they were in the Temple, preaching, so once again they were arrested and brought before the religious Council.

"Didn't we tell you to stop that preaching?" said the High Priest.

"Yes, but as we told you, we must obey our Lord—and he told us to tell everyone about him. And God has sent the Holy Spirit to help us do that."

Then their enemies were really furious with them. But one very wise man, called Gamaliel, said, "Let's calm down. If we are patient, we'll find out whether these men are telling the truth. Other people preach strange things, but after awhile they just disappear and nothing comes of their preaching. If these men are wrong, we'll know it after awhile."

The other leaders agreed, and they stopped being so mean to the disciples.

8

A Good Man Dies for His Faith

ACTS 6–7

A S THE GROUP of believers grew, the disciples became very busy. Their main job was to preach the gospel, so they chose seven good helpers to do other things, like looking after the money and feeding the poor. These helpers all loved Jesus and had been filled with the Holy Spirit.

One of them was Stephen. He did miracles to help people, and he could preach, too. This made the believers' enemies angry with him, so they found some excuse to arrest Stephen.

While they were questioning him, Stephen's face glowed with the joy of the Spirit. They asked him about Jesus, and Stephen preached a long message. He reminded them of everything God had done for his people. He said Jesus was the one who had come to fulfill the promises the prophets had made many years ago.

Then he accused the leaders of killing Jesus and rejecting the Good News. He said, "You are stubborn unbelievers!"

Well, you can imagine how angry that made them! They shouted terrible things at him, but Stephen looked up into the sky and said, "I see the Son of God at his Father's right hand in heaven!"

That only made things worse, so they dragged him out of the city. They took off their robes. A young man named Saul guarded their clothing as they threw heavy, sharp stones at Stephen. He was so badly hurt that he died.

As he was dying, he prayed, "Lord, don't blame them for this sin!" What a forgiving spirit he had!

354

STEPHEN'S death was the beginning of a new wave of cruelty against the believers in Jerusalem. Many had to move to other places so they wouldn't be arrested or killed.

Saul, who had watched the men's clothes as they stoned Stephen, was one of the worst enemies of the church. All the believers were afraid of him.

The believers told the Good News about Jesus wherever they went. The disciple Philip went into Samaria, and there he preached and healed people. Many people became Christians in spite of the scattering of Jesus' followers.

One day as Philip was traveling, he saw a man from Ethiopia riding in a chariot. The man was reading something, and he looked troubled. The Holy Spirit told Philip to speak to the man.

Philip said, "Can you understand what you are reading?"

The Ethiopian said, "No! Perhaps you can explain it."

He had been reading Isaiah's prophecies about Jesus. Philip explained what Isaiah had meant, and he told the Ethiopian all about Jesus.

The man asked if he could be baptized. "Yes," said Philip, "if you truly believe."

"I do believe that Jesus is the Son of God," he answered. So Philip baptized him in a nearby stream.

10

Saul Sees the Light!

ACTS 9

SAUL kept on trying to hurt the Christians. He decided to go to the city of Damascus and find believers to arrest. He wanted to bring them back to Jerusalem and put them in jail. He took some soldiers and started to Damascus.

As he traveled, something very strange happened. A brilliant light shone down out of heaven and a voice said, "Saul, why are you trying to hurt me?"

"Wh-who is that?" Saul stammered.

"I am Jesus, and you are acting like my enemy."

"What should I do, Lord?" Saul asked.

"Go on into Damascus and wait for instructions," the voice said.

The soldiers with Saul heard the voice but didn't see anyone. When the light and the voice were gone, Saul realized he was blind.

Then the Lord spoke to Ananias, a disciple in Damascus. "Go to the home of Judas, who lives on Straight Street. Ask for a man named Saul of Tarsus. I've told him you will come and give him back his sight."

"Oh, Lord, I'm afraid to! Saul is a terrible enemy of all believers. He's here to arrest us."

"Don't worry. I've chosen him to be my messenger not only to Jews but to Gentiles—even to kings!"

So Ananias obeyed. When he found Saul, he said, "The Lord has sent me so you can receive your sight and be filled with the Holy Spirit."

And that is what happened! From then on Saul was a faithful follower of the Lord Jesus and preached about him.

THE NEWS quickly spread among the Christians that their old enemy Saul was now saying he believed in Jesus. He was even preaching the gospel in Damascus.

Some were glad to hear this, but others said, "Don't you believe it! This is just a trick to get us to trust him. Then he will grab us and throw us into prison."

But Saul was a good preacher. Some Jews in Damascus became angry with him for saying Jesus was the Messiah—God's Son. They decided to kill him. They watched the city gate, planning to nab him if he tried to leave.

But the believers heard about that plot, and they helped Saul escape. They let him down over the city wall in a big basket!

Saul returned to Jerusalem and tried to join the believers' fellowship. But they were afraid to trust him.

One of their members, Barnabas, knew what had happened on the road to Damascus. He took Saul to the believers and said, "Listen! You know I would not trick you. Let me tell you how our brother Saul became a believer."

Then he told them the whole story about the bright light and the voice from heaven. He told how Saul had received his sight and had been filled with the Holy Spirit.

"He really is one of us," Barnabas said. From then on, the church accepted Saul. How exciting it was that one of Jesus' worst enemies became one of his most loving disciples!

DECEMBER

11

Can the Believers Trust Saul?

ACTS 9

DORCAS was a believer in Joppa who did kind things for poor people. When she died, her friends asked Peter to come quickly. They told him how much they would miss this good woman.

Peter asked them to leave the room. He prayed, then he said, "Dorcas, get up!" She came back to life and joined her friends. Everyone in town was happy, and many people believed in Jesus.

While Peter was still in Joppa, a Roman army officer in the city of Caesarea had an unusual experience. He was a good man named Cornelius. One night an angel appeared to him and said, "God knows you want to understand more about him. Send messengers to Joppa to find Simon Peter. Invite him to visit you."

Cornelius obeyed the angel's instructions. Meanwhile, in Joppa, Peter also had a vision. He was praying on the roof of the house where he was staying. Houses in that country had flat roofs, and people often sat up there, as we might sit on a porch or patio.

It was lunchtime, and Peter was hungry. Suddenly he saw a sheet coming down from the sky. On it were many kinds of animals, including snakes and birds. They were the kinds the Jews weren't allowed to eat.

A voice said, "Kill and eat whatever you want."

Peter said, "Oh, no! I would never eat unclean things."

The voice replied, "Don't argue. If God says the food is all right, believe him!"

The same thing happened three times. Peter wondered what this strange vision could possibly mean.

WHILE Peter was trying to understand his strange vision, Cornelius's messengers arrived at the front gate.

The Holy Spirit said to Peter, "Some men have come to take you to their master. I sent them, so it's all right for you to go."

Peter went downstairs and met the messengers. They told him all about Cornelius and his vision. "Our master is a good man, much respected by the Jews. An angel told him to send for you to help him learn more about God."

Peter invited them in for the night. The next morning they started to Caesarea, along with other Christians from Joppa.

When they arrived, Cornelius welcomed them into his home, where he had gathered friends and relatives. Cornelius fell down and worshiped Peter.

"Don't do that! I'm not a god," said Peter, so Cornelius got up.

Peter said, "Jews don't usually go into the homes of non-Jews. But God gave me a vision, and now I understand it. It meant I should never think of other people as unclean or worthless. God told me to come, and here I am. How can I help you?"

Cornelius told him how he wanted to be a believer, so Peter taught him about Jesus' life, death, and resurrection. He said, "Anyone who believes in him will have his sins forgiven."

Cornelius and his family believed, and the Holy Spirit filled them, just as he had filled the Jewish believers. When Peter saw that they were true believers, he baptized all of them.

THE JEWISH believers were shocked that Peter had baptized a Gentile, that is, a non-Jew. But Peter explained, and finally they accepted it. They said, "Praise God! He gives eternal life to both Jews and Gentiles!"

King Herod began to get tough with the believers. He killed John's brother James and put Peter in jail, planning to kill him too. All the believers prayed very hard for Peter.

The night before he was to be killed, Peter was sleeping in the prison. He was chained to two soldiers. An angel came and poked Peter in the ribs to wake him up.

The angel said, "Get up quickly and dress. Put on your shoes and follow me." The chains fell right off of Peter's arms, and he followed the angel.

Peter thought he must be dreaming! The angel led him through one cell block after another and out through the gates, which opened all by themselves! Then the angel disappeared, and Peter realized it was all true.

He hurried to the home where the believers were praying for him. He knocked, and when a girl named Rhoda saw him at the door, she ran back and shouted, "Peter is here!"

They said, "Impossible! You must have seen his ghost."

Peter kept on knocking, and finally they came and let him in. He told them what had happened, then he went away to a safer place.

THE HOLY SPIRIT chose disciples to travel, preaching the Good News about Jesus in different countries. Paul, who used to be called Saul, and Barnabas were two of the men chosen for this job. A young man named John Mark went with them as their assistant.

They visited some of the Greek cities and went into the country of Turkey. People believed in Jesus and asked him to forgive their sins.

In Turkey, John Mark decided to leave the other men and go home. Perhaps he got homesick or was afraid of what might happen to them in foreign countries.

The preaching of Paul and Barnabas upset the Jews who didn't believe in Jesus. They got jealous because these new speakers were so popular. But the non-Jews (remember, we usually call them Gentiles) were more interested in the Good News, and many of them became Christians.

When a group of people trusted Jesus, Paul and Barnabas organized them into a church and appointed a leader to help them understand more about Jesus.

Finally the two missionaries decided to go back and check up on all the new little churches they had started. Barnabas wanted to take John Mark on this trip, but Paul said, "No, indeed! He walked out on us last time. We can't depend on him."

They argued about this, and the argument separated Paul and Barnabas. Barnabas took John Mark and went to the island of Cyprus.

Paul teamed up with Silas and went to Syria to encourage the believers there.

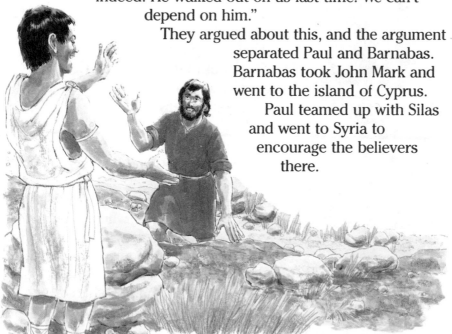

16

*The Church
Solves a
Problem*

ACTS 15

ALL the way back to the early part of the Bible, we read about how God taught his people to make animal sacrifices—that is, kill animals and offer them to God. These sacrifices were a kind of picture or preview of the sacrifice of God's Son, Jesus, who would come many years later.

Now that Jesus had come and had died as the sacrifice for the world's sin, did the Jews need to keep on making animal sacrifices? This was the question that the early Christians began to argue about.

Some said, "We have always made sacrifices, and we shouldn't stop."

Others said, "But Jesus' death was the final, real sacrifice. We don't need the 'picture' anymore."

And what about Gentiles who were becoming Christians? Did they need to follow Jewish customs? Finally the church leaders had a meeting. They prayed for wisdom and talked about these problems.

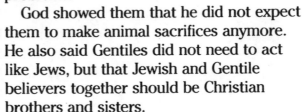

God showed them that he did not expect them to make animal sacrifices anymore. He also said Gentiles did not need to act like Jews, but that Jewish and Gentile believers together should be Christian brothers and sisters.

The leaders sent letters to all the new churches. How happy everyone was when they heard how God had led the church to solve the problem!

Paul and Silas went on traveling. They met new believers everywhere they went. Two of these became special friends of Paul's. Timothy, a young man in Lystra, became almost like a son to Paul. Lydia, a businesswoman in Philippi, shared her home with the apostles when they were in town.

LYDIA often met with a group of other Christians to pray beside a river in Philippi. While Paul and Silas were there, they joined that group for prayer.

As they went to the river, the apostles often saw a slave girl who was in the power of evil spirits. Her owners got a lot of money by using her as a fortune-teller. She followed the apostles, shouting, "These men are servants of God. They will tell you how to have your sins forgiven."

One day Paul turned to her and said to the evil spirit, "In the name of Jesus Christ, come out of this girl and leave her alone!"

The spirit obeyed, and the girl was free. But now she couldn't tell fortunes and earn money for her owners anymore, and this made them angry.

They dragged Paul and Silas to some judges who sat in the marketplace. They didn't admit they were angry about losing money. They accused the apostles of teaching things that were against Roman law.

The judges gave orders that the apostles be beaten with wooden sticks. Then they threw them into jail and told the jailer, "We'll kill you if these prisoners escape!"

Instead of being unhappy and discouraged, Paul and Silas spent the night praying and singing songs of praise. The other prisoners must have been surprised to hear joyful music in prison!

ABOUT midnight an earthquake shook the prison where Paul and Silas were. The building was badly damaged, and the doors flew open. All the prisoners' chains were broken.

When the jailer saw the prison standing wide open, he thought the prisoners had all escaped. He knew he would be killed for letting them get away, so he picked up his sword to kill himself.

Paul called quickly, "Don't harm yourself. We are all here!" Even though they could have run away, the prisoners had all stayed in their cells!

The jailer fell down before Paul and Silas and said, "What can I do to be saved?"

They answered, "Just believe on the Lord Jesus Christ, and you and your family will be saved."

Then they told him the Good News about Jesus, and the jailer and his family believed. They gave the apostles medicine for their injuries and fed them a good meal.

The judges then sent word that Paul and Silas could go free. But Paul said, "They beat us and imprisoned us without a trial. That was illegal because we are Roman citizens. We are not going to sneak out of town like criminals. Let them come and release us themselves!"

The judges had not realized the apostles were Roman citizens. They were worried that they would get into trouble because of the way they had treated them. They came and apologized and begged the apostles to get out of town. But Paul and Silas returned to Lydia's home and preached some more before they left.

DECEMBER

19

*Paul's
Preaching
Starts
Trouble*

ACTS 18–19

IN THE GREEK city of Corinth, Paul met a Christian man named Aquila and his wife, Priscilla. They were tentmakers, just as Paul was. They became friends, and Paul helped them with their tentmaking. This gave him a way to earn some money for his expenses.

Later Paul preached for awhile at Ephesus, doing miracles and leading many to believe in Jesus. Most of the people in Ephesus had worshiped the Greek goddess Diana. They bought silver idols of Diana and kept them in their homes. When they became Christians, of course, they didn't worship the idols anymore.

Soon the men who made the idols found they couldn't sell as many idols as they once did.

A businessman named Demetrius called the other silversmiths together and said, "We are losing much business because of Paul's preaching. We must get rid of this troublemaker."

The silversmiths started a big riot, and everyone shouted, "Great is Diana of the Ephesians!" The streets were filled with an angry crowd trying to find Paul to attack him. But Paul's friends kept him from being captured.

The mayor of Ephesus got everyone's attention and said, "Now see here. This isn't doing any good. If these Jews who are preaching are really breaking any laws, bring them before a court in the legal way. This riot will only get us into trouble with the Roman government. Calm down and go home."

The riot stopped, and the apostles were able to leave town in safety.

20

More Christians and More Trouble

ACTS 20–21

WHEREVER Paul preached the gospel, two things happened. Many people believed in Jesus and became Christians, and other people were angry and tried to stop Paul from preaching!

Once Paul was preaching on the third floor of a building. He talked until midnight, and a young man who had been sitting in an open window fell asleep and tumbled down to the ground below. Everyone thought he was dead, but Paul picked him up, and the young fellow was all right!

In Caesarea a prophet named Agabus warned Paul that if he returned to Jerusalem, he would be taken prisoner and tortured. Paul's friends tried to keep him from going, but Paul said he had to, even if he died.

In Jerusalem Paul's enemies tried to kill him, but a Roman army captain protected Paul from the mob. Paul told the captain how he had become a Christian. Then he told him he was a Roman citizen. The captain didn't hurt him, because a Roman citizen was supposed to get a fair trial if he was suspected of a crime.

Forty of Paul's worst enemies took a vow not to eat or drink until they had killed Paul. They made a plan to kidnap him from the Roman soldiers, but somehow Paul's nephew heard about their evil plot. He warned Paul and the captain.

The captain decided to send Paul to the Roman governor, Felix, in Caesarea. They went secretly, at night, to protect Paul from his enemies.

THE ROMAN captain sent a letter to Governor Felix, telling about Paul's trouble: "The Jews were about to kill him, but he is a Roman citizen, so he should have a fair trial. I've sent for his enemies to present their side of the case."

Felix read the letter and said to Paul, "When your accusers get here, I will listen to both sides of the story."

Several days later the High Priest arrived from Jerusalem, bringing other church leaders and a lawyer. They told Felix a lot of lies about Paul.

They said, "He's a terrible troublemaker. He led a rebellion against the Roman government and he defiled the Temple!"

Then it was Paul's turn. He told Felix that the High Priest had not told the truth. He said, "I believe in the Jewish law and I respect the Temple. I came into the Temple to pay a vow and to worship. My conscience is clear."

Felix kept Paul in prison but was kind to him. He let his friends come to visit him whenever they wished. Later Felix listened while Paul told how he had become a Christian when the Lord spoke to him on the road to Damascus.

This made Felix nervous and he sent Paul back to jail, although he brought him to his court to talk to him occasionally.

Two years later a new governor named Festus came in Felix's place, so Paul didn't see Felix anymore.

DECEMBER

21

Paul Talks to Felix

ACTS 23–24

PAUL'S enemies tried to get the new governor, Festus, to send Paul back to Jerusalem to be tried. They thought they might have a chance to kill him before a trial could take place! But Festus refused. He said, "No, the man is in Caesarea. That is where we will try him."

Again Paul's enemies came and told lies about Paul, and again Paul denied them. Festus asked him, "Do you want to go to Jerusalem to continue this trial?"

"Absolutely not!" Paul said. "I have a right to appear before Caesar, the Roman emperor."

"All right," Festus replied. "You have asked for an audience with Caesar; you shall have it!"

King Agrippa visited Festus a few days later, and Festus told him all about Paul and his desire to be tried before the emperor. Agrippa was a Jew, so he was interested in Paul's problem.

Again Paul was brought in and had a chance to tell his story. He told Agrippa all about his turning to Jesus Christ, and he preached the gospel to him. Paul hoped that the king himself would accept Jesus, but Agrippa was not convinced that the gospel was true. However, he could see that Paul was innocent of any crime, and that his enemies' accusations were untrue.

Agrippa said to Festus, "If Paul hadn't insisted on appearing before Caesar, I would have let him go free. But now he will have to go to Rome."

Immediately the governor made arrangements for Paul to sail across the Mediterranean Sea to Rome, carefully guarded by some soldiers.

FESTUS put an officer named Julius in charge of Paul on the voyage to Rome. Julius liked Paul and even let him go ashore to visit friends at one of the ports.

The weather got bad and the winds drove the ship off its course. The captain stopped at a place called Myra and transferred his passengers to another ship headed for Rome.

The weather kept getting worse, and the new ship's captain stopped at Fair Havens, where they stayed for several days. It was not a good time of year to make the trip across the sea, and Paul advised the captain to stay in Fair Havens until spring.

The captain disagreed with Paul and sailed away. The farther they went, the worse the storm got. The winds blew the ship far out to sea. For many days the crew fought to keep the ship from sinking. Finally they lost all hope.

Paul said, "You shouldn't have left Fair Havens, but the Lord has promised me that no one will die, even though we will be shipwrecked."

Two weeks after the storm hit them, the ship was driven toward some rocks near land. Paul urged all 276 passengers to eat something. Then it happened! The ship ran aground, and the rough waves began to tear it apart.

The soldiers thought Julius should kill the prisoners so they wouldn't escape, but he refused. Everyone jumped overboard and either swam or floated ashore on pieces of wood. Just as God had promised, they all reached shore alive!

WHEN the sailors and their passengers got to shore, they didn't even know where they were. Many people who lived there came to help them. They said, "Welcome! This is the island of Malta. We are glad you have all escaped death."

The citizens of Malta were very kind to the shipwrecked group. They started a big fire on the beach to warm them and dry their clothes.

Paul helped gather wood for the fire. Suddenly, as he picked up a bunch of sticks, a poisonous snake came out of the sticks, coiled itself around Paul's arm, and bit his hand.

"Aha!" cried the people. "This man must be a dangerous criminal— probably a murderer. Even though he was saved from the shipwreck, he is going to be punished by death from this snakebite."

They watched as Paul held his arm out over the bonfire and shook the snake loose. Everyone expected Paul's arm to swell with the poison. They could hardly believe their eyes when he showed no bad effects from the snakebite.

Then they said, "No, he's not a criminal. He has supernatural powers. Maybe he's some kind of god!"

The governor of Malta was Publius. He invited Paul and other passengers to stay at his house for several days. Paul saw that Publius' father was sick with a fever, so he put his hands on him and healed him.

DECEMBER

24

*A Snake
Bites
Paul*

ACTS 28

370

IN THE SPRING the ship's captain found another ship, and they continued their trip. They landed on the coast of Italy, then the soldiers had their prisoners walk to the city of Rome. Christians in Rome heard they were coming, so they hurried out to welcome Paul.

In Rome the guards turned their prisoners over to the Roman soldiers. For the next two years Paul lived in a house they provided for him. He didn't have to be in a prison cell, although he wasn't allowed to leave his house, and guards watched him all the time.

Paul asked the local Jewish leaders to visit him. He said, "The Jews in Jerusalem wanted to kill me, but the Roman officials wanted to set me free, because they could see I was innocent. But I demanded to be tried before Caesar, so they sent me here. I want to tell you about Jesus, so you will understand what I believe."

They said, "We hadn't heard anything about you, but we would like to hear what you have to say."

So Paul taught them about Jesus' love for them and his death and resurrection. A lot of them became Christians, although some didn't believe. He told them that if the Jews refused to accept the Good News of the gospel, it would be preached to the Gentiles and great numbers of them would become believers.

During the time he lived in Rome, Paul had many opportunities to preach and help people understand and accept the gospel.

DECEMBER

26

*Letters
from the
Apostles*

ROMANS;
1 AND 2 CORINTHIANS

PAUL and the other apostles couldn't stay and keep on teaching in each church they started, so they sent letters to encourage the believers and tell them how to live. We call those letters the "epistles," and they make up about half of the New Testament. Paul wrote most of the epistles.

Each epistle can help us today. For instance, when Paul wrote to the believers in Rome, he reminded them that all people are sinners. That might have discouraged them, but Paul didn't leave them with the bad news. He said that if they trusted in Jesus Christ, God would declare them "not guilty" and take away their sins.

Paul told the Romans to serve God and show love to each other and to their enemies. He taught them to obey the government and its laws.

When he wrote to the Corinthians, he said, "Don't quarrel and split up into unfriendly groups." He told them how to have strong marriages, being pure and loving to one another. And he said each believer had his or her own special abilities to help the church and serve other people.

One of the loveliest parts of the letters to the Corinthians is the "Love Chapter," which tells us that if we love others, we will be patient and kind. We won't be jealous, envious, boastful, proud, selfish, or rude. We will always be loyal and defend those we love!

In every one of Paul's letters he promised that the Holy Spirit would give believers the power to live the right kind of lives.

EVEN though Paul had a lot of trouble in Ephesus because of the silversmiths who made idols, he was able to start a church there.

When Paul wrote a letter to the Ephesian Christians, he reminded them that Satan is the worst enemy of God and of God's people. When we try to live for God, Satan does everything he can to keep us from doing right. It's like a long, hard war all through our lives.

Paul told the Ephesians something we should learn too. He said they would be able to defeat Satan if they would use some of the equipment soldiers had in those days.

First there was a wide belt that protected the middle part of the body. Paul said that truth is like that belt. And right living is like a breastplate—that is, metal armor that protects the heart.

Faith is the shield that stops the arrows Satan shoots at us. Salvation is the helmet that protects our heads from injury (just the way a motorbiker or football player is protected by a helmet).

He said we can move away from Satan quickly if we wear the shoes of the Good News of peace with God.

All those things are protective or defensive equipment. What can we use as a weapon against Satan? Paul said to the Ephesians that our best weapon is the sword of the Spirit: the Word of God, the Bible.

And then he told them one more good way to win the battle with Satan: Pray all the time!

DECEMBER
28

Jesus Is Coming Again

1 THESSALONIANS 4–5;
2 THESSALONIANS 2–3

REMEMBER how Jesus went up into heaven while his disciples watched? At that time an angel said, "Someday he will come back the same way he went away."

Well, Paul wrote two letters to the believers in Thessalonica, telling them more about that promise. He said that when Jesus is ready to return, he will appear in the sky and give a great shout of victory. An archangel will cry out loudly, and there will be a trumpet call.

Then the Christians who have already died will rise and be taken up into the sky to meet Jesus. After that, those on earth who love him will rise into the sky too.

All believers will then be given new bodies, perfect and pure in every way—they will never sin or get sick or die. And they will be with Jesus forever.

Paul said that these amazing things will happen very quickly—as fast as you can blink your eyes. Paul wanted everyone to know about the future so we will not worry about what happens to Christians who die. Although their bodies are dead and they are separated from their loved ones for awhile, they are safe in God's care.

Believers must never forget that Jesus is going to come back. Paul said, "Keep watching for him and obeying God as you wait for that wonderful day." More than two thousand years have gone by since those words were written, but they are just as true today as they were then.

The Runaway Slave

PHILEMON

ONCE when Paul was in prison, he had a visitor named Onesimus. Paul told him about Jesus, and Onesimus became a Christian. He did many kind things for Paul, bringing him food and telling him what was happening outside the prison.

Onesimus had a serious problem. He was a slave who had run away from his master. Paul was surprised to hear that the master was his friend Philemon. Long ago Paul had told Philemon about Jesus, and Philemon had become a believer.

Onesimus decided he should return to Philemon and be his slave again. Paul was afraid that Philemon might punish Onesimus severely because he had committed a crime by running away.

Paul wrote a letter for Onesimus to take to Philemon. In the letter Paul thanked Philemon for helping the church and letting the believers meet in his home. He asked Philemon to be kind and forgiving to Onesimus.

He said, "Now that Onesimus is a believer too, you and he should be like brothers. If Onesimus owes you any money, I will pay it." Then he reminded Philemon how much he owed Paul for helping him find God. Nothing could repay that debt!

At the end of the letter Paul said, "If I can get out of prison, I want to come to visit you, so keep a guest room ready for me!"

Do you suppose Philemon did forgive Onesimus and take him back into his home? We don't know for sure. How do you think the story ended?

ONE of the letters in the New Testament—the Book of Hebrews—was not signed by the writer. Many people think Paul wrote it, but no one can be sure, and it doesn't really matter.

The writer says Jesus Christ is like the High Priests of the Old Testament. The High Priest was allowed to go into the Most Holy Place in the Temple and offer the blood from sacrificed animals. Then God would forgive the sins of the people who had given those animals.

When Jesus died to become our Savior, animal sacrifices were no longer needed. He gave his own blood for our salvation, so we can go right into God's presence and speak to him in prayer.

The writer of Hebrews explained what real faith is. He said it is being sure something is going to happen, even though we are not able to see it happening right now.

In Hebrews we read a lot of great examples of people who had this kind of faith. All through this story book we have read about these people: Abel, Enoch, Noah, Abraham, Sarah, Jacob, Joseph, Moses and his parents, Israelites who followed Moses out of Egypt, and the soldiers who marched around Jericho.

The writer said we live our lives as if we were running a race in a stadium. All those heroes of faith are watching us. Isn't it wonderful to know we are being encouraged by other Christians, including those who lived long ago?

W HEN the apostle John was old, he was a prisoner on an island called Patmos. One morning he had a wonderful vision.

He saw Jesus in his glory. "His eyes were bright like flames of fire," John wrote. "His feet gleamed like polished bronze, and his voice was like thunder. His face shone like the sun."

Jesus said to John, "Don't be afraid. I am the Living One who died but is now alive. Come up into heaven, and I will show you what will happen in the future."

Instantly John's spirit was in heaven. He saw God sitting on a great throne. Light flashed from him, like rays from a jewel. Lightning and thunder came from the throne, and in front of it was a shining crystal sea. Then John heard millions of angels singing praise to God.

John saw terrible things happening on earth to people who refused to obey the Lord. But then he saw the Holy City.

He heard a voice shout, "Look! The home of God is now among people. He will live with them, and they will belong to him. There will be no more death or sorrow."

An angel said, "Nothing impure will ever be allowed there. No one who does wrong can enter. Only those whose sins have been washed away by the death of the Lord Jesus Christ can come in. Their names are written in God's Book of Life."

Is your name written in the Book of Life? It is if you believe in Jesus and your sins are forgiven!

TO THE READERS OF THIS BOOK:

You have now finished reading all the stories in this book. If you read them on the days indicated, you have come to the end of the year, too. Beginning on January 1, read through the book again during the coming year. None of us can ever read the Bible enough to get tired of its wonderful stories. We can always find something new to enjoy and remember about God and his great love for us.